Studies in Russian and East European History and Society

Series Editors: **R. W. Davies, E.A. Rees, M. J. Ilič** and **J. R. Smith** at the Centre for Russian and East European Studies, University of Birmingham

Recent titles include:

Lynne Attwood
CREATING THE NEW SOVIET WOMAN

Edwin Bacon and Mark Sandle (*editors*)
BREZHNEV RECONSIDERED

John Barber and Andrei Dzeniskevich (*editors*)
LIFE AND DEATH IN BESIEGED LENINGRAD, 1941–44

John Barber and Mark Harrison (*editors*)
THE SOVIET DEFENCE-INDUSTRY COMPLEX FROM STALIN TO KHRUSHCHEV

Vincent Barnett
KONDRATIEV AND THE DYNAMICS OF ECONOMIC DEVELOPMENT

R. W. Davies
SOVIET HISTORY IN THE YELTSIN ERA

Linda Edmondson (*editor*)
GENDER IN RUSSIAN HISTORY AND CULTURE

James Hughes
STALINISM IN A RUSSIAN PROVINCE

Melanie Ilič
WOMEN WORKERS IN THE SOVIET INTERWAR ECONOMY
WOMEN IN THE STALIN ERA (*editor*)

Melanie Ilič, Susan E. Reid and Lynne Attwood (*editors*)
WOMEN IN THE KHRUSHCHEV ERA

Peter Kirkow
RUSSIA'S PROVINCES

Maureen Perrie
THE CULT OF IVAN THE TERRIBLE IN STALIN'S RUSSIA

E. A. Rees (*editor*)
DECISION–MAKING IN THE STALINIST COMMAND ECONOMY
CENTRE-LOCAL RELATIONS IN THE STALINIST STATE, 1928–1941
THE NATURE OF STALIN'S DICTATORSHIP
The Politburo, 1924–1953

Lennart Samuelson
PLANS FOR STALIN'S WAR MACHINE
Tukhachevskii and Military-Economic Planning, 1925–1941

Vera Tolz
RUSSIAN ACADEMICIANS AND THE REVOLUTION

J.N. Westwood
SOVIET RAILWAYS TO RUSSIAN RAILWAYS

Stephen G. Wheatcroft (*editor*)
CHALLENGING TRADITIONAL VIEWS OF RUSSIAN HISTORY

Galina M. Yemelianova
RUSSIA AND ISLAM
A Historical Survey

Studies in Russian and East European History and Society
Series Standing Order ISBN 0-333-71239-0
(*outside North America only*)

You can receive future titles in this series as they are published by placing a standing order.
Please contact your bookseller or, in case of difficulty, write to us at the address below with
your name and address, the title of the series and the ISBN quoted above.

Customer Services Department, Macmillan Distribution Ltd, Houndmills, Basingstoke,
Hampshire RG21 6XS, England

Women in the Khrushchev Era

Edited by

Melanie Ilič
University of Gloucestershire and
Centre for Russian and East European Studies,
The University of Birmingham

Susan E. Reid
University of Sheffield

and

Lynne Attwood
University of Manchester

First published 2004 by
PALGRAVE MACMILLAN
Houndmills, Basingstoke, Hampshire RG21 6XS and
175 Fifth Avenue, New York, N. Y. 10010
Companies and representatives throughout the world

PALGRAVE MACMILLAN is the global academic imprint of the Palgrave
Macmillan division of St. Martin's Press, LLC and of Palgrave Macmillan Ltd.
Macmillan® is a registered trademark in the United States, United Kingdom
and other countries. Palgrave is a registered trademark in the European
Union and other countries.

ISBN 1–4039–2043–5 hardback

This book is printed on paper suitable for recycling and made from fully
managed and sustained forest sources.

A catalogue record for this book is available from the British Library.

Library of Congress Cataloging-in-Publication Data
Women in the Khrushchev era / edited by Melanie Ilič, Susan E. Reid, and
Lynne Attwood.
    p. cm.
  Includes bibliographical references and index.
  ISBN 1–4039–2043–5 (cloth)
    1. Women–Soviet Union–Social conditions. 2. Women–Soviet
Union–Economic conditions. 3. Women and communism–Soviet
Union–History. 4. Soviet Union–Social conditions–1945–1991.
5. Khrushchev, Nikita Sergeevich, 1894–1971. I. Ilič, Melanie, 1962– II. Reid,
Susan Emily. III. Attwood, Lynne.

HQ1662.W575 2004
305.42'0947–dc22   2003062677

10   9   8   7   6   5   4   3   2   1
13 12 11 10 09 08 07 06 05 04

Printed and bound in Great Britain by
Antony Rowe Ltd, Chippenham and Eastbourne

Contents

List of Illustrations

List of Tables

Acknowledgements

We would like to thank the following for their comments on initial draft chapters, which have helped to shape the final book: Bob Davies, Arfon Rees, Jeremy Smith, and the anonymous reader for a full and comprehensive report for Palgrave Macmillan. We acknowledge the permission granted by Cambridge University Press to reprint, in edited form, Donald Filtzer's chapter, 'The Position of Women Workers', originally in *Soviet Workers and De-Stalinization: the Consolidation of the Modern System of Soviet Production Relations, 1953–1964* (1992). We acknowledge also the financial support given by the following institutions towards the preparation of this book: the University of Gloucestershire; the British Academy for supporting research and illustration costs for Chapter 8, Susan E. Reid, 'Women in the Home'. The authors have made every attempt to contact copyright-holders. If any have inadvertently been overlooked, the necessary arrangements will be made at the first opportunity.

Much of the work contained here has been the subject of seminar and conference papers presented by individual authors around the world. We thank the panellists, discussants and audiences at these sessions for their comments and guidance in shaping the final versions contained in this book. In particular, Deborah Field thanks participants at the 1997 AAASS conference panel on 'Fathers in the Motherland: Soviet Masculinities in the Stalin and Khrushchev Eras', and is grateful to Susan Reid and Mark Schneyer for their comments. Susan Reid would like to thank Aleksandr Vatlin for his assistance, and the late Ol'ga Kazakova, who is dearly missed.

Finally, we offer our deepest thanks to the interviewees who have offered their testimonies to researchers so openly and freely, and whose experiences are detailed and analysed in the chapters that follow. The book is much enriched as a result of their participation.

Notes on the Contributors

Lynne Attwood is Senior Lecturer in Russian Studies at Manchester University. She is author of *The New Soviet Man and Woman: Sex-Role Socialization in the USSR* (Macmillan, 1990) and *Creating the New Soviet Woman: Women's Magazines as Engineers of Female Identity, 1922–53* (Macmillan, 1999), and editor of *Red Women on the Silver Screen: Soviet Women and Cinema from the Beginning to the End of the Communist Era* (Pandora, 1993).

Sue Bridger has published numerous articles on women in Russia. She is the author of *Women in the Soviet Countryside* (CUP, 1987), and co-author, with R. Kay and K. Pinnick, of *No More Heroines? Russia, Women and the Market* (Routledge, 1996). She is the editor of *Women and Political Change: Perspectives from East-Central Europe* (Macmillan, 1999) and co-editor, with F. Pine, of *Surviving Post-Socialism: Local Strategies and Regional Responses in Eastern Europe* (Routledge, 1998). She is currently working with R. Kay on men's experiences of, and responses to, change in post-Soviet Russia, and is writing a book on Soviet women cosmonauts.

Deborah A. Field received her PhD from the University of Michigan. She is currently Assistant Professor and chair of the History Department at Adrian College, Michigan. She has published articles on private life in the Khrushchev era.

Donald Filtzer is Professor of Russian History at the University of East London. He is author of *Soviet Workers and Stalinist Industrialization: the Formation of Modern Soviet Production Relations, 1928–1941* (M.E. Sharpe, 1986), *Soviet Workers and De-Stalinization: the Consolidation of the Modern System of Soviet Production Relations, 1953–1964* (CUP, 1992), *The Khrushchev Era: De-Stalinisation and the Limits of Reform in the USSR* (Macmillan, 1993), *Soviet Workers and the Collapse of Perestroika: the Soviet Labour Process and Gorbachev's Reforms, 1985–1991* (CUP, 1994) and *Soviet Workers and Late Stalinism: Labour and the Restoration of the Stalinist System after World War Two* (CUP, 2002).

John Haynes completed his PhD at the University of Manchester in 2000. He has taught at the School of Slavonic and East European Studies, UCL, and currently lectures in Film Studies in the History

Department at the University of Essex. His research interests include Soviet cinema and history, film and cultural theory, gender and psychoanalysis. He is the author of *New Soviet Man: Gender and Masculinity in Stalinist Soviet Cinema* (Manchester University Press, 2003), and is undertaking new research on representations of sport in popular national cinemas.

Melanie Ilič is Senior Lecturer in History and Women's Studies at the University of Gloucestershire, and Research Fellow at the Centre for Russian and East European Studies, The University of Birmingham. She is author of *Women Workers in the Soviet Interwar Economy: From 'Protection' to 'Equality'* (Macmillan, 1999) and editor of *Women in the Stalin Era* (Palgrave, 2001). In addition to her work on Soviet women's history, she is also researching the regional dimensions of Soviet political repression in the 1930s.

Marianne Liljeström is Professor of Women's Studies at the University of Turku, Finland. She is author of *Emancipated to Subordination: the Discursive Reproduction of the Soviet Gender System* (Turku,1995) and editor, with A. Rosenholm and I. Savkina, of *Models of Self: Russian Women's Autobiogaphical Texts* (Helsinki, 2000).

Irina Paert is Lecturer in European History at the University of Wales, Bangor. Between 2000 and 2001 she was a Simon Research Fellow at the University of Manchester (History Department). Her works on the history of the Russian Orthodox Church, popular religion, Old Believers, and gender and religion between the 1760s and 1940s have been published in both English and Russian. She is the author of *Old Believers, Religious Dissent and Gender in Russia* (Manchester University Press, 2003).

Michaela Pohl completed her PhD at Indiana University, and now teaches at Vassar College in New York. She has written on Russian youth culture, Soviet science fiction, rock music, folklore and the exile culture of the Chechens in Kazakhstan. She is currently writing a book about Khrushchev's Virgin Lands project.

Susan E. Reid is Lecturer in Russian Visual Arts at the University of Sheffield. She has published articles and chapters on various aspects of Soviet and post-Soviet visual culture, and is editor, with D. Crowley, of *Style and Socialism: Modernity and Material Culture in Post-War Eastern Europe* (Berg, 2000), and *Socialist Spaces: Sites of Everyday Life in the Eastern Bloc* (Berg, 2002).

Kristin Roth-Ey recently completed her PhD in history at Princeton University and is currently a postdoctoral fellow at the Harriman Institute, Columbia University. She is working on a monograph about mass media culture in the Khrushchev and Brezhnev eras.

Glossary of Russian Terms and Abbreviations

aul	remote village
bezdelnichestvo	idleness; loafing about
byt	everyday life
chastushki	folk verses, often humorous
CPSU	Communist Party of the Soviet Union
delegatki	female delegates
feministki	feminists
Gulag	*Glavnoe upravlenie lagerei*; (main administration of) labour camps
IPKh	*istinno-pravoslavnye khristiane*; truly Orthodox Christians
klikushestvo	demonic possession; hysterics
kolkhoz / kolkhozy	collective farm(s)
kommunalka	communal apartment (with shared kitchen and bathroom facilities)
Komsomol	(member of the) Communist Party's youth section
krai	territory
kul'turnost'	'culturedness'
MTS	machine tractor station
MVD	Ministry of Internal Affairs
NEP	New Economic Policy
oblast'	region
obshchestvennitsa / obshchestvennitsy	(woman engaged in the) volunteer wives' movement
ocherki / ocherkovyi	sketches; essayistic literature
orgnabor	recruitment bureau
psalomshchiki	psalm readers
raion	district
ravnopravki	'equal-rightsers'; women calling for equal rights
RSFSR	Russian Soviet Federative Socialist Republic
sborniki	anthologies
sel'sovet	rural soviet; rural council

shtab	staff
sovkhoz / sovkhozy	state farm(s)
Sovmin	Council of Ministers
SSSR	see USSR
stilyaga / stilyagi	style-monger(s); teddy boy(s)
svodki	official reports
tselina	Virgin Lands
tselinnitsa	female Virgin Lands settler
upolnomochennye	church representatives
USSR	Union of Soviet Socialist Republics
(V)LKSM	Vsesoyuznyi Leninskii Kommunisticheskii Soyuz Molodezhi; see also Komsomol
vospitanie	upbringing
vospominaniya	reminiscences
WFDY	World Federation of Democratic Youth
WIDF (MDFZh)	Women's International Democratic Federation (Mezhdunarodnaya demokraticheskaya federatsiya zhenshchin)
zhenotdel / zhenotdely	women's department(s)
zhensovet / zhensovety	women's council(s)

Archive acronyms used in the notes are detailed in full in the Bibliography.

Introduction

Melanie Ilič

Up to now, very little has been written in English-language studies about Soviet women and gender relations in the Khrushchev era.[1] The reason for this is unclear, especially given the attention paid to the revival of the 'woman question' in these years and the relatively easy access to primary sources for the study of this period. The in-depth studies offered by the various chapters contained in this book provide an indication of the wealth of information available, and much of it yet to be analysed, in this important period of Soviet women's history.

Mary Buckley has pointed to the tension in the Khrushchev era 'between ideological claims about the successful liberation of women under Soviet socialism and more realistic observations about women's lives'.[2] The contradictory nature of the Khrushchev era reforms is supported by studies that also identify the increased monitoring, surveillance and state interference in people's everyday lives in a period of supposed liberalisation and the conscious de-Stalinisation of Soviet society. Likewise, Khrushchev condemned Stalin's record on political repression, while simultaneously subjecting Soviet citizens to a new round of legal and cultural constraints, as well as increasing the numbers of people detained in prisons.[3]

Besides the contradictions inherent in the reforms of the Khrushchev period, a number of other key themes relating to this period of Soviet history are identified and explored in this volume of essays. The Khrushchev era is commonly associated with the following reformist trends: a strident effort to modernise and mechanise industrial and agricultural production; the boost given to public services, particularly housing construction, maternal welfare and childcare facilities, as well as to consumer production and material consumption; the promotion of hitherto under-represented groups to public office; a relatively liberal approach to social and cultural issues in comparison with Stalin's period of office; and a 'thaw' in international relations. Women's experiences and the gendered dimensions of Khrushchev's reforms are examined in detail in the chapters that follow.

In Chapter 1 Melanie Ilič outlines the demographic trends and the major economic, social and political policy initiatives of the Khrushchev era in respect of the role and status of women, providing a background and context for the more detailed studies that follow. The chapter also introduces contemporary Soviet debates on 'equality' and gender difference. The limits to Khrushchev's reforms are clearly indicated by reference to the complaints aired in the women's press and in the newspapers.

Donald Filtzer (Chapter 2) draws on evidence presented by the available statistical data and in largely unpublished Soviet doctoral dissertations examining the impact of the shift towards intensive production on the employment of women in industry. Filtzer argues that the maintenance of stable labour relations under Khrushchev was dependent, in part, on the continued marginalisation and exploitation of women in the workplace.

In Chapter 3 Michaela Pohl shifts our focus to the rural economy by examining the experiences of women who were recruited to take part in Khrushchev's Virgin Lands project. The harsh realities of women's everyday lives in the *tselina* are revealed in archival records and the oral testimonies of the settlers.

Kristin Roth-Ey (Chapter 4) examines various aspects of the youth culture of the thaw generation through a study of the 1957 Moscow International Youth Festival. This chapter provides insight into the ways in which Soviet sexual mores, the construction of female identity and gender relations were portrayed in contemporary popular media.

Deborah Field (Chapter 5) provides further evidence of what a number of recent historians have identified as a shift towards state paternalism under Khrushchev through her study of the contemporary pedagogic debates on child rearing and the examination of local court hearings on questions relating to child protection.

Taking as examples *The Cranes are Flying* and *Ballad of a Soldier*, John Haynes in Chapter 6 investigates the reconstruction of Soviet motherhood in the cinema of the Khrushchev era and argues that the cultural context of gender construction was less dogmatically masculine in these years.

The memoir and autobiographical literatures of the Khrushchev era, Marianne Liljeström argues in Chapter 7, also provided a forum for the renewed discourse on sexual equality, as well as providing the opportunity for women to reassess their own personal and revolutionary identities within the currently defined gender boundaries.

Susan Reid (Chapter 8) moves our focus to the domestic interior by examining the impact of the improvement in living standards on shifting Soviet definitions of taste and design in furnishing the home, the responsibility for which was regarded as lying almost exclusively within women's realm.

With the home still in mind, Lynne Attwood in Chapter 9 examines the differential access to accommodation and household goods in the Khrushchev era, a period in which there was a gradual shift towards the single-family apartment. The particularities of Soviet housing policy and design, she argues, complicated the traditionally gendered distinction between the public and the private.

Chapter 10 by Irina Paert offers a focused study of Khrushchev's anti-religious campaigns with specific references to their impact on women believers. The anti-religious campaigns are studied as evidence of the further secularisation and Sovietisation of society under Khrushchev.

Sue Bridger in Chapter 11 completes our studies with an examination of the first space flight piloted by a woman. Valentina Tereshkova's achievements are examined in the light of their propaganda value in the age of Cold War, the international arena of the arms and space races, and the Soviet promotion of women as symbols of peace.

Notes

1   For English-language, book-length studies that offer coverage of women in the Khrushchev era, see: S. Bridger, *Women in the Soviet Countryside: Women's Roles in Rural Development in the Soviet Union* (Cambridge, 1987); D. Brown (ed.), *The Role and Status of Women in the Soviet Union* (New York, 1968); G. Browning, *Women and Politics in the USSR: Consciousness Raising and Soviet Women's Groups* (London, 1987); M. Buckley, *Women and Ideology in the Soviet Union* (London, 1989); N. T. Dodge, *Women in the Soviet Economy: Their Role in Economic, Scientific, and Technical Development* (Baltimore, 1966); G. W. Lapidus, *Women in Soviet Society: Equality, Development, and Social Change* (Berkeley, 1978); A. McAuley, *Women's Work and Wages in the Soviet Union* (London, 1981); D. L. Ransel, *Village Mothers: Three Generations of Change in Russia and Tataria* (Bloomington, 2000). Some of the journal literature is identified in the notes to the chapters and the bibliography contained in this book. For some of the legal changes introduced in this period, see *Soviet Legislation on Women's Rights: Collection of Normative Acts* (Moscow, 1978).

2 Buckley, op. cit., p. 140.
3 These contradictions are explored more fully later in the book – see particularly Chapters 7 and 8. See V. Buchli, *An Archaeology of Socialism* (Oxford, 1999), P. H. Juviler, *Revolutionary Law and Order* (New York, 1976), O. Kharkhodin, *The Collective and the Individual in Russia: a Study of Practices* (Berkeley, 1999), and A. Troitsky, *Back in the USSR* (Boston, 1988).

1
Women in the Khrushchev Era: an Overview

Melanie Ilič

This chapter provides an overview of the changing roles and status of women in the Soviet Union in the Khrushchev era (1956–64), incorporating many of the issues that will be discussed in more detail in subsequent chapters.[1] In this period of tentative de-Stalinisation, Khrushchev gave new impetus to the 'woman question' and reversed a number of important legal decisions concerning women and the family that had been introduced in the 1930s and 1940s.[2] The outcome of the population losses and demographic imbalance resulting from the Second World War was that considerable emphasis was now placed on the health and welfare of women, in particular concerning their reproductive rights and maternal responsibilities. The relative economic prosperity of the post-war years provided additional material benefits and home comforts for all Soviet citizens, as well as bringing about changes in the conditions of employment in both industry and agriculture. The scope of production was now extended to the newly developing territories and settlements of the 'Virgin Lands'. These changes inevitably impacted on the lives of women.

A new lease of life was given to women's social and political organisations, and women's representation in the various organs of government and administration increased substantially. Soviet women participated in, and convened, a number of important international conferences in these years. Whole generations of women, who had been active in, or eyewitness to, the events of the Russian revolutions of 1905 and 1917, were reaching old age by the 1950s, and they were now encouraged to record and publish their memoirs (see Chapter 7). In the public as well as the private realm, then, the Khrushchev era saw Soviet women once more propelled into the limelight, and, most startlingly of all, even into space.

In preparing this chapter, I have drawn heavily on a number of Soviet women's magazines that enjoyed mass circulation in the Khrushchev era. Most notable amongst these are *Rabotnitsa* (Woman Worker), *Krest'yanka* (Peasant Woman) and *Zhenshchiny mira* (Women of the World, published by the Russian Women's International Democratic Federation). During the Khrushchevian 'thaw' in international relations the Soviet Union explored and extended its communications with other countries, sometimes with the aid of the foreign language press. The magazine *Soviet Woman*, the monthly publication of the Soviet Women's Anti-Fascist Committee and the All-Union Central Council of Trade Unions, was circulated widely in the Western world and developing countries. Newspaper reports have provided interesting and important additional sources of information.[3] The press media are an important source for exploring both the dissemination of official policy directives and the airing of popular opinion, taking into account the editorial constraints of the magazines and newspapers under review.

Statistical indicators[4]

In the years following the Second World War, the Soviet Union experienced a critical demographic imbalance in that the number of women vastly outstripped the number of men. The sex (and age) imbalance of the population was not fully rectified even by the end of the Khrushchev era in 1964. The consequences of this were that, in a society where marriage was the overwhelming norm, many older women were left widowed and younger women were less likely to find a husband. Single motherhood, therefore, was not uncommon in these years, and it did not carry with it the same negative social stigma as it did in the West. In view of the population losses suffered during the war, the Soviet government was keen to increase the overall birth rate. Regular monthly social welfare benefits were paid to mothers of large families, defined as those with four or more children, and financial assistance was offered to single mothers. In addition, mothers of large families were awarded honorific titles and medals. Efforts were also made to expand state-funded childcare provision.

Despite this, there was no increase in the birth rate during the Khrushchev era – in reality, the birth rate dropped a little. However, the levels of recorded infant mortality did decline dramatically, and this was doubtless partly the result of the increases in financial aid and improvements in the medical services provided for expectant women and new mothers during the Khrushchev period. Average life expectancy increased, especially among women, who were predicted to live several years longer than men. For those born in 1963–64, average life expectancy for the Soviet population as a whole was cited as 70 years, and for women in particular 73 years.

According to official census data, women constituted 52.1 per cent of the Soviet population in 1939, but this had risen to 55 per cent by 1959. The sex imbalance of the Soviet population was most evident in the older age groups. Hereafter, however, the imbalance began to show signs of correction. A steady fall in the proportion of women in the Soviet population was registered from the beginning of the 1960s, as the number of men outstripped women in the under-35 age cohort. Despite this, even by 1 January 1965 women still constituted 54.3 per cent of the Soviet population. Overall for the USSR, the demographic imbalance was slightly more evident in rural than urban areas. Women were less geographically mobile than men, and they remained tied to the land and to the agricultural economy in ways that men were not.

Since the 1930s, the Soviet Union had had a notable and successful record of drawing women into paid employment. By the outbreak of the Second World War in 1941, women constituted roughly 40 per cent of paid workers in the Soviet Union, and this had risen to 55 per cent by the end of the war. This proportion inevitably fell as men returned from the front. Nevertheless, by the beginning of the Khrushchev era, in 1956 women still equalled 45 per cent of those in paid employment, and this proportion rose steadily for many years thereafter. By 1964 women constituted 49 per cent of the Soviet labour force. The increasing trend of female employment was most advanced in the European republics of the Soviet Union, and specific policies were introduced to encourage women into paid employment in other areas of the country.

Outside of agriculture, where women continued to dominate in collective farm production, the greatest numbers of women, by far, were employed in the industrial sector, and here they remained concentrated in the light industries (for example, in textiles and sewing, other clothing manufacture and food preparation). More notable about the Khrushchev era, though, is the trend towards the increasing feminisation of particular areas of employment. Building on a pattern of development evident for many years, health care was heavily feminised by 1964. By this time women also predominated in trade and public services, such as catering, in communications, the administration of finance, in education and lower-level scientific work, and women were beginning to predominate in civil service-type jobs. Needless to say, this increasing trend towards women's employment and the feminisation of certain areas of work was less marked in the higher echelons of executive office and management. Where women did hold senior management positions, this was more likely to be in the health care sector or in educational facilities where women already formed the bulk of employees.

The increasing proportional employment of women, and in white-collar jobs in particular, was facilitated in part by the improvements in the levels of educational attainment recorded among women. By the end of 1964, women constituted 63 per cent of students with specialist further education, and they were 53 per cent of graduates in higher education. Again, though, at the highest levels of educational attainment, women were less in evidence. Women were far less likely than men to hold the post of professor or to be awarded an academic doctorate. In contrast, by 1964, 74 per cent of medical doctors were women, and this marked a decline from 76 per cent in 1958.

The final area of the statistical indicators that concerns us here is the election of women to public office and their membership of political and social organisations. In 1962, 390 women were elected as deputies to the USSR Supreme Soviet. This meant that women constituted 27 per cent of the elected representatives at the highest level of legislative decision-making. They were elected in higher proportions to the various subordinate government and administrative bodies. In 1963, women were elected to around one-third of the Supreme Soviets of the Union and Autonomous Republics. At the lower levels of government and administration, women constituted 42.7 per cent of deputies on local soviets and workers' councils in 1965.

In the organisations of the Communist Party of the Soviet Union (CPSU), of members with voting rights at the extraordinary XXI Congress of the CPSU in 1959, still only 17.5 per cent were women. In contrast, girls and younger women made up 44.5 per cent of Komsomol (the Youth Communist League) recruits. Women also made up roughly one-half of trade union members. However, we should also note here that women were far less likely than men to be recognised for their active political participation, public service or outstanding economic performance by the award of honorific titles and medals. Only approximately one-third of such awards were made to women in total up to 1963, and women were only one-quarter of those who had been awarded the Order of Lenin.

Maternity[5]

One of the concerns of the early Khrushchev administration appears to have been a desire to tackle the demographic crisis and the social position of women head on. One of the stated directives of the 1956 XX Party Congress for the period of the sixth Five-Year Plan was a commitment to 'improving in every way the working and living conditions of women workers and providing additional benefits for working mothers; in particular, longer leaves for pregnancy and childbirth'.[6] The congress also discussed the need to increase childcare provision, especially in rural areas, and the possibility of reducing the length of the working day for pregnant women and mothers with young children. These suggestions were greeted with much applause.[7] The law prohibiting abortion, introduced in 1936, had already been revoked in the previous year with the aim of reducing levels of infant mortality and improving women's health.

Accordingly, the Presidium of the USSR Supreme Soviet introduced regulations, applicable from 1 April 1956, which increased state-paid maternity leave from 77 to 112 days (the equivalent of eight weeks before plus eight weeks after confinement). Seventy days (ten weeks) of postnatal leave was granted for difficult and abnormal births. In effect, this marked a return to the maternity entitlements granted to women soon after the October Revolution in 1917, which had subsequently been foreshortened in the run-up to the war in the late 1930s.[8] Administrators, though, were keen to prevent any abuse of the system, either through pregnant women taking an excess amount of leave before the birth, however unwittingly, or through new mothers being pressurised to return to work before they had taken their full entitlement of 112 days' maternity leave.[9]

Despite promised increases and improvements in state-funded childcare, working women in particular still complained that not enough was being done to ease their situation. For example, in letters to *Rabotnitsa* women complained that the crèches and nurseries were not open at times that matched work schedules. If a woman did not finish work until six o'clock in the evening, how was she supposed to be able to collect her child from a nursery that also shut at six?[10] What were working mothers to do if crèches closed even earlier?[11] These issues remained unresolved. The Soviet family was sustained through many decades via reliance on the network of the extended family. The grandmother (*babushka*) was an essential component of domestic childcare arrangements. Other long-standing complaints were also now re-aired in the press. Pregnant women and new mothers were still being illegally dismissed from their jobs, and they were still being denied their full entitlements to maternity leave and holiday, as well as financial payments while on leave.[12] Insufficient attention was still being paid to the rights and statutory working conditions of nursing mothers.[13]

On the other hand, the joys of motherhood, and especially large families, were now exalted in the press.[14] There was also some discussion on the situation of single mothers.[15] Advice was offered to women on how to care for themselves before and during pregnancy, how to care for their babies after the birth, and about their legal entitlements as mothers.[16] The mother's role in childcare and general upbringing and education was also an issue raised in the women's press.[17] In some cases, and especially where teenage children were concerned, a generation gap was much in evidence.[18] Personal experiences of abortion and infertility now found their way into women's magazines.[19] The issue of women's health was of concern to the writers and readers of women's magazines. The medical advice offered by the magazines was supposed to replace the 'old wives' tales' and interference of unqualified local midwives in the care of babies and young children.[20]

The designation of 'illegitimacy' was discussed and challenged, with some observers calling for a revision of the 8 July 1944 family law, which had introduced a legal distinction between children born within and outside of wedlock, largely because unregistered 'marriages' were no longer recognised. The space for the name of the father was left blank on the official documentation of 'illegitimate' children. The 1944 law had also restricted access to divorce. The issues of child abandonment, institutionalised childcare and adoption were also occasionally raised in the press.[21] During the Khrushchev era, the difficulties experienced by women in combining motherhood, household responsibilities and professional commitments (the 'triple burden') were taken seriously by policy makers and were widely debated in the press, often spearheaded by the cultural–literary newspaper, *Literaturnaya gazeta*.[22]

Managing the home

The spheres of the family and the home were constructed as a predominantly female realm (see Chapter 8). One article in *Rabotnitsa* put it this way: 'what housewife does not want to see in her apartment nice, pretty, affordable furniture? But you can never find it in the shops', clearly attributing responsibility for furnishing the home to the female domestic manager.[23] The newspaper *Izvestiya* asked rhetorically in June 1960, 'and who but the wife can best look after the cleanliness and neatness of the house?'[24] On the subject of domestic labour, though, the Soviet Union (intoning Lenin) continued to boast of 'the gradual liberation of women from housework'. This was to be achieved, on the one hand, through the expansion of public services (canteens, child-care, laundries, etc.) and improvements in the technologies of domestic goods, and, on the other hand, via the redistribution of household tasks among family members. The Seven-Year Plan (1958–65) placed great emphasis on raising living standards and improving the material situation of the Soviet population, and this goal became one of the major features of the Khrushchev era. Women's domestic chores would be eased, in theory at least, by the expansion and increase in production of basic foodstuffs and clothing materials, and the manufacture of household appliances, such as refrigerators and sewing machines.[25] In October 1959, the USSR Council of Ministers and the Central Committee of the CPSU introduced a decree 'on measures to raise production, expand the range and improve the quality of products of cultural-daily life significance [MI: that is, radios, televisions, etc.] and household appliances'.[26] These promised goods, however, were slow to materialise and women were left, as ever, doing arduous household chores, such as the laundry, by hand.[27]

Despite these public pronouncements, time budget surveys revealed, as they had done in the 1920s, that women continued to spend considerably more of their 'free time' on housework and food preparation, and less time sleeping, than men. The outcome of this, of course, was that women had less time to spend on improving their qualifications, cultural activities, hobbies and sports.[28] Yet in assigning women responsibility for household management, the Soviet government also sought ways to alleviate the domestic burden. For example, the newly constructed apartment blocks in the south-east region of Moscow were to be fitted out with canteens where ready prepared food could be purchased cheaply and served up at home.[29] A self-service launderette was set up in house number 33 on Moscow's prestigious Leningradskii Prospekt, equipped with five 'snow white automatic washing machines'. Here, all of the laundry could supposedly be done in half an hour.[30] Women were encouraged to make use of such facilities in order to save the time and trouble of doing the work themselves at home.[31]

Another recognised way of lifting the burden on women was the redistribution of household tasks among other family members.

Literaturnaya gazeta even asked 'why ... is the opinion that the main burden of caring for a child should fall on the mother so persistent among us?' The newspaper called on fathers to play a more active role in child rearing.[32] *Rabotnitsa* received an enthusiastic response to its call to men to take greater responsibility around the house and to share more equally in domestic tasks. The type of husband who expected his wife to make personal sacrifices so that she could wait on him around the house and service the home was criticised in the women's press.[33]

Nevertheless, the idea of the female-dominated domestic sphere remained deeply embedded. A further area in which the state-sponsored press sought to educate its female readership was in household management and domestic economy. Reports began to appear that were critical of women's disdain for housework and their ignorance of basic tasks around the home. This was regarded to be the case especially among younger and more highly educated women.[34] Publications began to appear offering women advice on running the home and basic cooking, as well as on personal hygiene.[35] The two-volume *Short Encyclopaedia of Housekeeping* was hailed by *Pravda* as a 'fine gift to women'.[36] Despite all of the attention paid to female domesticity, in reality this was still a realm in which women had responsibility rather than authority. The husband and father was still considered to be the head of the household – and accommodation was assigned accordingly (see Chapter 9).[37]

Domestic bliss and marital discord

With the aim of cultivating better manners and improving the moral standing of its citizens, the Soviet state found no difficulties in making pronouncements on the conduct of personal relationships (see also Chapter 5). In December 1961 and January 1962, *Komsomol'skaya pravda*, the official newspaper of the communist youth organisation, published the results of a public opinion survey among young people to canvass their views on love, marriage and the family. The answers to many of the survey questions were much as would be expected: marriage at a young age and after a relatively short engagement carried pitfalls; insufficient state and social support was being offered to young families, especially working mothers; people were marrying for the wrong reasons; and so on. From one male respondent, however, there was a particularly strident response:

> Is it true that the woman has the inferior status in the family? It seems to me that it will soon be necessary to talk of the 'emancipation' of

men... . In my opinion, it is time to stop shouting about helping women.

He claimed to know a number of families where the husband participated extensively in housework, but the wife did little. He concluded,
'the break-up of young families I explain by the absence of the
necessary domestic skills in the wife'.[38]

In the opinion of one journalist writing in *Pravda Ukrainy*, 'in our
socialist milieu the marriage that is not for love is almost extinct'. She
was, however, most interested in the causes of marital disharmony. She
argued that bad relationships were the result of impetuous youth,
housing shortages, stress at work and an imbalance in the division of
domestic labour. Such pressures could be the cause of serious arguments. Many arguments, she claimed, depended on the whim of the
wife, and she blamed these disputes on 'survivals of the capitalist past
... – ... vodka and jealousy'. She concluded her article by entreating
wives not to undermine their husbands in front of friends, and to serve
as their defenders rather than their prosecutors.[39]

In contrast, the readers and editors of the women's magazines
identified a different range of causes for marital unrest. The letters
pages often reported incidences of domestic strife caused by such
factors as male alcoholism, the husband's failure to help around the
house and with childcare (which many men continued to see as
'women's business'), or by men's reluctance to offer any of their wages
towards housekeeping expenses, preferring instead to spend the money
on drink and cigarettes.[40] The broader issue of male violence was also
now openly discussed in the press, and this included actual cases of
domestic violence resulting in the murder of the wife.[41] One example
of domestic violence came from the Kirghiz republic, where a young
woman complained of having been abducted and forcibly married to a
man she had never met before. Her family offered her no support
when she ran away and asked them for help.[42] Similar stories appeared,
offering insights into marriage customs and practices in the predominantly Muslim Central Asian republics.[43] The press also condemned
the religious practices of all denominations and belief in superstitions
that maintained the inequality of women.[44]

One solution to marital difficulties was believed to lie in the revision
of the divorce laws, including the possibility of divorce by mutual
consent, but this, on the whole, received relatively little attention in the
press.[45] Further evidence of crimes of violence against women and
sexual abuse began to be discussed more openly. This included reporting

on the court cases of rape trials, for example.[46] Towards the end of the Khrushchev era there were also debates in the press on issues such as premature and premarital sex (see also Chapter 4).[47]

Women in the Soviet countryside[48]

One of the initiatives introduced by Khrushchev at the XX Party Congress in 1956 was a programme of extensive agricultural reform.[49] The Khrushchev era is closely associated with a radical shake-up of the rural economy, the mechanisation of agricultural production, the mass planting of maize as a staple crop and the 'Virgin Lands' scheme (see Chapter 3). Even so, many rural areas, even by the early 1960s, were poorly supplied with the most basic amenities and public services. It could be argued, then, that it was in such underdeveloped areas that women's lives were the harshest. Peasant women were expected to contribute to work on the collective farms, as well as having the virtually exclusive care of the family's private plot and livestock, the children and the household. Soviet rural women had a relatively restricted education; they worked from an early age, married young and tended to have more children than their urban counterparts. Their familial responsibilities could become an overwhelming burden.[50]

In reality, the promise to mechanise agricultural production benefited men rather than women. The new machines were in very short supply.[51] Men were still given priority in access to and use of mechanised equipment, and women were left with the routine, repetitive and often laborious manual tasks.[52] For example, the introduction of mechanised equipment for harvesting cotton, the 'white gold' of Central Asia, was met with 'inertia and conservatism'. *Pravda* reported that 'the officials of many farms believe that women are unable to operate machines', and one collective farm chairman argued, 'what do I need women drivers for? The farm has 25 male machine operators. The women are just a lot of bother.'[53] The article noted that in many areas women had little access to training courses; once trained, they often did not find work with machines, and if they did, the machinery was often in a poor state of repair.[54]

Nevertheless, occasional reports did appear in the magazines of minor success stories by women in mechanised agricultural production. A key feature in these stories, as had been the case two decades earlier, were women's achievements as tractor drivers.[55] Their achievements in the use of mechanised agricultural equipment in general were celebrated in Moscow in June 1964 at a three-day All-Union conference-seminar of

women mechanisers.[56] Yet, as would be expected, machine
and especially tractor driving remained dominated by m¢
report in *Krest'yanka* noted that some men felt that physical
farms was beneath them. As a consequence, men dominated, too, in the
running and management of collective farms.[58] The absence of female
leadership on the collective farms was often commented on in the
press.[59] The situation is clearly illustrated in a cartoon that appeared in
Krest'yanka: an official is depicted examining the photos of the progressive workers in collective farm labour. He asks in surprise, 'All women
... but where are the men?' 'Here they are!' comes the reply as his host
points to the row of men facing the display, and they are all carrying
briefcases labelled 'chairman', 'deputy', 'director'.[60] A further issue,
raised by the readers of *Rabotnitsa*, was the emphasis placed on the
manufacture of machinery to aid crop production in the fields. Where
was the machinery to assist in livestock production, where women were
mostly employed?[61] Heavy manual labour by women, then, remained a
characteristic feature of Soviet agricultural production throughout the
Khrushchev era.

Women in industrial employment

By the 1950s, many millions of women were employed in Soviet industrial enterprises (see Chapter 2). Yet despite the fact that the industrial
employment of women had become common practice, some commentators raised objections against it. One observer, V. I. Nemtsov, gave his
views on 'respect for women' in a series of articles published in
Literaturnaya gazeta in 1958, offering at the same time a critique of
recent fictional portrayals of women workers. Nemtsov argued that
heavy physical labour stripped women of their femininity and diverted
them from the path of motherhood. He claimed that younger women,
with no familial responsibilities, were misguided in wanting to hold
down relatively highly paid jobs. He criticised their aspirations to pur-
chase fine fabrics: 'is velvet or fine wool really the most important
thing in girls' lives?'[62] Like many before and after him, his discussion
drew on what he believed to be natural divisions: 'readers' letters
include many just observations about girls who, doing a man's job that
is not natural for them, try to keep up with the men in other respects
and take to smoking and even drinking vodka'.[63] The official response
to this series of articles was an announcement by the Ministry of Public
Health that, in collaboration with the trade unions, the lists of jobs
determining the scope of women's employment were already under

review.[64] The decree that had allowed women to work underground in mining during the war had already been revoked in 1957, and women were subsequently banned from work on fishing fleets from 1960.[65]

When the preliminary returns of the 1959 census became available, it became evident to Soviet planners that the country had significant untapped labour reserves. If the economy was to expand as intended, a higher proportion of the working-age population needed to be drawn into 'social production'. These included 'persons engaged in house-work and personal auxiliary farming'.[66] In practice, these were predominantly women of working age not currently in paid employment, estimated to constitute up to one-quarter of potential workers in some areas of the country. It was also claimed that the collective farms were overstaffed. In order to draw more people into industrial employment, and women in particular, it was recognised that vast improvements had to be made in public services: in particular, childcare facilities, including the number of spaces available at boarding schools; and public catering, which would 'play an important part in freeing women from the household'.[67]

Here, then, were two rather contradictory approaches to women's industrial employment. The argument that heavy industrial labour was inappropriate for women created a problem for economic planners, who saw the expansion of industrial production as being dependent on the recruitment of hitherto unutilised labour reserves, most of whom were women. The possible solution lay in the proposals put forward at the XXI Party Congress for the mechanisation of the production process. Mechanisation, it was argued, would eliminate heavy manual labour. Furthermore, the expansion of public services would liberate women from the demands of household labour. In the opinion of Olimpiada Nefedova, a senior representative of the textiles and light industry workers on the Central Committee of Trade Unions, such a process would allow Soviet women to enjoy equality not only on paper, but also in reality.[68]

The Khrushchev era, then, promised significant advances in the mechanisation of industrial production and improvements in the working conditions of women. In the success stories reported in the press, mechanisation brought many benefits to women, including the opportunity to earn higher wages and a reduction in manual labour.[69] In reality, as was the case in the agricultural sector, in many women's experiences these changes were slow to materialise and many industrial processes continued to be very labour intensive.[70] Mariya Alekseevna Sokolova complained to *Rabotnitsa* that every morning she listened to the radio and read the newspapers, and her heart raced: 'but you go to work ... and see that everything is as it was twenty years ago. Can manual labour be replaced by machines, or is this impossible?'[71] She was particularly concerned because she worked in a small-scale workshop, where mechanisation was having little impact.

Improvements in women's working conditions were also little in evidence. Soviet newspapers and magazines were quick to pick up on violations of the labour code, especially as they impacted on women. There was considerable discussion of cases involving illegal sackings and the widespread employment of women in violation of the terms set out in the labour code.[72] The trade union newspaper, *Trud*, however, was forthright in its defence of Soviet work practices in the face of international criticism. *Trud* argued that reported violations of labour laws were 'isolated examples'.[73] In reality, though, it is likely that minor infringements were extremely common. Women's lives were made more difficult by the fact that there were sometimes no proper bathroom facilities at their place of work, and laundries, household goods shops and food stores were not located near to the factory or their homes.[74] Little was actually being done, it was argued, to improve women's working conditions.[75] The press led the call for changes. If there were to be any reduction in the length of the workday, then it should be applied in the first instance to women.[76]

Other issues raised in the press included: improvements in workplace services, such as canteens; the role of Soviet trade unions in protecting women's interests at work; equal pay for equal work; and the shortage of job opportunities for women in communities dominated by mining and metallurgical industries, and the unfavourable living conditions in these areas.[77] One suggestion here was that light industries should be relocated or established in these areas to provide work opportunities for the women who already lived there. *Rabotnitsa* also discussed the problems arising from the failure to supply adequate protective clothing to women workers, such as shoes of the correct size, since many such items were manufactured with male workers in mind.[78]

Women in politics and social activism

On paper, the 1936 constitution of the USSR guaranteed Soviet women equal rights with men in all areas of economic, state, cultural and sociopolitical life. The Khrushchev era saw much encouragement given to the revival of women's political and social activism and to their participation in decision-making at all levels. Much publicity was given to women's representation on official state and party bodies, and to their participation in local government, sociopolitical organisations and volunteer work. The first woman to be appointed to the Presidium, Yekaterina Furtseva, took up her office in 1957 and held the post until 1961. The Committee of Soviet Women, under the presidency of Nina Vasil'evna Popova from February 1958, was an important political body in the Khrushchev era. The committee had a prominent diplomatic role and promoted the ideas of world peace and equal rights for women.[79] In March 1958, 366 women (26.4 per cent of the total) were elected to the USSR Supreme Soviet. This was reported as testament to 'Soviet democracy and the genuine equality of women in our country'.[80] In 1959, 222 women from all walks of life and from all over the country served as delegates at the XXI Congress of the CPSU.[81] At the lower levels of decision-making and organisation, by the late 1950s women's councils (*zhensovety*) had been revived, and women were actively encouraged to become volunteer activists (*obshchestvennitsy*) in their local communities.

The *zhensovety* campaigned for improvements in services for women, and there were calls for them to be established particularly in rural areas by the early 1960s.[82] Their remit extended to commenting on local childcare provision and the supply of goods to their neighbourhood shops.[83] A snapshot of the work of the women's council in Chelyabinsk in 1963 was presented in *Rabotnitsa*. Seventeen women sat on the city *zhensovet*, but thousands more women were active in the factories and the apartment blocks in the region. At the Chelyabinsk tractor factory, the local *zhensovet* monitored the conditions of women's employment. In the central region, the *zhensovet* organised social–cultural evenings for women resident in the area, inviting along guest speakers and providing the opportunity for women to sing and dance together. In rural areas, educational lectures were delivered on maternity and childcare issues.[84] In rural areas in other parts of the country, the *zhensovety* were instrumental in establishing childcare facilities to meet the needs of working women, sometimes, by necessity, on a seasonal basis when women were required to work in the fields. *Krest'yanka* called on women to let the magazine know of their efforts.[85] Their successes were reported in subsequent issues.[86] Housewives were again encouraged, as they had been in the 1930s, to tackle social issues arising in their neighbourhoods.[87] *Rabotnitsa* ran a special page (*stranitsa obshchestvennitsy*) to report on their activities, as well as those of the *zhensovety*.[88]

In areas of the country where women were traditionally less active in public life, special campaigns were launched to mobilise women, not only into employment, but also into public office. Special women's congresses were convened in the various Central Asian republics, for example.[89]

Celebrating women's achievements at home and abroad[90]

The traditional day in the Soviet calendar for recognising and celebrating women's achievements was 8 March, International Women's Day. This was a designated public holiday, but by the Khrushchev era celebrations on this day had become something akin to, at best, Mothers' Day or Valentine's Day in the West. On an official level, congratulations were offered and awards were made to women and these were often reported in the press.[91] Popular celebrations of the day, however, took many different forms. Most involved offering token gifts – cards, flowers or chocolates – to wives, mothers and girlfriends. An eight-page special commemorative supplement for the fiftieth anniversary of International Women's Day was issued with *Rabotnitsa* in 1960.

At its worst, though, the day had become an opportunity for excess eating and drinking and male bonding, mostly serviced by women in the kitchen. The widespread male hypocrisy surrounding the celebration of International Women's Day was lambasted in the satirical magazine, *Krokodil*. In one cartoon, at a meeting to discuss preparations for the 8 March celebrations, the only woman in the audience is berated by her neighbour: 'but why are you still here? Go home, bake some pies: there's a holiday tomorrow!'[92] In another cartoon, sitting at a table laden with food and drink, drunken men raise their glasses to congratulate the women, who are rushing in and out of the room with freshly prepared dishes and dirty plates. In the same issue, a man is depicted asking his wife to deliver a box of chocolates to his boss's wife.[93]

Despite the denigration of International Women's Day at home, the post-war years offered many opportunities for Soviet women to forge international allegiances abroad. Khrushchev spearheaded a 'thaw' of the Cold War in international relations and a period of 'peaceful coexistence' with the Western powers. The Soviet Union opened its borders to foreign visitors and entered into constructive dialogue with Western and developing nations. In the 1950s and 1960s, women the world over, including Soviet women, came together as part of the Women's International Democratic Federation (WIDF, formed in 1945) to voice their opposition to world conflict.[94] They opposed an escalation of the arms race, and the use of atomic weaponry in particular.[95] The WIDF claimed over 200 million members worldwide by 1960.[96] Its activities were widely reported in the Soviet women's press.[97] The Soviet organisation of the WIDF also convened its own meetings.[98] Khrushchev spoke at one of these in October 1959.[99]

Moscow was host to the World Conference of Women, 24–29 June 1963. The congress was sponsored by the WIDF, now with Nina Popova as its vice-chair, and was attended by almost 2000 people from 114 countries. The event was also widely reported in the press.[100] Khrushchev's address to the congress indicated his belief in the critical role that women had to play in maintaining world peace: '... to yearn for peace is not enough. What is needed is energetic, truly heroic activity on a mass scale to avert a world war. You women have an especially great role to play here!'[101]

Equality

In many ways the Khrushchev era saw a reinvigoration of debates on 'equality' in the Soviet Union, partly centred on workplace practices, government and politics, but also involving other spheres of activity. Conferences were convened and books were published on this important topic. An international seminar on the 'Equality of Women in the USSR', with delegates from 37 countries, was held in Moscow in 1956.[102] The major reports were published as a book in the following year.[103] By the late 1950s and 1960s, Soviet representatives were taking part in a number of international congresses discussing women's rights, including those organised by the United Nations.[104] Soviet women attended the first International Congress of Working Women in Budapest, 14–17 June 1956.[105]

In effect, Soviet discourse on equality in these years called, as it had done earlier, for women to be fully involved in both the productive economy and the domestic sphere, as well as in the decision-making process. To a large extent, this was both an accommodationist strategy, as women had to fit themselves into predominantly male work practices, and a highly instrumental policy, because women were by now an essential component of the labour-intensive Soviet agricultural and industrial economies. The subtext of Yekaterina's Furtseva's speech (as deputy to the USSR Supreme Soviet) to an Indian women's conference in Madras in 1960 was that Soviet women's equality could be measured by the numerical absorption of women into traditional male spheres of activity – politics and employment, for example – and by granting them legal concessions and better access to public services. She stated that:

> Soviet society has put an end forever to the humiliation of women, wiped out once and for all everything that encroached on her dignity as a human being. Our women are inspired by the knowledge that they are playing a tremendous role in the life of society, that they are truly equals of men, that they enjoy the esteem and respect of the people.[106]

In some of the popular debates on the issue of equality the belief in the natural division of the sexes was much in evidence: 'One should not forget the qualities with which nature has endowed women. After all, a man likes to busy himself with an axe, a plane and a file, while a woman is more inclined toward needlework and sewing.'[107] This observer, though, did progress in her address to call for 'the final elimination of the unequal position of women in daily life, but most of all, for the liquidation of the underrating of their business qualities and abilities'.[108] The physiological differences between the sexes were especially emphasised during the first Soviet space flight piloted by a woman, Valentina Vladimirovna Tereshkova, on 16 June 1963[109] (see Chapter 11). V. Parin, from the USSR Academy of Medical Sciences, wrote that:

> I am sure the time will come when the crew of a spaceship will consist not of men alone but of both men and women. It is, after all, no accident that nature has united these quite different creatures: in their physiological qualities, in their abilities to perform various actions and in many habits and capabilities, men and women complement each other. The moral harmony tested by many years of 'earthly' experience will also serve its purpose in space.[110]

The chief designer of the spacecraft heralded the flight as 'one of the clearest indications of the equal rights of Soviet women, their activeness and their valour'.[111]

Many Soviet women were well aware of contemporary international debates on women's rights and sex equality. At a time when the post-war 'cult of domesticity' predominated in the West, they were willing to answer questions about why so many women worked in the Soviet

Union.[112] Olimpiada Nefedova called for women's rights and 'equality' to be implemented in reality as well as being enshrined in the law. What use was it to guarantee women's right to work, for example, as many Western countries had declared, if help was not provided for them to make this a reality? From the perspective of this campaigner, women's equality could best be guaranteed by improving their conditions of employment rather than eliminating them from the workplace altogether, which was a recognised common practice in the West.[113]

Conclusion

From the outline provided by this chapter of the major policy directives and initiatives introduced during Khrushchev's time in power, it is clear that the late 1950s and early 1960s saw the reopening of the 'woman question' in the Soviet Union. If we were to look at these policies on the role and status of women in isolation, we might easily be persuaded of their much-publicised achievements. A close examination of the women's press and mass-circulation newspapers (still under strict party/state control) in these years, however, provides an indication of the limits of these reforms in their conception, implementation and outcomes. The Khrushchev era reinvigorated the 'woman question' in the Soviet Union, but it by no means solved it. The scope and limitations of the Khrushchev era reforms in relation to women are discussed in more detail in the in-depth studies that follow.

Notes

1   For introductions to the Khrushchev era in Soviet history see D. Filtzer, *The Khrushchev Era: De-Stalinisation and the Limits of Reform in the USSR* (Basingstoke, 1993), M. McCauley (ed.), *Khrushchev and Khrushchevism* (Basingstoke, 1987), and W. Taubman et al. (eds), *Nikita Khrushchev* (Yale, 2000). These books have little to say about women. On women, see D. Brown, *Role and Status of Women in the Soviet Union* (1968), and D. Filtzer, *Soviet Workers and De-Stalinization* (Cambridge, 1992). Filtzer's detailed study of the labour conditions of women workers is reprinted in edited form in this volume.

2   The 'woman question' had been declared solved under Stalin in 1930, and the Women's Department of the Communist Party of the Soviet Union, the *Zhenotdel*, had been closed down. For a more detailed examination of Soviet women in the period from the 1920s to the 1940s, see M. Ilič (ed.), *Women in the Stalin Era* (Basingstoke, 2001).

3   Useful English-language summaries of Soviet newspaper and journal reports are to be found in *Current Digest of the Soviet Press* (hereafter *CDSP*).

4   The statistical data on which this section is based are drawn from: 'Zhenshchini v SSSR', *Vestnik statistiki*, no. 1, 1966, pp. 86–96; *Women in the USSR: Brief Statistics* (Moscow, 1960); *Women and Children in the USSR: Brief Statistical Returns* (Moscow, 1963); and 'Women in the USSR – Facts and Figures', *CDSP*, no. 12, 1960, pp. 22–5 (complete text from *Partiinaya zhizn'*, no. 4, 1960, pp. 58–61). See also 'Defenders of Peace, Progress and the Happiness of Children', *CDSP*, no. 10, 1957, pp. 33–4 (excerpt from *Pravda*, 8 March 1957).

5   The cinematic representations of maternity and the family are discussed in more detail in Chapter 6.

6   See 'The Speeches at the Party Congress – Concluded', *CDSP*, no. 20, 1956, p. 23 (complete text from *Pravda*, 26 February 1956).

7   Ibid.

8   See M. Ilič, *Women Workers in the Soviet Interwar Economy: From 'Protection' to 'Equality'* (Basingstoke, 1999), Ch. 5.

9   See, for example, 'Change the System of Pregnancy and Childbirth Leaves', *CDSP*, no. 51, 1956, p. 23 (condensed text from *Meditsinsky rabotnik*, 20 November 1956).

10   N. Amburg, 'Chto volnuet materei?', *Rabotnitsa*, no. 2, 1956, p. 29.

11   Z. Savchenko, 'Pros'ba materei', *Rabotnitsa*, no. 7, 1956, p. 27.

12   'Otvechaem chitatelyam', *Rabotnitsa*, no. 9, 1957, p. 29; 'Yuridicheskaya konsul'tatsiya', *Rabotnitsa*, no. 9, 1960, p. 29.

13   'Otvechaem chitatelyam', *Rabotnitsa*, no. 1, 1957, p. 29.

14   S. Dzerzhinskaya, 'Uchite zhit' dlya drugikh', *Rabotnitsa*, no. 11, 1956, p. 11; M. Volodyaeva, 'Zapiski mnogodetnoi materi', *Rabotnitsa*, no. 8, 1958, pp. 25–7. See also 'A Big Family', *CDSP*, no. 16, 1959, p. 31 (condensed text from *Komsomol'skaya pravda*, 13 March 1959).

15   'Oni ne odinochki!', *Rabotnitsa*, no. 1, 1957, p. 15.

16   Ye. I. Kvater, 'Yesli vy gotovites' stat' mater'yu ...', *Rabotnitsa*, no. 8, 1959, pp. 27–8; K. Bazhenova, 'Vy zhdete rebenka ...', *Rabotnitsa*, no. 10, 1960, p. 29; 'Dlya materei', *Rabotnitsa*, no. 5, 1962, p. 29; Yu. Grigor'ev, 'Dlya budushchei materi', *Rabotnitsa*, no. 10, 1963, p. 31; I. Rozovskii, 'Chto nado znat' beremennoi zhenshchine', *Krest'yanka*, no. 5, 1962, pp. 30–1; I. Lyandres, 'Mastit', *Krest'yanka*, no. 8, 1962, p. 31.

17   'Govoryat materi', *Krest'yanka*, no. 8, 1956, p. 24.

18   '"I Hate Mother" – a Girl's Letter and Some Replies', *CDSP*, no. 24, 1964, pp. 18–20 (condensed text from *Komsomol'skaya pravda*, 17 May 1964).

19   See, for example, Ye. P. Maizel', 'Ne lishaite sebya materinstva!', *Rabotnitsa*, no. 11, 1957, p. 31; 'Pochemy ya ne mogu byt' mater'yu?', *Rabotnitsa*, no. 9, 1958, p. 30; I. Rozovskii, 'Abort', *Krest'yanka*, no. 8, 1961, p. 31.

20   V. Tankinov, 'O sueverii i predrassudakh', *Krest'yanka*, no. 4, 1956, p. 24; G. Akulenko, 'Po sledam odnogo pis'ma', *Krest'yanka*, no. 4, 1957, p. 25. See also D. Ransell, *Village Mothers: Three Generations of Change in Russia and Tataria* (Bloomington, Ind., 2000).

21   See, for example, 'Divorce Laws and the Status of Illegitimate Children', *CDSP*, no. 21, 1958, pp. 20–1 (complete text from *Izvestiya*, 22 May 1958); 'In the Interests of the Family', *CDSP*, no. 26, 1958, pp. 19–20 (complete text from *Izvestiya*, 26 June 1958); 'State and Law', *CDSP*, no.

23, 1959, p. 19 (complete text from *Izvestiya*, 9 June 1959); 'Right to a Family', *CDSP*, no. 17, 1960, pp. 27–8 (complete text from *Izvestiya*, 19 April 1960); 'Marriage Law and Illegitimacy's Stigma: a Dispute', *CDSP*, no. 21, 1960, pp. 13–14 (condensed text from *Literaturnaya gazeta*, 2 April 1960); 'Bigot in a Scholar's Toga', *CDSP*, no. 30, 1960, pp. 31–2 (complete text from *Literaturnaya gazeta*, 16 July 1960).

22   See, for example, 'Who is Right?', *CDSP*, no. 9, 1959, pp. 66–7 (complete text from *Literaturnaya gazeta*, 10 January 1959); 'Who Should Stand at the Stove?', *CDSP*, no, 25, 1960, pp. 29–30 (complete text from *Izvestiya*, 19 June 1960).

23   A. Dinov, 'Pervye shagi', *Rabotnitsa*, no. 9, 1958, pp. 18–19.

24   'Who Should Stand at the Stove?', *CDSP*, no. 25, 1960, p. 29.

25   *Zhenshchiny mira*, no. 12, 1958, pp. 4–6 outlined the plans, including those for housing construction. For a progress report after five years, see 'Shagaet pyatyi', *Rabotnitsa*, no. 1, 1963, pp. 4–5.

26   For more details, see I. I. Gordeevym, 'Dlya vas, zhenshchiny!', *Rabotnitsa*, no. 11, 1959, p. 22.

27   See the earlier complaints in L. Travkin, 'Gde vystirat' bel'e?', *Rabotnitsa*, no. 4, 1959, p. 26.

28   'An Analysis of How Workers Spend Off-Work Time', *CDSP*, no. 33, 1963, pp. 3–7 (complete text from *Voprosy ekonomiki*, no. 6, June 1963, pp. 32–41).

29   P. Kozhanyi, 'Domovaya kukhnya', *Rabotnitsa*, no. 5, 1958, p. 29.

30   A. Levina, 'Sluzhba byta, deistvui!', *Rabotnitsa*, no. 10, 1962, pp. 20–1.

31   See, for example, 'At Home', *CDSP*, no. 51, 1960, pp. 38–9 (condensed text from *Literaturnaya gazeta*, 10 December 1960).

32   Ibid., p. 38.

33   'Otkrovennyi razgovor', *Rabotnitsa*, no. 3, 1956, p. 30.

34   'Vitya asks for Porridge', *CDSP*, no. 21, 1957, pp. 34–5 (complete text from *Pravda*, 26 May 1957).

35   See, for example, A. G. Pap et al., *Gigiena zhenshchiny* (Kiev, 1964).

36   'A Fine Gift to Women', *CDSP*, no. 10, 1959, p. 31 (condensed text from *Pravda*, 9 March 1959).

37   For an example of a woman complaining about this, see 'Mozhet li zhenshchina byt' glavoi sem'i?', *Rabotnitsa*, no. 10, 1958, p. 23.

38   'Komsomol'skaya Opinion Poll on Family and Marriage', *CDSP*, no. 9, 1962, pp. 17–19 (complete texts from *Komsomol'skaya pravda*, 17 December 1961; condensed text from *Komsomol'skaya pravda*, 24 December 1961; complete and condensed texts from *Komsomol'skaya pravda*, 6 January 1962).

39   'You are a Wife', *CDSP*, no. 14, 1960, pp. 31–2 (complete text from *Pravda Ukrainy*, 27 March 1960).

40   See, for example, *Krest'yanka*, no. 9, 1957, letters page; Ye. Kononenko, 'Razgovor o semeinom schast'e', *Krest'yanka*, no. 3, 1958, pp. 7–8.

41   See, for example, A. Pershin, 'Chto sluchilos' v Yefremove ...', *Rabotnitsa*, no. 12, 1956, p. 29; 'Pust' penyaet na sebya tot, komu vodka dorozhe sem'i', *Rabotnitsa*, no. 9, 1958, p. 30.

42   'This is Your Fault, Fellow Villagers', *CDSP*, no. 48, 1962, pp. 30–1 (complete text from *Pravda*, 2 December 1962).

43 See, for example, N. Grigor'eva, 'Tri glavy', *Krest'yanka*, no. 3, 1963, pp. 2–5.

44 F. Olezhchuk, 'Religiya i zhenshchina', *Rabotnitsa*, no. 4, 1956, pp. 21–2; K. Voropaeva, 'Religiya unizhaet zhenshchinu', *Krest'yanka*, no. 8, 1958, pp. 25–6; R. Berkovich-Gurina, 'Ne obrashchaites' za pomoshch'yu k babkam!', *Krest'yanka*, no. 12, 1958, p. 29. For more on Khrushchev's anti-religious campaigns, see also Chapter 10.

45 'Divorce is a Serious Matter', *CDSP*, no. 21, 1958, pp. 21–2 (complete text from *Literaturnaya gazeta*, 24 May 1958). See also D. Field, 'Irreconcilable Differences: Divorce and Conceptions of Private Life in the Khrushchev Era', *Russian Review*, vol. 57, no. 4, 1998, pp. 599–613.

46 See, for example, 'Bitter End, Bitter Lesson', *CDSP*, no. 38, 1963, pp. 27–8 (condensed text from *Literaturnaya gazeta*, 17 August 1963).

47 'Should Newspapers Discuss Topic of Premarital Sex?', *CDSP*, no. 21, 1964, pp. 19–20 (complete text from *Sovetskaya pechat*, no. 4, April 1964, pp. 19–20).

48 See also S. Bridger, *Women in the Soviet Countryside: Women's Roles in Rural Development in the Soviet Union* (Cambridge, 1987).

49 This is outlined in 'Pyatiletka krutogo pod''ema sel'skogo khozyaistva', *Krest'yanka*, no. 4, 1956, pp. 9–10.

50 See the life story of Raya Sitnik outlined in 'The Dying Star', *CDSP*, no. 31, 1959, pp. 20–1 (complete text from *Izvestiya*, 4 August 1959), and *CDSP*, no. 41, 1959, pp. 25–6 (complete text from *Izvestiya*, 9 October 1959).

51 See the complaint in 'Posle sessii', *Krest'yanka*, no. 5, 1958, p. 2.

52 On manual labour, see G. Radov, 'Uvazhenie k rukam zhenskim', *Rabotnitsa*, no. 8, 1959, pp. 7–8.

53 'Advocates of Old Traditions', *CDSP*, no. 36, 1962, pp. 23–4 (complete text from *Pravda*, 4 September 1962).

54 For an earlier and more optimistic account of Central Asian women's access to farm machinery, see Z. Rakhimbabaeva, 'Ketmen' ukhodit v proshloe', *Krest'yanka*, no. 8, 1958, pp. 7–8.

55 L. Zhukhovitskii, 'Osobyi narod', *Krest'yanka*, no. 1, 1959, pp. 9–12; L. Petrova, 'Khorosho byt' traktoristkoi', *Krest'yanka*, no. 5, 1960, p. 31; K. Barantseva, 'Rabotaem po-novomu', *Krest'yanka*, no. 7, 1960, p. 14; 'Razgovor prodolzhaet chitatel'', *Krest'yanka*, no. 10, 1962, pp. 10–11. See also M. Ilič, '*Traktoristka*: Representations and Realities', in Ilič (ed.), *Women in the Stalin Era*, pp. 110–30.

56 For a report from the seminar, see *Krest'yanka*, no. 7, 1964, pp. 1–2.

57 'Nash trud budet proizvoditel'nee', *Krest'yanka*, no. 6, 1960, p. 29.

58 A. Korytova, 'Smelee vydvigat' zhenshchin', *Krest'yanka*, no. 1, 1957, p. 23.

59 D. L. Yenina and M. Lisova, 'O vnimanii i ravnodushii', *Krest'yanka*, no. 2, 1956, p. 27; M. Nazarov-Gashin, 'Nesostoyatel'naya teoriya', *Krest'yanka*, no. 1, 1963, pp. 16–17; V. Gofaizen, 'Nashi komandiry', *Krest'yanka*, no. 3, 1963, pp. 22–3 (for an illustration of a woman in a leadership position); 'Yest' kogo vydvigat'', *Krest'yanka*, no. 5, 1963, pp. 28–9. See also 'More Boldness, More Trust!', *CDSP*, no. 29, 1957, pp. 24–5 (condensed text from *Turkmenskaya iskra*, 4 July 1957).

60   *Krest'yanka*, no. 11, 1963, p. 27.
61   'Doyarka i ptichnitsa – professii industrial'nye', *Rabotnitsa*, no. 7, 1963, p. 9.
62   'A Word about Our Women', *CDSP*, no. 37, 1958, p. 6 (condensed text from *Literaturnaya gazeta*, 10 July 1958).
63   Ibid., p. 7.
64   'On Respect for Women', *CDSP*, no. 45, 1958, p. 24 (complete text from *Literaturnaya gazeta*, 17 June 1958).
65   N. Dodge, *Women in the Soviet Economy: Their Role in Economic, Scientific and Technical Development* (Baltimore, 1966), p. 70.
66   'Plans to Shift Women from Gardens, Kitchens to Jobs', *CDSP*, no. 5, 1961, p. 25 (condensed text from *Ekonomicheskaya gazeta*, 7 February 1961).
67   Ibid.
68   'Ravnopravie de-yure i de-fakto', *Zhenshchiny mira*, no. 2, 1960, pp. 20–1.
69   A. Khmelnitskaya, 'Does Mechanization Help the Worker?', *Soviet Woman*, no. 9, 1958, pp. 16–18; G. Yermolova, 'Avtomaty oblegchayut trud', *Rabotnitsa*, no. 10, 1956, p. 5.
70   'Nam nuzhna mekhanizatsiya', *Rabotnitsa*, no. 5, 1956, p. 20; 'Nam nuzhna mekhanizatsiya', *Rabotnitsa*, no. 11, 1956, p. 25; 'I podsobnye raboty nado mekhanizirovat'', *Rabotnitsa*, no. 5, 1958, p. 25; 'Mekhanizatsiya po-kustarnomu', *Rabotnitsa*, no. 7, 1959, p. 15.
71   'Shveinym atel'e – novuyu tekhniku', *Rabotnitsa*, no. 7, 1959, p. 14.
72   See the letter sent to the editor of *Rabotnitsa*, no. 2, 1958, pp. 25–6; 'Perevod na druguyu rabotu', *Rabotnitsa*, no. 6, 1958, p. 31; 'Uvol'nenie po sokrashcheniyu shtatov', *Rabotnitsa*, no. 11, 1959, p. 30; A. Petrova, 'When the Trade Union Has to Take Action ...', *Soviet Woman*, no. 2, 1956, p. 18.
73   'A Poor Effort', *CDSP*, no. 17, 1957, pp. 33–4 (condensed text from *Trud*, 25 April 1957).
74   Z. Shukyurova, 'V interesakh rabotnits', *Rabotnitsa*, no. 9, 1958, p. 13.
75   'Kogda zabyvayut ob okhrane truda ...', *Rabotnitsa*, no. 8, 1960, p. 26; 'Kogda zabyvayut ob okhrane truda', *Rabotnitsa*, no. 11, 1960, p. 32.
76   'Make Work Easier for Women in Production and Everyday Life', *CDSP*, no. 1, 1959, p. 27 (condensed text from *Pravda*, 3 January 1959).
77   I. Varlamova, 'Zametnye izmeneniya', *Rabotnitsa*, no. 7, 1956, pp. 12–13; L. Pozdnyakova, 'Zheny shakterov', *Rabotnitsa*, no. 3, 1957, p. 24; 'Eto tvoi profsoyuz, rabotnitsa!', *Rabotnitsa*, no. 1, 1958, p. 6; P. Sergeeva, 'Za ravnuyu oplatu truda', *Rabotnitsa*, no. 2, 1960, pp. 19–20; interview with V. V. Grishin, 'The Soviet Trade Unions and Women's Interests', *Soviet Woman*, no. 3, 1958, p. 8; 'Concerning Women's Work', *CDSP*, no. 49, 1958, p. 55 (condensed text from *Izvestiya*, 5 December 1958); 'Young Women Live in a Dormitory', *CDSP*, no. 28, 1964, pp. 13–15 (complete text from *Pravda*, 4 July 1964).
78   'Rabotnitsam – udobnuyu spetsodezhdu!', *Rabotnitsa*, no. 10, 1958, pp. 22–3; 'Shinitsy', *Rabotnitsa*, no. 11, 1960, p. 9; A. Levina, 'Khalat "Voobshche"', *Rabotnitsa*, no. 4, 1962, pp. 18–19; 'Khalat "Voobshche"', *Rabotnitsa*, no. 7, 1962, p. 9.
79   'Plenum komiteta sovetskikh zhenshchin', *Rabotnitsa*, no. 3, 1958, p. 15.

80 '366 Women Elected to the Supreme Soviet', *Soviet Woman*, no. 4, 1958, p. 4.

81 'Delegatki XXI s"ezda', *Rabotnitsa*, no. 2, 1959, pp. 16–17.

82 A. Blazhenkova, 'Ochen' nuzhen zhensovet', *Krest'yanka*, no. 6, 1960, p. 30; A. Shkarubo, 'Dobroe delo', *Krest'yanka*, no. 5, 1961, p. 23.

83 See, for example, Z. Bakhmach, 'Zhensovet deistvuet', *Rabotnitsa*, no. 5, 1958, p. 30.

84 'Sily v nikh kroyutsya neischislimye', *Rabotnitsa*, no. 2, 1963, p. 8.

85 'Pod kontrol' zhenskoi obshchestvennosti!', *Krest'yanka*, no. 5, 1962, p. 21.

86 See, for example, T. Kvitko, 'Vsekh del ne perechest'', *Krest'yanka*, no. 5, 1964, pp. 8–9.

87 M. Baranchikova, 'Zapiski obshchestvennitsy', *Rabotnitsa*, no. 12, 1956, pp. 26–7. See also M. Buckley, 'The Untold Story of the *Obshchestvennitsa* in the 1930s', in Ilič (ed.), *Women in the Stalin Era*, pp. 151–72.

88 See, for example, 'Pravil'no, Polina Ivanovna! – govoryat zhenshchiny-obshchestvennitsy', *Rabotnitsa*, no. 4, 1957, p. 11; 'Stranitsa obshchestvennitsy', *Rabotnitsa*, no. 9, 1957, pp. 19–20 (for an earlier report from Chelyabinsk); 'Stranitsa obshchestvennitsy', *Rabotnitsa*, no. 8, 1959, p. 12; Z. Samokina, 'Budni odnogo zhensoveta', *Rabotnitsa*, no. 4, 1964, p. 28.

89 V. Vavalina, 'S"ezd zhenshchin Uzbekistana', *Rabotnitsa*, no. 5, 1958, pp. 6–8; V. Vavalina, 'Khozyaiki strany', *Rabotnitsa*, no. 8, 1960, pp. 16–19 (Dagestan and Tadjikistan); Ye. Leont'eva, 'Na s"ezde zhenshchin Uzbekistana', *Krest'yanka*, no. 5, 1958, pp. 7–8; 'Congress of Women of Kazakhstan', *CDSP*, no. 30, 1961, p. 31 (complete text from *Pravda*, 25 July 1961).

90 For historical background, see C. Chatterjee, *Celebrating Women: Gender, Festival Culture, and Bolshevik Ideology, 1910–1939* (Pittsburgh, 2002).

91 See, for example, 'To Soviet Women', *CDSP*, no. 10, 1961, p. 32 (excerpts from *Pravda*, 8 March 1961), and 'Tireless Toilers, Active Fighters for Peace', *CDSP*, no. 10, 1963, p. 35 (excerpts from *Pravda*, 8 March 1963).

92 *Krokodil*, no. 7, 1956, p. 7.

93 *Krokodil*, no. 6, 1963, pp. 10, 15.

94 On the work of the Women's International Democratic Federation, see M. G. Gryzunova, *Mezhdunarodnaya demokraticheskaya federatsiya zhenshchin, 1945–1975* (Moscow, 1975).

95 E. Kotton, 'Sovetskim podrugam', *Rabotnitsa*, no. 3, 1956, p. 7. For background on Soviet women's involvement in international peace organisations, see V. Bil'shai, 'Zhenshchiny v bor'be za mir', *Krest'yanka*, no. 6, 1963, pp. 2–3, and N. Popova, 'For a World without Arms and Wars, a World without Slavery and Oppression', *Soviet Woman*, no. 12, 1960, pp. 2–3.

96 K. Dzanti, 'Nas 200 millionov!', *Rabotnitsa*, no. 12, 1960, p. 26.

97 See, for example, S. Kotova, 'Mat', Grazhdanka, Truzhenitsa', *Rabotnitsa*, no. 7, 1958, pp. 1–4; N. Popova, 'Navstrechu IV kongressu', *Krest'yanka*, no. 6, 1958, pp. 2–3; 'Manifest IV kongressa MDFZh', *Krest'yanka*, no. 7, 1958, pp. 2–3; Z. Fedorova, 'Golos zhenshchin Azii i Afriki', *Krest'yanka*, no. 4, 1961, p. 11; Z. Lebedeva, 'V bol'shoi pokhod za mir!', *Krest'yanka*,

no. 5, 1962, p. 2; L. Balakhovskaya, 'Navstrechu vsemirnomu kongressu zhenshchin', *Krest'yanka*, no. 2, 1963, p. 9; 'Sovetskie zhenshchiny vystupayut protiv atomnoi opasnosti', *Zhenshchiny mira*, no. 11, 1958, p. 9.

98   'Budem zashchishchat' mir!', *Krest'yanka*, no. 8, 1958, pp. 5–6.

99   L. Petrova, 'Khrushchev govoril ot imeni vsekh materei', *Rabotnitsa*, no. 12, 1959, p. 6.

100   L. Petrova, 'Vsemirnyi kongress zhenshchin budet v Moskve', *Rabotnitsa*, no. 2, 1963, p. 15; 'Navstrechu vsemirnomu kongressu zhenshchin v Moskve', *Rabotnitsa*, no. 5, 1963, p. 19; O. Khvalebnova, 'Pered vsemirnym kongressom zhenshchin', *Krest'yanka*, no. 4, 1963, pp. 4–5; 'Skoro kongress', *Krest'yanka*, no. 5, 1963, p. 11; M. Grineva, 'Moskva zhdet gostei', *Krest'yanka*, no. 6, 1963, pp. 14–15; 'K zhenshchinam vsekh kontinentov', *Krest'yanka*, no. 8, 1963, pp. 3–4; *Zhenshchiny mira*, no. 8, 1963, pp. 6–8, 22–3; 'World Women's Congress Ends without Unanimity', *CDSP*, no. 26, 1963, pp. 3–4 (condensed text from *Pravda* and *Izvestiya*, 25 June 1963); 'Erroneous Position', *CDSP*, no. 30, 1963, p. 10 (complete text from *Izvestiya*, 26 July 1963).

101   'World Women's Congress', p. 3.

102   M. Orlova and L. Rechvina, 'Mezhdunarodnyi seminar', *Rabotnitsa*, no. 10, 1956, pp. 1–2; Ye. Leont'eva, 'Na mezhdunarodnom seminare', *Krest'yanka*, no. 11, 1956, pp. 9–10; 'Eighty Thousand Questions? Quite Possible!', *Soviet Woman*, no. 1, 1957, p. 27, and '80,000 Questions? Quite Possible ...', *Soviet Woman*, no. 2, 1957, p. 38; 'International Seminar on "Equality of Women in the USSR" Ends', *CDSP*, no. 40, 1956, p. 20 (excerpts from *Pravda*, 2 October 1956).

103   *Equality of Women in the USSR: Materials of International Seminar (Moscow, September 15–October 1, 1956)*, compiled by L. Petrova and S. Gilevskaya (Moscow, 1957).

104   For a report on one of these, see Z. Mironova, 'V zashchitu prav zhenshchiny', *Rabotnitsa*, no. 6, 1963, pp. 4–5.

105   T. Dmitrieva, 'Vstrecha v Budapeshte', *Rabotnitsa*, no. 6, 1956, p. 1, and Ye. Kononenko, 'Yedinstvo truzhenits mira', *Rabotnitsa*, no. 7, 1956, pp. 4–6; L. Ivanova, 'Konferentsiya v Budapeshte', *Krest'yanka*, no. 6, 1956, p. 15.

106   'Our Women', *Soviet Woman*, no. 3, 1960, pp. 3–4. See also 'Exciting Meeting with Indian Women', *CDSP*, no. 4, 1960, p. 19 (excerpts from *Pravda*, 26 January 1960).

107   'Women are Active Builders of Socialism', *CDSP*, no. 32, 1961, p. 24 (complete text from *Pravda*, 7 August 1961).

108   Ibid.

109   'Pervaya!', *Rabotnitsa*, no. 6, 1963, p. 3; Yu. Ivanova, 'Nasha chaika', *Krest'yanka*, no. 7, 1963, p. 4; V. Chernosvitova, 'Zhenshchina v kosmose', *Krest'yanka*, no. 8, 1963, pp. 13–14.

110   'We are Domesticating the Universe', *CDSP*, no. 24, 1963, p. 20 (complete text from *Izvestiya*, 18 June 1963).

111   'The Way to the Far Reaches of the Universe', *CDSP*, no. 25, 1963, pp. 22–3 (complete text from *Pravda*, 23 June 1963).

112   Z. A. Lebedeva, 'Dlya sovetskoi zhenshchiny trud stanovitsya potrebnost'yu', *Zhenshchiny mira*, no. 4, 1963, pp. 24–5.

113   Interview with Olimpiada Nefedova, *Zhenshchiny mira*, no. 2, 1960, pp. 20–1.

2
Women Workers in the Khrushchev Era

Donald Filtzer

As under capitalism, patriarchy played an important role in consolidating the class relations of Soviet society. Millions of women entered social production, but were marginalised into the most unskilled and lowest-paid jobs. Women became proletarianised, while their domestic burdens remained unabated or grew heavier. They retained almost total responsibility for looking after the home while doing a full day's labour. In all aspects women were relegated to a subordinate position within Soviet society, a position simultaneously reproduced within the home and at work. It is common to refer to this as women's double burden, but this terminology is misleading because it implies that these are discrete phenomena, the one merely an accretion to the other. They are not. Rather, women's positions at work and in the home mutually determined one another. Their subordinate status in the home profoundly affected the attitudes of male workers and managers, so that discrimination against women in jobs and pay seemed completely natural. Conversely, the perpetuation of women in low-paid, unskilled and heavy manual labour reinforced male prejudice (and women's own aspirations) about women's ability to do skilled work or to assume positions of authority, be it in society, the workplace or the household. In more practical terms, the burdens of domestic labour and the drudgery of most female industrial jobs combined to make it difficult for women to find the time or energy to upgrade their skills and earn promotions.

From the mid-1960s Soviet sociologists began to examine a range of issues dealing with social inequality. A small group of sociologists and labour economists, most of them women, began to investigate the position of women workers, supporting their studies with their own surveys of women in particular industries and localities. They took a detailed look at the marginalisation of women into particular trades and industries, wage discrimination and the specific content and conditions of female labour. These studies were far more detailed than any of male workers carried out at this time. Other than in short articles, much of this work was presented only in dissertations, and was not officially published. These Soviet investigators understood the need to examine the position of women in production, and to develop from this a critique of the position of women within Soviet society. Even where the main contribution was simply to present unpublished statistics on job discrimination and wages, the choice of these data presupposed a definite political outlook radically at variance with the prevailing official line on women's role in Soviet society. This is not to overlook the real political limitations imposed by their 'Sovietised' Marxism. They saw the phenomena they uncovered as inadequacies that could be overcome within the bounds of the system, rather than as expressions of its immanent nature whose solution demanded its radical overthrow.

Whatever the strengths of these studies, they did not address the real issue, namely the political economy of female labour, and its specific role in regulating the Soviet economy. This goes far beyond the issue of the reproduction of labour power. Women workers were subjected to relations within production that in important ways deviated from those generally prevailing within industry, particularly among male workers. Women constituted a reserve army of workers marginalised for the most part into two types of jobs. First were those where technology allowed management to exercise relatively tight control over the labour process. The intensity of labour was high and wages poor. The most important of these were in the textile industry, but women on conveyor work in engineering and other areas of light industry found themselves in similar conditions. Second, women formed the overwhelming majority of auxiliary workers doing heavy, manual and usually unskilled or semi-skilled labour. Their working conditions were harsh and their pay often quite low, although as manual workers they had greater control over the pace of work. The existence of each of these two sectors was predicated on the other. It was only possible to induce women to enter the textile mills because the alternative was potentially more unattractive, namely manual labour in auxiliary shops. Together these two spheres of employment gave the elite an important lever for recouping part of the control over production that it was forced to cede to male workers in heavy industry. First, these women were taking jobs that male workers could not be persuaded to do. Second, as a low-wage workforce subject generally to a high intensity of labour, the surplus product they produced afforded the elite a certain buffer allowing it to tolerate the concessions over earnings and the intensity of labour which managers were forced to grant other, usually male, workers in less easy-to-control sectors.

The position of women in the home and in industry altered little over the course of the 1950s and 1960s. Indeed, the problems of low pay, marginalisation into manual and low-skilled jobs, harsh working conditions and the unequal sexual division of labour within the home were just as pressing at the end of the Soviet Union as they had been 25 years before.[1]

The structure of female employment

At the end of the Khrushchev period there were roughly 11.6 million women workers (excluding clerical personnel) in Soviet industry and construction; these women accounted for 31 per cent of all female employment outside the collective farms.[2] Women's share of industrial workers was obviously much higher: 44 per cent in 1960 and 46 per cent in 1967. Of the roughly 10.2 million women industrial workers, two-thirds were employed in four industries: engineering, food, textiles and the garment industry. In addition, the 1.4 million women working in construction represented an increase of over 60 per cent since 1958 (see Table 2.1).

Table 2.1 Women workers in industry and construction, 1965 (total and as percentage of all workers)

	Total	*as % of all workers in sector*
All industry	10,159,000	45
including:		
Engineering	2,998,000	40
Food (1962 estimate)	1,243,000	55
Textiles	1,239,000	73
Garment	1,206,000	84
Building materials (1960 data)	707,000	54
Footwear	270,000	67
Construction	1,419,000	29

Sources: Calculated from *Trud v SSSR* (Moscow, 1968), pp. 84–5, 121; *Zhenshchiny i deti v SSSR* (Moscow, 1969), pp. 72–3, 86, 107; *Itogi vsesoyuznoi perepisi* (Moscow, 1962), p. 167; *Rabochii klass SSSR (1951–1965gg.)* (Moscow, 1969), p. 139; M. A. Korobitsyna, 'Zhenskii trud v sisteme obshchestvennogo truda pri sotsializme' (Candidate Dissertation, Sverdlovsk, 1966), p. 38; S. V. Brova, 'Sotsial'nye problemy zhenskogo truda v promyshlennosti. Po materialam sotsiologicheskikh issledovanii na predpriyatiyakh Sverdlovskoi i Chelyabinskoi oblastei' (Candidate Dissertation, Sverdlovsk, 1968), p. 103.

There were nearly as many women employed in engineering as there were in the three main branches of light industry combined (food, textiles and garments). It is also significant that in the non-Slavic republics (that is, excluding the Russian Federation, Belorussia and Ukraine) the share of native women among native workers was almost uniformly smaller than the total percentage of women among workers in these republics, a fact which reflects the agrarian, and in many cases also the Muslim, character of their populations, both of which created serious obstacles to the entry of native women into industrial work.[3]

Women also made up the largest share – about three-quarters – of the 'non-productive' sector, that is, services, trade, health, education and science, and administration. By 1965 this sphere employed around 17.6 million women workers and clerical employees, or slightly less than half of all women outside of the collective farms.[4] According to the 1959 census, there were also more than 16 million non-working women of working age, accounting for 90 per cent of the non-working able-bodied population.[5]

Not surprisingly, the distribution of women workers among different industries showed sharp regional variations. The Urals deviated significantly from the general pattern. The almost total absence of light industry in that region produced a higher than average concentration of women in heavy industry. Fourteen per cent of women industrial workers in Sverdlovsk oblast' held jobs in iron and steel, as opposed to just 2.5 per cent in the USSR as a whole. A further 10 per cent of women workers in that oblast' worked in non-ferrous metals, an industry with comparably difficult working conditions, so that metallurgy as a whole accounted for a quarter of female industrial employment. A further third of women worked in engineering – again, higher than the national average of 30 per cent. At the other end of the scale, some 12 per cent of all women industrial workers in the USSR worked in the textile industry, but in Sverdlovsk oblast' the figure was just 3 per cent.[6]

The marginalisation of women into manual labour

One of the distinguishing features of Soviet industrialisation was the attraction of women into branches of heavy industry from which they were normally excluded under capitalism. Once there, however, they found themselves pushed primarily into low-paid, manual work. In 1965, over a third of women workers were in low-paying branches of light industry (food, textiles, garments and footwear). Access to other industries, such as engineering, had not, however, provided them with more skilled or better-paying jobs. Within production they tended to perform routine, often monotonous jobs as machine operators. As auxiliary workers, where women predominated, they found themselves concentrated in low-skilled, and often heavy manual jobs such as quality controllers, weighers, sorters and packers, warehousing and storeroom attendants, and ancillary jobs in lifting and transport. At the other extreme, women were almost universally excluded from highly skilled jobs such as tool-setters and electricians, even within industries such as textiles, where they made up the vast majority of production workers.

According to the 1959 census, women were 15 per cent of turners, 48 per cent of other machine tool operators, and 64 per cent of press and stamp operators. At the same time, they were a mere 10 per cent of welders, 10 per cent of tool and pattern makers, 6 per cent of fitters, mechanics and assemblers, and 6 per cent of tool-setters and tuners.[7] By the late 1960s this situation remained virtually unchanged: women were 80 per cent of ancillary workers in industry, 86 per cent of sorters, 98 per cent of packagers, and 80 per cent of packers. By the same token, they continued to be an insignificant percentage of skilled tool-setters, including those industries with a largely female workforce.[8]

More comprehensive all-Union data are not available because the 1959 census gave only a partial list of the percentage of women in different industrial trades; similarly, the Occupational Censuses of 1959, 1962 and 1965 were never published, except for their most general sections. Fortunately, considerable material from the Occupational Censuses carried out in different regions and industries was presented in dissertations, from which we can piece together a more detailed picture of women's employment.

In Ukraine, for instance, women were 35.6 per cent of industrial workers. Although they were 40 per cent of machine tool operators, most of these women tended relatively simple equipment; women were only 20 per cent of milling machine operators and 15 per cent of metal turners. The disparities are even more dramatic if we consider that women were 74 per cent of quality controllers, 76 per cent of storeroom attendants, 64 per cent of ancillary workers, but only 10 per cent of electricians, and such a small number of electrical fitters that they did not register in the statistics.[9]

In the Urals there was a similarly clear pattern, by which women were marginalised into certain trades: control and measuring; sorting and packing; warehousing; and manual ancillary jobs. In addition, they were over 80 per cent of sand mixers, and over 90 per cent of core makers in foundries; 97 per cent of signal workers on factory railway networks; and 80 per cent of manual workers in the meat industry (much of which was extremely heavy work).[10]

The same pattern was true of the engineering industry (see Table 2.2). The pattern here is unmistakable. Women were shunted either into routine, mostly manual auxiliary jobs, or the less skilled production trades. The more skilled, better-paid and rewarding the work, the fewer women there were doing it.

Perhaps even more striking was the situation in the textile industry, where women made up three-quarters of the workforce and nearly 100 per cent of basic production trades, such as spinners, weavers, winders, twisters and knitters. As in engineering, however, they were an infinitesimal share of skilled tool-setters, deputy foremen (whose main job was also tool-setting) and tuners. This had not always been the case, however, as Table 2.3 makes clear.

Thus as late as 1959 women had been a quarter to a half of skilled manual trades, *from which they were systematically displaced*. A very similar, though less drastic, pattern was repeated in the engineering industry of Sverdlovsk oblast', where the share of women model makers declined from 6.5 per cent in 1959 to 0.5 per cent in 1965; their share of tool-setters from 13.1 to 11.5 per cent (which was still twice the national average); and their share of fitters-tool makers from

Table 2.2   Women as a percentage of selected trades in engineering, 2 August 1965

All workers	39.0
Storeroom attendants	90.0
Manual ancillary workers	73.0
Capstan-lathe operators	66.0
Painters	57.5
Milling-machine operators	21.0
Turners – metal-cutting machine tools	19.5
Fitters on machining-assembly jobs	16.0
Tool-setters, machine-tool tuners, instrument adjusters	7.8
Tool-setters of automatic machine tools	4.7
Maintenance electricians	3.8
Fitter-tool-makers, fitter-pattern-makers	1.6
Fitter-assemblers	1.3
Maintenance fitters	0.7

Source: V. I. Starodub, 'Tekhnicheskii progress i trud zhenshchin' (Candidate Dissertation, Leningrad, 1966), pp. 57, 84, citing the unpublished Occupational Census of August 1965.

Table 2.3 Women as a percentage of tool-setters and related trades: textiles, 1959–65

	1 August 1959	*1 August 1962*	*1 August 1965*
Tool-setters of automatic machines	48.1	20.0	3.0
Tool-setters, machine-tool tuners, and instrument adjusters	25.3	9.7	9.2
Deputy foremen	17.0	n/d	11.0
Deputy foremen on mechanical ribbon looms	4.0	1.2	1.0
Foremen on automatic weaving machines	1.6	0.5	0.4

Sources: V. I. Starodub, 'Tekhnicheskii progress i trud zhenshchin' (Candidate Dissertation, Leningrad, 1966), pp. 57–8; N. P. Maloletova, 'Rabochie legkoi promyshlennosti SSSR v 1945–1965gg. (chislennost' i sostav)' (Candidate Dissertation, Moscow, 1970), pp. 210–11.

2.8 to 1.2 per cent. The trend was much more pronounced in wood-working, where the percentage of women machine tuners fell from 11.7 per cent in 1959 to 1.7 per cent in 1965. The proportion of women was falling in other skilled manual trades: instrument adjusters, fitters, electrical fitters and electricians.[11]

It is likely that three processes were taking place here. First, some skilled women manual workers were being pushed out of these jobs, partially through the enforcement of protective legislation. Second, as women who had entered these trades during the war reached retirement, their jobs were given not to a new generation of skilled women workers, but to men. Third, and probably more significant was the fact that, as the absolute number of tool-setters and similar occupations expanded with automation and increased mechanisation, these jobs, too, were going almost exclusively to men, so that the proportion of women fell.[12] The cumulative result of these three trends was a *relative deskilling of female labour*.

The process of actually excluding women from skilled trades in which they once participated appears to have been most pronounced in ferrous and non-ferrous metallurgy, where a ban on women from a number of heavy and hazardous jobs which they had moved into during the war was clearly used as a pretext to remove them from work they could easily have carried on performing. In Sverdlovsk oblast', the number of women manual metal cutters fell from 79.2 per cent of the trade to 18.3 per cent; the number of teamsters in mines from 67 to 6.5 per cent; hot metal stampers from 36.6 to 19.5 per cent; and workers with refractory materials in iron and steel from 40.6 per cent to zero. These were indeed dangerous and heavy jobs. At the same time, however, the share of women control panel operators on furnaces and rolling presses also fell, from well over half to less than a quarter, a change that could in no way be justified on the grounds of labour safety.[13] A similar process occurred in ore mining, where, in 1957, women were removed from underground work, with many being shifted to lower-paying and less skilled jobs.[14]

Especially pronounced was the tendency for skilled jobs created as a by-product of automation (tool-setters and machine tuners; repair and maintenance) to go almost exclusively to men. This is illustrated by the case of Sverdlovsk oblast', the data for which are presented in Table 2.4. These show a fall in the share of men doing unskilled manual labour and a corresponding rise in the share doing skilled manual jobs. Brova, who presented these data, used the following categories, at that time standard in Soviet sociology:

Group I: Automated jobs, involving numerous control functions.
Group II: Mechanised jobs using machinery and mechanical devices.
Group III: Manual labour carried out on machinery and mechanical devices. This group included workers on specialised machinery, individual machines or conveyors.
Group IV: Manual labour without the aid of machinery or mechanical devices. Workers in this group carried out heavy physical labour.

Table 2.4   Male and female workers by degree of mechanisation, Sverdlovsk oblast', 1959–65 (percentage of workers in each occupational group)

	Year	Group				
		I	*II*	*III*	*IV*	*V*
Male workers	1959	0.3	36.8	9.2	37.7	16.0
	1962	0.5	40.4	8.7	32.6	17.8
	1965	0.4	39.2	9.6	30.2	20.6
Female workers	1959	0.5	37.5	9.2	52.0	0.8
	1962	0.8	38.5	9.4	50.4	0.9
	1965	0.8	39.5	9.2	49.1	1.4

Source: S. V. Brova, 'Sotsial'nye problemy zhenskogo truda v promyshlennosti. Po materialam sotsiologicheskikh issledovanii na predpriyatiyakh Sverdlovskoi i Chelyabinskoi oblastei' (Candidate Dissertation, Sverdlovsk, 1968), p. 106, using data from the 1959, 1962 and 1965 Occupational Censuses of Sverdlovsk oblast'.

Group V: Workers carrying out repair and maintenance on machinery and mechanical devices. This work combined manual and mental labour.

The percentages of women and men in the first three groups were roughly equal. The real disparity was at the extremes of the skill scale: women were far more likely than men to do heavy unmechanised labour, while men had virtually exclusive access to skilled manual trades.

This picture was repeated in virtually every industry in the oblast'. In iron and steel women were one-third of all workers in 1965, but 42.5 per cent of those on heavy manual labour – this was over half of all women workers in the industry. Conversely, they were less than 5 per cent of skilled maintenance workers. In chemicals, where they were half the workforce, women were two-thirds of those doing heavy manual work (again over half of all women) and 2 per cent of skilled manual workers. In textiles, women had been 100 per cent of workers in Group I in 1959, but were only a third of such workers in 1965. Meanwhile, the share of women on heavy manual work climbed from 60 to 70 per cent in the same period. Here, as elsewhere, they were a mere 5 per cent of skilled maintenance trades. With the exception of textiles, light industry and food, where the entire workforce was overwhelmingly female, women were a far higher percentage of those performing heavy manual work than they were of the workforce as a whole; at least half – and usually well over half – of all women workers were confined to these types of jobs.[15]

There is also anecdotal evidence to suggest that when heavy manual jobs were mechanised women were removed from them and these jobs were given to men.[16] If true, this would explain why the trend in the USSR was quite different from that usually observed under capitalism, where mechanisation is often accompanied by a simplification of tasks and the displacement of skilled male workers by lower-paid women. Such a tendency was excluded in the USSR by the political impossibility of creating large-scale male unemployment. What was politically excluded for the regime became a determinant of economic necessity for industrial managers, who depended on their ability to carry out informal bargaining with workers on the shop floor in order to keep the enterprise functioning relatively smoothly. Here male workers were doubly privileged: they were able to protect themselves from displacement or deskilling in a way that women could not, and they received preferential reassignment to jobs where working conditions had been substantially improved. They enjoyed such advantages not just because of male 'solidarity' and prejudice, but also because managers required their cooperation in other areas of factory life.

The issue was not simply that women were pushed out of skilled production into auxiliary jobs, but that these latter jobs remained unmechanised.[17] This was perpetuated by the managerial practice of concentrating investments and efforts at mechanisation in production shops, neglecting auxiliary sections of the enterprise. While the main pressure for this undoubtedly came from the planning system, the fact that women were virtually a captive workforce in the auxiliary sector left managers free to feel that they could continue to ignore the problem. This profoundly influenced the job motivations of women workers: a Leningrad study published in 1965 found that, with the exception of women tool-setters and control panel operators, the most prevalent factor affecting women's choice of occupation was the absence of any alternative. Their selection of a job was a means to an end: earning their subsistence; minimising distances between home and work; the opportunity to work only one shift; the availability of dormitory space for single women; or just taking a job wherever they found one. Most women felt that the combination of their jobs and their domestic situation offered them no prospects for upgrading their skills. This contrasted sharply with male workers, who were much more likely to take up a particular trade because it interested them (although a large minority of men also had entered their current job because they felt there was little choice).[18] The other side of this was that many women agreed to take jobs with hazardous and heavy working conditions because these offered better pay and were the only way out of the trap of low wages.[19]

Working conditions

Despite the reduction in the numbers of women on heavy or hazardous jobs, women still made up a substantial proportion of such workers. In non-ferrous metallurgy in Kazakhstan, for instance, they were nearly half of ore crushers and almost all of transport workers on ore enrichment. In recognition of the difficulties of this work the women who did it were accorded accelerated pension rights: ore crushers and some underground workers could retire at age 45; transporters in ore enrichment could take their pension at age 50.[20] In the Urals women were a substantial minority of workers carrying out various difficult manual foundry operations (including about one-third of stokers and nearly half of loaders working by hand). Here, too, women were willing to take these jobs because of material compensations, in this case the higher pay that heavy and hazardous jobs brought with them.[21]

There were a number of jobs which technically complied with existing health and safety standards, but where the work was nonetheless extremely heavy. This was especially true of lifting jobs, since regulations limited the maximum weight of any one load that women could lift and transport, but placed no limit on the cumulative weight that could be carried over the course of a shift. Brick making was a particularly graphic example. Women brick moulders would lift up to 5000 raw bricks in a shift, each weighing from 4 to 6 kilograms. Although this conformed to the law, the women were lifting 25 tons a shift. When it came to unloading finished bricks conditions were even worse, since in addition to the excessive weight the women had to cope with the intense heat of bricks that had not yet cooled down after coming out of the ovens. Women packers and loaders in the soap industry faced similar conditions, lifting and carting from 5 to 7 tons a shift. In the paint and varnish industry the poor design of conveyors forced women in some factories to lift 40 kilogram drums on to the conveyor 100 or more times a day.[22] This is not to say that managers did not also violate regulations. A 1964 survey of over 200 Leningrad factories allegedly uncovered a vast number of violations, with women having to cart 400 kilogram loads in wheelbarrows or haul 25 kilograms up a flight of stairs.[23]

The persistence of such heavy labour was directly connected with the undermechanisation of primarily female auxiliary jobs. To some extent this was a by-product of managers' general unwillingness to apply innovations or new technology. This trend – while encouraged by the planning system – was reinforced by the fact that managers saw no reason to mechanise jobs done by cheap female labour.

The physical toll of heavy and intense work made itself felt in high turnover, often associated with women leaving the industry where they worked altogether. At a time when the regime was still finding it difficult to recruit non-working women into the workforce, the fact that women were not staying in such traditional industries as textiles or light engineering until retirement age must have seemed particularly alarming. A survey of spinners found almost two-thirds under the age of 30, and a mere 4 per cent working past the age of 45. Among weavers, over 80 per cent were younger than 40, and only 4 per cent over 50.[24] The same pattern also emerged at the Svetlana electrical appliance factory in Leningrad, where half of women were under 30, and nearly 80 per cent under 40.[25] These figures can in no way be attributed to women's family circumstances. Had this been the case, women would have dropped out of the workforce when they were younger and their children were of pre-school age, and then re-entered it after the age of 40, when they had the time and independence to resume work. Instead, we observe an exodus of women who, in terms of experience and ability, should have been at the prime of their working life. This could only have been due to working conditions.[26]

For many women a major problem was monotony. Whether they carried out heavy manual labour or worked on a conveyor, a large proportion of women's jobs involved highly repetitive operations that allowed little variation in the work routine. The work was further impoverished by the fact that it was often broken down into sub-operations. In the Sverdlovsk garment industry, for example, the women were so highly specialised in what they did that when a worker was absent it was difficult to find someone to replace her.[27] Conveyor work was especially bad in this regard, because the repetitiveness was compounded by the workers' lack of control over the speed and rhythm of the job, which remained more or less constant throughout the day, and were the same for all workers, irrespective of abilities. The same applied to press operators, nearly two-thirds of whom were women. Their work involved just three basic operations: inserting the piece, stamping and removing it. Given the technology prevailing in the 1960s, in the course of a shift a worker would carry out between 13,000 and 15,000 identical, monotonous movements. In addition, the work demanded speed, accuracy, quick reactions and intense concentration.[28] As one would expect in these conditions, it was also very dangerous.

Yet women were able to find definite compensations in monotonous jobs. Some felt that, although their work was tedious and boring, it was nonetheless socially useful, which gave them an indirect satisfaction.[29] More common was the feeling that the work was undemanding and left women time and space to think about themselves and their problems and to interact with their friends.[30]

Conditions in the textile industry

Detailed studies of working conditions for women in the textile industry revealed a portrait of high intensity and stress in what were frequently unsafe or unhealthy working conditions. In 1965 there were more than 1.2 million women in textiles. This was more than one in 20 of all industrial workers, and nearly one in eight women. Taking the textile and garment industries together, they accounted for nearly a quarter of all women industrial workers.

Work in textiles was noisy, dusty, hot and humid. About one-third of a worker's time was spent repairing broken threads, an operation demanding speed, dexterity and high concentration. It was estimated that the average weaver covered from 15 to 20 kilometres a shift walking between machines. The average spinner did less walking – a 'mere' 6–9 kilometres. In addition, the design and construction of spinning machines were poor, so that spinners had to work in uncomfortable positions. Mending broken threads, for example, had to be done stooping. As spinners performed this operation some 1500–2000 times a shift, or between 35 and 38 per cent of their work time, this meant about three hours a day constantly bending over and straightening up. The work rate was also intense. Women were on the job more than 95 per cent of the time, with only one short break of eight to 10 minutes. This was a far higher use of work time than in any other industry. Work in textiles was also unhygienic, and associated with numerous health problems, including cardiovascular disease, deafness, back trouble, varicose veins and rheumatic ailments.[31] A comparative study of textile and iron and steel workers found that the incidence of cardiovascular and rheumatic disease was actually higher in textiles.[32]

The stress and intensity of the work were, in Kalinina's words, 'right at the physiological limit of human capabilities'.[33] Equipment utilisation in textiles was nearly 100 per cent, versus barely 50 per cent in engineering. Yet for all this workers in light industry received less annual leave than workers in any other industry.[34] In addition to the strains of carrying out basic operations, there was also that caused by the threat of injury and the need to avoid it (shuttles flying off, burning one's fingers on high-speed spindles). Moreover, women had the additional burdens of childcare and housework, which took up nearly as much time as their work in production.

It was the technology of production itself, however, which placed women in textiles under the greatest strain, a problem which appears to have grown worse with mechanisation. Quality controllers, for example, performed movements of only 0.5 to 3 seconds in duration, repeated some 70–79 times a minute, or 27,000 times a shift. This demanded considerable concentration and placed great strain on the eyes. In addition, they spent 11 per cent of their time doing heavy lifting. Most controllers did their entire job standing, with just

20 minutes' rest over the course of a 7-hour day. Spinners and winders took 5–6 seconds to repair a thread break, 1.5 seconds to remove a cop of spun thread and 7–9 seconds for a cop of wound thread. For weavers it took from 16 to 60 seconds to repair a broken thread. All of these operations were repeated hundreds, if not thousands, of times in the course of a shift, involving the constant repetition of brief movements and terrible monotony. Thus a winder doing thread rewinding, who had less than 14 minutes' rest over an entire shift, performed more than 2000 monotonous operations, involving over 200 repetitive physical movements a minute – all while standing up in a semi-bent position.[35]

Some, if not most, of this stress could have been alleviated had equipment been better designed and manufactured. New automatic weaving looms introduced into the woollen industry in 1958 were designed so that in order to carry out quality control, a controller had to lie on the floor in the space between the looms, carrying out the inspection under ambient light.[36] Kalinina estimated that much of the bending done by spinners and weavers could be eliminated if the main work area of machines was raised a further 15 centimetres from the floor. Under then current construction, spindle bars were too low, requiring women to bend at a 60 degree angle when mending broken threads.[37] Similarly, the poor quality of raw cotton or wool increased thread breaks, and thus imposed even greater strain on spinners and weavers.[38]

Fatigue was made worse by prevailing shift schedules, which compelled many women to work night shifts, usually in combination with a six-day week. The problems with night work were legion. Productivity and quality were notoriously worse than on day shifts. The physical toll on the women was severe: they had less sleep, did more housework and had a higher accident rate while on the job.[39] Night shifts were understandably unpopular, so much so that in Moscow women were prepared to move from factories on a three-shift system to one with just two shifts even if this meant a cut in pay.[40]

Conditions in the mills were poor. Temperatures in the summer months routinely reached 30–42 degrees centigrade, causing even greater fatigue, which in turn increased the danger of accidents. The machinery generated vibration and noise. In addition to deafness, these also affected neurological functions and slowed down motor reactions. The result was both reduced productivity and increased risk of accidents, not the least because women were unable to hear the warnings of other workers when dangerous situations developed.[41]

Lighting and ventilation were also bad. A number of production and quality control jobs caused eye strain, which was made worse by the fact that lighting conditions in a number of mills were below officially set standards, sometimes providing as little as one-third, or even one-fifth the permitted minimum.[42] Dust levels created a number of hazards. The main contaminants were natural fibre particles, together with admixtures of earth and sand, and their concentrations at times exceeded statutory maxima by as much as 50-fold. In addition, sizing and dyeing operations involved the use of toxic substances – sulphuric, hydrochloric and acetic acids, as well as caustic soda – which gave off harmful vapours. The problem was compounded by the poor state of ventilation systems. Many ventilation systems only blew air into the workplace and did not extract it. They did nothing to alleviate high temperatures in the summer months or high dust levels.[43]

The nature of the textile industry was that it imposed a very different type of work regime than existed in most areas of heavy industry. If the characteristic feature of Soviet production was that the worker was generally able to appropriate a large degree of control over the labour process, such opportunities were much reduced – if not almost non-existent – in textile production. The intensity of labour, and the attendant degree of concentration and stress, were higher even than in those areas of light engineering and automobiles where the pace of work was largely dictated by the conveyor, but where workers still could 'conceal' certain 'reserves' (to use Soviet parlance) and expect breaks in their routine due to problems with supplies and equipment breakdowns. Conditions in the textile industry changed little during the decades after Khrushchev's fall. In the 1960s the mills undoubtedly seemed a more attractive alternative to unskilled manual work in heavy industry.

Conclusion – the contradictions of female labour

With the exception of wartime, one of the major functions of women industrial workers under capitalism has been as so-called 'dilutees', where mechanisation has allowed management to replace skilled male workers with non-skilled and lower-paid women. This has either occurred as direct displacement, or by creating new industries or industrial processes staffed by women, and which supplanted older industries or processes that employed men.[44] This pattern was only partially repeated in the USSR. Prior to the Revolution, men made up almost half of all textile workers, but by the end of the First Five-Year Plan this industry was almost exclusively female.[45] Women also made up the bulk of the workforce in new conveyor and assembly-based industries, especially light engineering. Yet there were also important differences from capitalism. With Stalinist industrialisation women entered many 'male' trades, especially as machinists in engineering, but also in the building trades, where they faced a different kind of discrimination. They were kept in lower wage and skill grades, so that they received less money and found it difficult to win promotion. Parallel with this trend, women became – and remained – the bulk of workers in manual, unmechanised and largely (although not exclusively) low-paid auxiliary jobs on internal transport, loading, packing, sorting and quality control.

The role of the family in determining the structure of female employment also differed under capitalism and in the USSR. Under capitalism, women have been the flexible element in the workforce, a pool of labour able to be drawn into production at times of a labour shortage, and readily expelled when their labour power was no longer needed. As Beechey has noted, women, unlike men, can be made redundant at little cost to the state. When they lose their jobs they are reabsorbed back into the domestic economy.[46] Parallel with this, women have been readily recruitable into low-wage areas, because earnings were still higher than unpaid domestic labour. Women workers in the Soviet Union were in a quite different position. The problem was not how to use women as an easily unemployable workforce, but, on the contrary, how to attract them back into the labour market. In fact, during the Khrushchev period, the problem was how to overcome the economic incentives that many women had to remain within the domestic economy, where their labour was more advantageous to the family budget than work in industry or services.[47] Moreover, once recruited, there was no question of women being made redundant, although they could be displaced from certain mechanised jobs if management felt compelled to offer this work to men.

Thus the decision by Soviet women to enter social production brought with it a multidimensional exploitation, based on the fact that they held down a full-time job and shouldered almost the entire burden of domestic labour. In fact, this was both official policy and the dominant ideology shared by both women and men. Most married women decided to stay in employment because the family needed the extra wage, even though it was significantly lower than their husbands'. Women also valued work in its own right and found various social compensations even in the most monotonous and tedious jobs.

The role of the family was crucial because it established structural limits to women's acquisition of skills (little free time, exhaustion) and concurrently reproduced a patriarchal ideology that also circumscribed their occupational opportunities.

In general, we can identify a duality in female industrial employment in the USSR. In industries such as textiles, the garment industry, and light engineering and other processes based on conveyors and assembly lines, women held jobs which were relatively tightly regulated in terms of the intensity of labour and the use of work time, and they subsequently found it far harder than their male counterparts in heavy industry to extract concessions from management over work organisation or earnings. On the contrary, the percentage of utilised work time was high – far higher than for industry as a whole – while wages were low. This, then, was a sector where the elite was relatively successful in controlling the extraction and disposal of the surplus product, a fact which was indirectly reflected in the high profits generated by light industry, which were skimmed off into the state coffers. There, instead of providing resources for new investment in light industry and an expansion of consumer goods, they allowed the elite a certain degree of leeway to tolerate its relative lack of control over the labour process in other sectors of industry – most notably the lax use of work time and the collusion between line managers and workers to bust regulations designed to limit earnings. This does not mean that heavy industry was being 'subsidised' by 'super-profits' extracted from light industry. It does mean, however, that the limits on the surplus due to excessive waste and the elite's imperfect control over the labour process were partially compensated and kept within bounds that allowed the economy to continue to carry out expanded reproduction, albeit in crisis-ridden form.

The other main area of female employment was in non-skilled, manual auxiliary jobs. These jobs were generally heavy and unpleasant, and usually low-paid. Productivity was low, partly because these jobs were unmechanised, and partly because the prevalence of manual labour gave these workers greater control over the intensity and pace of their labour. This area of employment engendered its own contradictions, rooted in the conflict between the needs of the economy as a whole and those of the individual enterprise. This was partly recognised by Starodub:

> At the current state of development of our society a clear contradiction is taking place. On the one hand, our country possesses highly-

mechanised enterprises, where the process of production places growing demands to raise the level of general education and skills among workers. On the other hand, about half of industrial workers – the majority of them women – are still employed on manual labour, which at times does not permit them to raise their cultural–technical level. The existence of low-skilled jobs lowers the average level of labour productivity. Since it is mainly women who work at low-skilled jobs, it is precisely owing to them that the general level of labour productivity is falling.[48]

This very well connects two basic problems: the impact of undermechanisation on the performance of the economy as a whole, and its impact on women workers. The duality of female employment meant that, thanks to the existence of jobs where the labour process was tightly controlled and wages were low, the elite could tolerate concessions to more strategically important sections of the workforce, primarily men. At the same time, women constituted a pool of unskilled, low-productivity workers whose labour was harder to control and which undermined the performance of the entire economy and of the enterprise itself. The undermechanisation of auxiliary jobs was a major source of bottlenecks and disruptions to production, lowering overall productivity and in many cases negating the results of the more mechanised labour of workers in direct production.

On the surface, the retention of this sector appears wholly irrational, and due solely to the structural rigidities of the planning system. This, however, overlooks two important economic functions that it served. First, from the enterprise's point of view, it was possible, indeed probable, that individual managers found it economically more expedient to maintain an inefficient, but low-wage auxiliary sector – despite its impact on overall production results – than to invest in the equipment needed to mechanise these operations. Here the expectations and assumptions about low female wages surely played a key role.

Second, there was another, deeper level at which the maintenance of this army of unskilled women workers remained crucial to the regulation of the Soviet economy, even while it acted to undermine its efficiency and to erode the production of the surplus. This in turn had two aspects to it. First, this 'reserve army' of low-skilled manual workers (which, beginning in the late 1960s, was made up not just of women, but of migrant workers of both sexes from rural areas) did jobs that men refused to do, at least under prevailing working conditions and wages. Second, this reserve army was vital in getting women to take jobs in tightly controlled areas of production where the rate of exploitation and extraction of the surplus was higher than in most male-dominated sectors or trades. If women had possessed a real choice, if they had not been effectively barred from skilled and highly skilled production jobs, if auxiliary jobs in industry had been better paid with acceptable working conditions, it would have been extremely difficult to recruit and hold women in high-intensity industries. Women preferred to enter the service sector, where the pay was also bad, but conditions were far less strenuous. In so far as the existence of this high-intensity sector played an important role in helping the elite to regulate the economy, maintaining a steady flow of low-paid women workers was a central economic task. Yet this supply of labour was in large part dependent upon the existence of the reserve army of low-paid manual workers, who in effect acted as a disciplining factor by limiting women's employment alternatives.

In this sense the concessions granted to workers in heavy industry (most, but not all, of whose beneficiaries were men), while being largely reproduced by the actions of the workers themselves, were to a significant extent also made possible by the subordinate position of women workers in high-intensity areas of production and the unskilled auxiliary sector. Thus the privileges men enjoyed in the home were mirrored in those they received at work. The position of women workers was, therefore, even more contradictory than our discussion may have indicated. Their specific role in production involved an enormous waste of human resources and potential, and acted to perpetuate the relatively backward structure of the Soviet economy. At the same time it provided the elite with the means partially to compensate for one of the principal results of that backwardness, that is, the loss of control over production caused by the shop floor bargaining power of male workers. To this extent, the perpetuation of that power was conditional upon the heightened exploitation of their wives, sisters and mothers. Politically, the relative privileges that men derived in the home and at work at the expense of women acted further to atomise the workforce and undermine any potential re-emergence as a class for itself, able to act as a self-conscious collective historical agent and to challenge the elite for power. The position of women thus impinged upon the most basic contradiction of all in Soviet society: the need for the elite to maintain the atomisation of the working class as a means of ensuring its own domination, versus the inherent instability of the system that arose from that atomisation.

Notes

1 This chapter is a condensed version of 'The Position of Women Workers', Ch. 7 of D. Filtzer, *Soviet Workers and De-Stalinization: the Consolidation of the Modern System of Soviet Production Relations, 1953–1964* (Cambridge, 1992). This extract focuses on women's industrial employment. For further information on the issues raised here, and for women's domestic labour, see the full-length chapter.

2 In 1965 there were approximately 37.7 million female workers and clerical employees employed in all sections of the economy, excluding the collective farms. *Narodnoe khozyaistvo SSSR za 60 let* (Moscow, 1977), p. 469.

3 S. L. Senyavskii, *Rost rabochego klassa SSSR (1951–1965gg.)* (Moscow, 1966), p. 223. The one exception was Kirghizia, where, in 1959, 38.5 per cent of native workers were women, whereas women were only 36.4 per cent of all workers.

4 In 1965 trade (which Soviet statistics usually included in the productive sector), services, health, education and other non-productive areas employed 23.8 million people. According to V. I. Starodub, 'Tekhnicheskii progress i trud zhenshchin' (Candidate Dissertation, Leningrad, 1966), p. 65, in 1964, 74 per cent of workers and clerical employees in these branches were women. This comes to 17.6 million, or 47 per cent of all women workers and clerical employees (excluding collective farms). *Narodnoe khozyaistvo SSSR za 60 let*, pp. 463, 469. Both the size of the non-productive sector and the importance of women within it grew rapidly over the course of the Khrushchev period. Excluding trade and public catering, it accounted for 15.9 per cent of total employment (including *kolkhozy*) in 1958, and 20 per cent in 1965. If we include trade and public catering, the 1965 figure rises to 25 per cent. In 1961 'only' 70 per cent of workers and clerical employees in this sphere were women, versus 74 per cent in 1964. Starodub, op. cit., p. 65; *Narodnoe khozyaistvo SSSR za 60 let*, pp. 459–60.

5 *Itogi vsesoyuznoi perepisi* (Moscow, 1962), pp. 98–9.

6 The figures for Sverdlovsk oblast' are from M. A. Korobitsyna, 'Zhenskii trud v sisteme obshchestvennogo truda pri sotsializme' (Candidate Dissertation, Sverdlovsk, 1966), p. 41. The All-Union data come from the following. The figure for textiles is calculated from Table 2.1. In 1960 there were 886,000 workers in Soviet iron and steel; in 1961, 29 per cent of iron and steel workers were women, from which we can estimate a total of 257,000 women, or 2.5 per cent of all women industrial workers. *Trud v SSSR: statisticheskii sbornik* (Moscow, 1968), pp. 84–5; *Zhenshchiny i deti v SSSR* (Moscow, 1969), p. 107.

7 *Itogi vsesoyuznoi perepisi*, p. 167.

8 V. B. Mikhailyuk, *Ispol'zovanie zhenskogo truda v narodnom khozyaistve* (Moscow, 1970), pp. 67–8.

9 N. A. Sakharova, 'Zhenskie rezervy trudovykh resursov gorodov i rabochikh poselkov Ukrainskoi SSR' (Candidate Dissertation, Kiev, 1962), pp. 98–101. The year for these data is not given, but they are probably from the 1959 population census. Elsewhere she gives figures from the Occupational Census of August 1959, showing women to be a slightly higher share of

some trades: 47 per cent of machine tool operators (including 17 per cent of metal turners), 28 per cent of milling machine operators, and 11 per cent of electricians. Ibid., p. 92.

10 Korobitsyna, op. cit., pp. 42, 44.

11 Ibid., pp. 50–1. In light industry the fate of women tool-setters followed a peculiar pattern. In the food industry, where women were a majority of workers, women were 3.9 per cent of tool-setters and tuners in 1959, this rose to 7.0 per cent in 1962, and yet by 1965 there were no women in this trade at all. It was the same in light industry, where the share of women tool-setters jumped from 16.6 per cent in 1959, to a surprising 26.5 per cent in 1962, then falling to 11.7 per cent in 1965. Ibid., p. 50.

12 This was certainly the trend in engineering, where between 1948 and 1959 the number of tool-setters increased 2.3 times, while the share of women in this trade remained extremely small. Mikhailyuk, op. cit., p. 67.

13 Korobitsyna, op. cit., p. 48. The share of women on fully automated jobs in iron and steel actually rose in this period, so that by 1965 they were more than half of workers in this category. Yet this accounted for so few jobs in the industry that these women still made up less than 1 per cent of all female steel workers. This same process occurred in non-ferrous metals. S. V. Brova, 'Sotsial'nye problemy zhenskogo truda v promyshlennosti. Po materialam sotsiologicheskikh issledovanii ne predpriyatiyakh Sverdlovskoi i Chelyabinskoi oblastei' (Candidate Dissertation, Sverdlovsk, 1968), pp. 108, 110–11. At the same time women were excluded from virtually all skilled trades in Ukrainian iron and steel (where in 1959 they made up 31 per cent of all workers) which did not involve especially heavy or dangerous work: welders, tool-setters, moulders, lathe operators and metal turners (Sakharova, op. cit., p. 103).

14 According to Mikhailyuk, op. cit., p. 83, for the whole of the USSR 150,000 women were displaced from ore mining, but many were re-employed on heavy physical labour.

15 Brova, op. cit., pp. 108, 110–11. Although the data for Sverdlovsk oblast' are the most complete, this trend for women to be marginalised into heavy manual jobs was practically universal. In the engineering industry in 1965, for example, women were 39 per cent of workers, yet they were 55 per cent of manual carters and transport workers and 73 per cent of manual ancillaries. In Leningrad industry in 1962, women made up three-quarters of manual workers on loading and hauling, and 86 per cent of manual ancillary workers. Starodub, op. cit., pp. 60–61.

16 Brova, op. cit., p. 115; Starodub, op. cit., pp. 63–4, citing *Rabotnitsa*, no. 7, 1966, p. 10.

17 A survey of auxiliary jobs in light industry gives the following proportions of auxiliary workers whose jobs were totally unmechanised: loaders – 6 out of 7; controllers – 4 out of 5; factory cleaners – 15 out of 16; transporters – 7 out of 10; packers – 3 out of 4. N. P. Maloletova, 'Rabochie legkoi promyshlennosti SSSR v 1945–1965gg. (chislennost' i sostave)' (Candidate Dissertation, Moscow, 1970), p. 240.

18 *Trud i razvitie lichnosti* (Leningrad, 1965), pp. 82–4, 86, 94–5.

19 Brova, Abstract, p. 10. One of the additional attractions of construction was that it had no night shifts and offered many of its workers accommodation

in dormitories. N. M. Shishkan, *Trud zhenshchin v usloviyakh razvitogo sotsialisma* (Kishinev, 1976), p. 116.

20 R. M. Sagimbaeva, 'Problemy ispol'zovaniya resursov zhenskogo truda (na materialakh Kazakhskoi SSR)' (Candidate Dissertation, Moscow, 1968), p. 17.

21 Korobitsyna, op. cit, p. 49.

22 Starodub, op. cit, pp. 55–6, 111.

23 Ibid., pp. 149–50. Women industrial workers were not the only ones having to cope with these kinds of conditions. A great deal of work in services was also hard and boring (for example, cleaners, dish washers, pot scrubbers). Ibid., pp. 111–12.

24 Ibid., pp. 51–2.

25 Ibid., p. 51.

26 'Analysis of the age composition of working women in a number of trades shows that a huge number of them over 40 years old are no longer able to carry on working in their own trade and have to transfer to other, lighter, but lower-paid jobs.' Ibid., p. 52. In support of her claim, Starodub (pp. 118–19) cites the examples of enterprises in light industry and engineering where improved conditions – particularly noise levels and lighting – were matched by increases in labour productivity.

27 *Ural'skii rabochii*, 27 October 1962.

28 *Rabochii klass i tekhnicheskii progress. Issledovanie izmenenii v sotsial'noi strukture rabochego klassa* (Moscow, 1965), p. 131; E. Z. Danilova, *Sotsial'nye problemy truda zhenshchiny-rabotnitsy* (Moscow, 1968), p. 24.

29 Ibid., p. 25.

30 *Rabochii klass i tekhnicheskii progress*, pp. 131–2; N. G. Valentinova, 'O psikhicheskikh osobennostyakh lichnosti rabochego, svyazannykh s soderzhaniem truda', in *Sotsiologiya v SSSR*, vol. 2 (Moscow, 1965), p. 110; A. G. Zdravomyslov and V. A. Yadov, 'Vliyanie razlichii v soderzhanii i kharaktere truda na otnoshenie k trudu', in *Opyt i metodika konkretnykh sotsiologicheskikh issledovanii* (Moscow, 1965), pp. 188–9.

31 Danilova, op. cit., pp. 26–7; N. P. Kalinina, *Usloviya truda i osnovnye napravleniya ikh uluchsheniya na predpriyatiyakh tekstil'noi promyshlennosti* (Moscow, 1969) pp. 12-13; Starodub, op. cit., pp. 114–17. In one shop of Leningrad's Kirov textile combine carders tending three machines covered 4 kilometres an hour (ibid., p. 115).

32 G. N. Cherkasov, *Sotsial'no-ekonomicheskie problemy intensivnosti truda v SSSR* (Moscow, 1966), p. 204.

33 Kalinina, op. cit., p. 20.

34 Danilova, op. cit., pp. 28–9; Starodub, op. cit., pp. 199–201. This prompted Starodub to call for women in textiles and related branches of light industry to receive the same amount of additional leave time as did workers in iron and steel, non-ferrous metallurgy, and other industries with heavy and hazardous conditions.

35 Kalinina, op. cit., pp. 10–11, 22–4.

36 V. I. Starodub, 'Tekhnicheskii progress – uslovie rasshireniya sfery primeneniya truda zhenshchin', in *Nauchnye zapiski* (Leningradskii Finansovo-ekonomicheskii Institut im. N. A. Voznesenskogo), vypusk 27 (1965), p. 225.

37 Kalinina, op. cit., pp. 13–14.

38 *Moskovskaya pravda*, 10 August 1956; *Rabochii krai*, 23 January 1962, 3 April 1962.

39 Kalinina, op. cit., pp. 63–4; *Statistika byudzhetov vremeni trudyashchikhsya* (Moscow, 1967), p. 108. At the Bryansk worsted combine the accident rate on night shifts was 30–50 per cent higher than on day shifts (Kalinina, op. cit., p. 64).

40 *Puti likvidatsii tekuchesti kadrov v promyshlennosti SSSR* (Moscow, 1965), p. 84. In an attempt to cut the amount of night work in textiles the regime introduced the so-called 'Ivanovo Schedule' in the early 1960s. This was supposed to cut night shifts from seven per month to two.

41 Kalinina, op. cit., pp. 39–40.

42 Ibid., pp. 27–8; *Rabochii krai*, 2 April 1964.

43 Starodub, Dissertation, pp. 115, 134.

44 V. Beechey, 'The Sexual Division of Labour and the Labour Process: a Critical Assessment of Braverman', in S. Wood (ed.), *The Degradation of Work? Skill, Deskilling and the Labour Process* (London, 1982), p. 67.

45 *Zhenshchiny i deti v SSSR* (1969), p. 86.

46 Beechey, op. cit., p. 70.

47 In a number of industrial regions skilled male workers earned sufficiently high wages that women could contribute more to the household budget if they stayed home and tended the private plot than if they took up a low-paying job. Filtzer, op. cit., p. 64.

48 Starodub, Dissertation, p. 93.

3
Women and Girls in the Virgin Lands

Michaela Pohl

Nikita Khrushchev's first large-scale project, the 'mass opening of the Virgin Lands', was designed primarily to increase Soviet grain production. Starting in 1954, it brought hundreds of thousands of Slavic settlers to the northern regions of Kazakhstan. Celebrated as a 'great achievement of the party and people' during the Soviet period, the project was dismissed as a 'disaster' for the Kazakh nation after 1991.[1] The Communist Party sent people to 'remote' steppes, to a 'backward' region, but Kazakhstan was not empty when the settlers arrived. They encountered a multitude of the victims of Stalin's terror: prisoners, exiles, as well as the Kazakhs themselves, decimated after a terrible famine in 1931–33, and deprived of nearly all their leaders after the Stalin-era purges. In the 1930s the north of Kazakhstan had been turned into one of the main sites of the Gulag and into a place of exile for a great number of groups and nations deported by Stalin – *kulaks* ('rich' peasants expropriated and arrested during collectivisation), followed by Poles, Koreans and Ukrainians. The two largest groups that were brought to the region by force were Germans and Chechens during the Second World War.[2] Ten years later the region became the headquarters of the Virgin Lands.

The Virgin Lands opening is one of the most interesting and contradictory episodes of the Khrushchev period. Not merely a chapter in the history of agricultural politics in the Soviet Union, it was an important social process that initiated the de-Stalinisation and rehabilitation of a vast region that had served as a dumping ground for punished peoples and for labour camps. Over the next two decades the project brought up to 2 million additional people to Kazakhstan, creating one of the largest Russian-speaking diasporas in an area which, after the collapse of the Soviet Union, would become Russia's 'near abroad'.

The Virgin Lands project yields unique insights into how women responded to Khrushchev's reforms. Tens of thousands of Russian, Ukrainian and Belorussian women, including collective farmers, students, workers and housewives, relocated to the north of Kazakhstan each year throughout the 1950s and 1960s. Women and girls were addressed in all Virgin Lands appeals that went out to young people and the population as a whole, and they were recruited separately in several 'girls' recruitment campaigns in 1954 and 1958–59. This chapter discusses the intentions of the party in recruiting women. It also explores the experiences of the women on site, their living and working conditions, their conflicts with bosses and local people, their courtship and marriage, the opportunities the Virgin Lands afforded them, and the contribution women made to frontier life. The chapter is based primarily on the women's own testimonies, both in interviews and in the archives. The oral testimonies are drawn from about 30 interviews with Russian, Ukrainian, Moldovan, Belorussian, German, Kazakh and Chechen women, life histories that I collected on fieldwork trips to the Akmola region in Kazakhstan between 1994 and 2000. My questions varied depending on nationality and background, but I followed a similar set of questions for both men and women.[3] Kazakh and Russian archives contain hundreds of recently declassified letters from the settlers in addition to the correspondence of Komsomol leaders Aleksandr Shelepin and Vladimir Semichastnyi.[4] These documents reveal aspects of life in Kazakhstan that informants were sometimes hesitant to discuss frankly in interviews, for instance hunger conditions or violent incidents.

As Natalya Kosmarskaya has shown, on the basis of her interviews with several hundred Russian-speaking respondents in Kyrgyzstan, women have been 'more active and influential agents of interethnic relations' in Russia's former borderlands, given that 'it is mainly women who find themselves in the very demanding role of "contact person"'.[5] Women's testimonies allow us to explore ethnic 'contact routines', in contrast to the more dramatic male-initiated riots and disturbances that I have explored elsewhere.[6] They illuminate in sharper detail processes of social, economic and cultural transformation at the domestic level, and, as Cynthia Simmons has argued for the siege of Leningrad, in some cases their story is the more accurate version of events.[7] Many of the women whom I interviewed came to Kazakhstan to get married and they emphasised that they stayed in Kazakhstan primarily because they started a family. The chapter ends with their conclusions on Khrushchev's reforms and on what women contributed to frontier life, to the economy and to the transformation of culture in Kazakhstan.

Caring hands

Official image-makers and propagandists in the Komsomol and Communist Party did not consistently pursue a clearly defined separate image for women in the Virgin Lands. They created official ideals of women in the Virgin Lands, and promoted them in newsreels, feature films and print media, but the result was not a '*tselinnitsa*' (female Virgin Lander). There is no specifically named 1950s female Virgin Lands activist to add to the Stalinist images and role models of *traktoristka*, *komsomolka* and *obshchestvennitsa* (female tractor driver, Komsomol member, social activist) that have been discussed in recent literature about women's experiences in the Soviet Union, although these role models clearly continued to function in the Virgin Lands.[8] The reason is that the party was not interested in recruiting women in the Virgin Lands into mechanised professions such as tractor driving. Rather, it specifically wanted them to move to Kazakhstan to get married, in order to set up households and gardens, and to work in animal husbandry (to milk the cows, traditionally a female role). One of the main slogans used to recruit women to the new Virgin Lands settlements was 'Your caring hands are needed everywhere.'[9]

Year after year, in appeals, speeches, newspaper articles and internal documents, party bosses simply referred to women settlers in Kazakhstan as 'girls' (*devushki*) – from Khrushchev and Brezhnev on down to the planners who drafted tables of how many 'girls' were needed in individual regions and state farms. These men saw women primarily as a source of wives and housewives, and their testimonies on this issue are nearly identical. Both Khrushchev and Brezhnev took credit in their memoirs for solving 'the guys' problems' in the Virgin Lands, emphasising that they 'sent girls' because they listened to complaints and to what Soviet workers had to say to them on their inspection trips.[10] Brezhnev, who served as First Secretary of the Kazakh Communist Party during the first two years of the Virgin Lands programme (1954–55) called this 'solving demographic problems in a civilised way':

> Try to think how you can keep people on the farm. First, invite some girls here. Dairy-workers, seeder operators, telephonists, cooks, doctors, teachers. There's plenty of work for them here already.

Invite the girls and many of the lads will stay on for good. [...] Neither the state nor society can find everybody their 'chosen' one ... but we must see to it that there are no purely 'male' regions or 'female' towns. And if the demographic problems are dealt with competently, the young people will find each other and be happy. And happy they must be because without that the country cannot prosper.[11]

According to Dmitrii Esipenko, chief of the Rural Youth Sector of the Komsomol Central Committee 1953–59 and one of the key members of the Komsomol's Virgin Lands Recruitment Commission, the 'girls' idea' arose to give a jump start to poultry and milk production on the *tselina*. Esipenko took part in the work of an editorial team (together with editors and journalists) that wrote up appeals to women. They distributed them in rural regions and in industries that had large female workforces, such as textile mills.[12] Esipenko's team authored a famous appeal, frequently mentioned in books and articles on the Virgin Lands, 'Join us, girls, in the Virgin Lands' (*'Priezzhaite, devushki, k nam, na tselinnye zemli'*), which was published in *Pravda* on 17 July 1954, and received nationwide attention for years afterwards. The 'Marinovskii appeal', as it is known, was ostensibly written by six young women at the Marinovskii sovkhoz in the Akmolinsk region in the first Virgin Lands summer of 1954.[13] It consists of three columns of text. The first two describe the construction of the Marinovskii Virgin Lands state farm, 'one of those new farms which are growing in front of our eyes, and which have a great future ahead of them'; the third reads as follows:

A lot of men are working in the Virgin Lands, and there are few girls and women. In our state farm for instance, we count 37 women, about a sixth of the total number of workers. In the meantime, active female workers are needed in the state farms. The farms need agriculture specialists, mechanisers, construction workers, milkmaids, doctors, nurses, teachers, accountants, and radio operators. ... Girls of many specialities are finding a challenge for their strengths and knowledge in the new state farms. Their caring hands are needed everywhere, in all branches of production. Girls who come to our state farms are actively working in tractor-field brigades, in construction, in the accountant's office, at the medical office, in the lunch hall. However, in daily life, and in many branches of production we are experiencing a serious shortage of women. For instance, we only have one female tractorist. The state farm has received forty cows to provide milk for the workers, but there are not enough experienced hands to take care of them and to milk them. There are also not enough girls to work in the gardens. Expressing not only our opinion, but the wishes of all the workers on the new state farms, we call on girls to come participate in the opening of the virgin and fallow lands, in order to take personal part in the struggle for the fulfillment of patriotic duties posed by our party and government. The girls and women of our country have always been active participants of all patriotic endeavors. Dear [girl] friends! Answer our call, come work in the Virgin Lands regions![14]

According to the party literature, the Marinovskii state farm was flooded with over 60,000 letters from potential volunteers in response to the appeal, the director temporarily turning into a kind of postmaster.[15] Internal recruitment tables show that far fewer female volunteers were needed and expected, a total of 17,894 for the republic as a whole.[16] The campaign was poorly organised. Almost a week after the first groups of women and girls were already on their way to Kazakhstan, among them 49 volunteers from Moscow factories, no one had issued directions on where exactly to send them. The volunteers of 1954 were unevenly distributed in only a few state farms and villages in northern Kazakhstan, in large groups of several thousand women who were all from the same central region.[17] After that, interest waned for several years. Later in the decade, under the pressure of severe labour shortages due to the yearly return migration of up to two-thirds of Virgin Lands settlers, women were recruited separately in two drives to Kazakhstan, in 1958 and 1959; 28,754 women and girls came to Kazakhstan as a result in 1959. About 20,000 stayed, while a little over 8000 left by 1960.[18] The separate women's campaigns ceased after that, perhaps because women were actively recruited through all other channels as well, and in addition thousands of them came and went spontaneously (*samotek*), especially women who did not meet the age requirements to be recruited as 'girls' (roughly over 25).[19]

'A tiny corner and work'

What initially motivated settlers to come to the Virgin Lands? Obviously there are many different answers, but my interviewees (men and women) unanimously pointed to the grinding post-war poverty as something they all desperately tried to leave behind. Rima Rodionova, a collective farm woman who made a modest career as an accountant, said she believed Kazakhstan was a 'rich country' when she was a girl of 17, living in the province of Ivanovo, in central Russia. Her older sister (who had come to Akmolinsk in 1954) told her it was easier to live in Kazakhstan, that one could find work and that the wages were good. 'I thought the bread grew in loaves here', she said, and burst out laughing. Growing serious, she recalled another frequently mentioned reason why people responded to the party's appeals. It gave them the chance to leave the collective farm and to receive an internal passport, without the Virgin Lands opening an impossible dream for thousands of youth stuck in bleak, war-damaged collective farms, especially in the western regions of the Soviet Union. Rodionova recalled that the labour days (*trudodni*) accumulated in kolkhozy amounted to nothing more than 'little sticks' (*palochki*): they were counted, but one received no money for them, only grain at the end of year. Meanwhile, in the state farms of Kazakhstan, one could earn money wages.[20]

The archives contain hundreds of letters such as the following, dated 11 February 1956, from a 35-year-old woman in the Poltava region. This kind of letter was never published in the press, because its author, a single mother with a child, did not fit the mould of the conventional volunteer:

> Dear Comrade Director! I would very much like to apply for permanent work in your state farm. I already know much about your farm from the letters of my acquaintances who live there. I am glad about your achievements, and I regret that I did not participate in these first accomplishments ... I can do any work according to your discretion. Where could I be of the greatest utility? True, I am not so young anymore (birth date 1921), and I have a seven-year-old son. I am asking you to please write whether I could receive the tiniest corner (a room) and work. Everything else will come of its own. I also have good neighbours: the husband is a combine driver, the wife a medical worker. They would also like to resettle.[21]

Female Komsomol members or students initially arrived with greater confidence, demanding more than 'tiny corners'. Regardless of age or background, however, most women ended up doing similar work in Kazakhstan. The great majority worked in the worst paid and most physically demanding jobs: non-mechanised fieldwork and animal husbandry, construction and food preparation. Only professionals directly recruited into management positions (soil scientists, veterinary surgeons) and a few educated women found white-collar jobs right away, although the chance of getting such a job improved the longer one stuck it out. To give an example, of just over 6400 women who arrived in the Akmola region in August 1958, 2760 were initially sent into haymaking, 2107 worked as milkmaids and pig farmers, 935 were sent to construction sites, 894 attended various short-term training courses (150 of 6400 attended tractor-driving courses), and less than 450 found work based on their previous experience as accountants, sales clerks, teachers and medical personnel.[22]

Non-mechanised fieldwork was extremely arduous. No norms and wage guidelines were set up for haymaking, procuring straw and reeds, milking cows, raising chickens, digging, weeding, and watering vegetable plots, and for harvesting produce. Only latecomers took these jobs, and they were usually women and girls, in part because the women's campaigns were planned belatedly and hastily (in each of the 'girls' campaigns' in 1954 and 1958–59 the women were recruited in the summer, rather than the spring seasons). Several of my informants worked as milkmaids in Kazakhstan, both before and after the Virgin Lands started. One of them remembered that her income was 40 rubles per month during the 1950s, while her husband, working as a tractor assistant, earned 200–300 rubles per month. (Tractor drivers' earnings ranged from 400–500 to several thousand rubles per month, especially during summer months.)[23] Komsomol boss Aleksandr Shelepin sharply criticised the lack of attention to poor conditions and insignificant wages in women's jobs in the summer of 1954,[24] only to repeat similar criticisms one year later.[25] At the end of the decade he continued to receive reports such as this from the Virgin Lands: '[T]he girls are sent to third-rate and poorly paid jobs and often they have no work at all ... in some districts 160–300 of the girls don't work at all.'[26]

As an alternative to poorly paid farm work, many women initially worked in construction units. Workers in state farm construction brigades were considered unskilled labourers and they earned between 200 and 300 rubles per month. This was still much less than the typical earnings of (usually male) mechanisers, who could make that much in two to three days, but construction work was better paid than fieldwork.[27] I collected testimonies from a small group of Virgin Landers in the village of Manshuk, about 100 kilometres south of former Akmolinsk (now Astana). They were the last of a large group of several hundred youth who came to this Virgin Lands settlement in 1955, almost all from the province of Ivanovo in central Russia. All of the women remembered working in rock and sand quarries near

Manshuk, and in construction. Antonina Azeeva insisted that despite the hardships of those years, a sense of community prevailed that was lost after the collapse of the Soviet Union:

AA I worked in construction. Three years I worked in construction. We built houses. We used to have these panel houses, prefabricated Finnish houses. There was plenty of work to go around. It was an untouched land, and everything had to be done by hand. [...] We [the women] were auxiliary workers. We prepared the mortar. ... Right here stood two wooden troughs. We fill in sand, fill in cement, pour water, and mix it. We had blood coming from our noses! We weren't used to the heat. It was up to forty degrees, thirty-five degrees every day. That's how we worked! And today, do you think people work?! You can't force them! [Loudly, with shrill voice.] And we?? We ran to help, we were Komsomols, we built everything! For whom? For whom? Who even considers us human beings nowadays? [Voice breaks, quietly.] Nobody. [Long pause.]

MP What made you work so hard?

AA [Resignedly, then louder.] I don't know. I guess our consciousness was like that. That's how it was. All of Russia is built on the shoulders of the Komsomol! After the war! Everything! All the cities! ... And we transported the sand, I mean, we did everything by hand. Kenbydaik, it's about eighteen kilometers from here, to the sand quarry. We had these shovels, trowels, today you wouldn't do anything with them. They sent Ivan Ivanovich, the foreman. 'Girls, you won't go to lunch today. The trucks will go back and forth.' And, indeed, we were three girls, two from Ukraine and me, we were in the eighth brigade. We went, with our shovels, the trucks go back and forth, transporting the sand, and we filled them by hand. I worked so much during those three years! Up to here! [Gestures.] I was in work up to my neck! I don't even want to remember it. [Pause.] And cement, we went to Tselinograd to load cement and we loaded slate, what all we didn't load. And in the winter, how much snow we cleared! They were so strict in those years, it was unbearable! Forty degrees frost, in the winter, how could you go out? But they sent us out into that weather, to work. Every day we had to register at work. ... If there was a building, with walls erected, it meant you had to do something inside. ... Or you had to load something [...] The pay was low.

> Everything depended on your seniority, how much you had already worked there. I don't even want to remember. And look how we ended up. Why don't they value people like that any longer?[28]

Opportunities increased during good harvest years, for workers who stayed for several years, and for those who had a minimal education. In 1956, a record harvest year, an assistant accountant (accountants were usually female) earned 400–600 rubles per month, while women workers loading grain at a grain mill earned over 600 rubles.[29] Those of the women construction workers in Manshuk who had a seventh-grade education all found work in accounting by the mid-1960s, including Azeeva.

The initial living conditions were terribly difficult, for both men and women, especially during the first few years of the so-called 'mass opening'. The party made an enormous effort to supply the Virgin Lands regions with technology, building materials and foodstuffs, but initially many of the materials piled up at railroad stations, far from the new state farms, and the workers experienced severe and prolonged shortages of all basic food supplies. In extreme instances workers went hungry for days, as in this example described in a letter by Aleksandra Lukanina, a young woman from Moscow recruited to work in Ust-Kozha, in the Altai region:

Hello from Siberia, 30 May 1956
Be greeted dear parents. ... In the first lines of my letter I want to let you know that I haven't received a letter from you yet, and now I want to write a few words about how we are living now. We're having a strike right now, the workers aren't going to work, and the reason I'm writing is that they haven't paid us for two months now. ... So, Mama, don't expect us at home. [...] We're sitting here hungry for four days now, not just us, me and Lesha, but the girls are all lying in bed without eating. The wind gets to them and their legs won't carry them. That's how far we've come. Can it be that there's no help in the Soviet Union and no one cares how the Virgin Landers live. Mamochka, I feel so sorry for the girls, they all have a temperature from hunger, and it's a shame to live in such a time in the Soviet Union and where is our Government and where is it looking, how can they allow people to sit hungry, in our time. [...] Mama, don't cry and don't get upset, I'm not the only one like that here, there's a lot of us, so don't just cry about me, I ask of you, and

about coming home, I just can't right now, it's not 40 km after all, but 6,000 km. [...] It's my own fault, I didn't listen to my elders, and now it can't be fixed. Mama, please send me a small parcel, even if it's just bread [...] but don't send flour, we don't have anywhere to bake it, we don't have ovens. ... Mamochka, please don't be angry that I'm asking you for help, I don't have the strength not to ... I understand you don't have it easy, either. [...] Mama, we really ask you to please go to the Stalin district committee, and to one other place, Papa knows where to go, our girls are asking you. Our letters aren't getting there, so we ask you to go with this one ... and send us the results, what they say, we're waiting for an answer. Sorry this is without a stamp, but we don't have money for bread.[30]

Complaints about shortages in Kazakhstan came in by the hundreds each month, but this letter caused considerable alarm in Moscow, not only because of the famine condition, but because it mentioned a strike. A representative from the Komsomol Central Committee investigated the case. The investigation revealed that the situation was exactly as described in the letter. The girls mentioned in Lukanina's letter were all from the same orphanage in Moscow. Ignored by the state farm, earning extremely little money, they had been forced to sell their things to survive (their meagre orphanage belongings!), and, feeble from hunger, had spent entire weeks lying on their cots, unable to go to work.[31] It was an extreme case, but not an isolated one. The documents of the investigation show clearly that the situation was made worse by corruption (as in many other state farms), as a cynical farm boss and administration personnel lined their pockets from the sale of supplies intended for the settlers. Furthermore, the regions of Kazakhstan where the Virgin Lands were ploughed up were deeply marked by the presence of labour camps and of deported populations. The atmosphere was repressive, and few bosses cared about the conditions for workers. Many of the bosses who were brought in were demobilised officers, while local farm directors were used to working with camp prisoners and deportees, and they treated the volunteers in the same way.

'We Moscow girls are not asking, we are demanding!'

Local bosses were likely to dismiss most complaints as exaggerations, but especially those from Moscow volunteers. Volunteers from the capital acquired a particular reputation in the Virgin Lands. They had no experience in agricultural work, but they were perceived as wild and troublesome, 'loafers' who drank to excess but asked for medical excuses at the most inexcusable times and who complained loudly about everything. Their weak work performance in the fields did not endear them to other settlers either. Members of a tractor brigade in the Kokchetav region, for instance, wrote to *Komsomol'skaya pravda* to complain about the strange Moscow youth (boys and girls) who wore 'sweaters down to their knees', danced 'in style' (*tantsuyut stilem*, meaning 'Western style' or rock'n'roll) and sang songs 'not in the repertoire of Russian songs nor of the union republics'.[32] They singled out girls from Moscow for indecency, even though the bosses did not provide separate tents or barracks for them:

> When we talk to them, they say 'you don't understand us, we're just being sociable'. But we don't think it's very tactful for a young girl to be around in underwear and a bra, living in a brigade with 20–30 men including men up to 50 years of age. Dear editors, we ask you please to explain are we right or did we just not understand the people from Moscow?[33]

Local people saw a lot of wild behaviour over the years, and some perceived Moscow youth as 'loose' or 'immoral'. These notions were especially intensely projected on to women. In addition, people who had more attractive options (a job offer elsewhere, an education, relatives in Moscow or any other large city) ended up leaving the *tselina*, and some hostility towards more privileged volunteers who had this option, again, especially women, was even still expressed by my informants in the 1990s, as in this outburst by an elderly man in Manshuk:

> Why did the professor's daughter, the daughter of a colonel come here to the *tselina*? She came to eat *kasha*. While at home they fed her delicacies. She came to sit out the season, and in the winter she went home! And there were many like that! Why did someone like that come here? To find excitement, to say they took part. ... Every day in the summer, they sent them packages, full of oranges and little bottles of cognac.[34]

Komsomol First Secretary Vladimir Semichastnyi addressed the issue of 'girls in the *tselina*' at a plenum in 1956, in passing. He was aware of the wide distribution of negative stereotypes of women in the Virgin Lands, but was primarily interested in them as signs of a 'backward' or 'old-style' (Stalinist) management style in rural regions. Semichastnyi mocked a typical report on youth behaviour received from a small town in the Virgin Lands:

> Very often they [rural Komsomol secretaries] talk of the poor behaviour of some of the arriving youth, and then they mention one particular girl, and they judge her for frequently going to dances. [Annotation in original: Laughter.] They accuse her of behaving poorly. [...] [O]nce again [we] denounce improper behaviour, punish and scold the arriving youth. [...] Once again we pour dirt on our youth, paint a picture of them as loafers, hooligans, alcoholics. The Central Committee of the Kazakhstan [V]LKSM seriously has to deal with these matters, comrades.[35]

Semichastnyi scolded the backward Kazakh youth organisation for their punitive approach, and approved the youth's demands in the Virgin Lands for better material and 'cultural' conditions as 'justified', but he did not return to the issue of women in this or other speeches. The Komsomol leadership in Moscow was ultimately unable to reform the 'leadership style' of the rural organisations, and there is no evidence in the documents that rural attitudes to women changed at all in response to efforts from outside.

The first Virgin Lands decade was marked by frequent criminal and ethnic violence, and occasionally by rioting.[36] Most frequently violence erupted between the arriving Virgin Landers and deported Caucasians, Chechens or Ingush. My analysis of collective violence in the Akmola region has shown that the great majority of active participants in public confrontations and in mass fights were young males, but of course women were deeply affected by the violent atmosphere in Kazakhstan. They were the victims of beatings, rapes and many accidents caused by the careless attitude towards human life in general. Smaller fights are often described as having started 'over girls', or because either settlers or local men 'tried to squeeze' or 'made advances' towards women, or 'tried to enter the girls' tent'. The word 'rape' or 'attempted rape' is used very infrequently in reports, even those that are otherwise explicit about beatings, shootings, riots and accidents, but several of my informants indicated that rapes took place frequently.[37] It is also clear that some of the so-called 'instant weddings' criticised in Komsomol directives (see below) were abusive situations in which drunken women consented to sexual activities that they later regretted, but I have not found any systematic documentation on this issue.[38] Women who experienced rapes and beatings were almost certainly unlikely to find help or sympathy on the part of indifferent farm bosses or even among people in the villages, many of whom stereotyped the victims as loose women who had come to live and drink with unknown men.

Kazakhs, and other families who had lived in Kazakhstan for a while, regardless of national origin or faith, kept girls and young women tightly controlled until they were married, around age 14–16 among Muslims (Kazakhs, Chechens, Ingush, Tatars) and age 16–18 among Russians, Poles and Germans. Nearly everyone also practised the strict control of young daughters-in-law, who had to move to the husband's household after marriage. In some villages in the Akmola region, Polish girls were forbidden by their families to go to the rural club, which had a 'wild' reputation, but still, some German and Polish girls attended special lectures and joined the Komsomol, while Muslim women were hardly represented in these organisations at all. [39] In keeping with practices and guidelines established in Central Asia since the 1930s, the party organisation in Kazakhstan was concerned about the 'feudal-religious attitudes' by which young Muslim women were 'held hostage', and about their parents, who 'observe old customs and do not allow the girls to take part in public life'.[40] The Communist Party routinely prosecuted those among its own members who practised bride abduction, marriage to minors and polygamy – year after year, dozens of cases were reported by the regional committee in reports to Moscow – but it barely made a dent in deeply rooted practices in the villages.[41]

Gender roles and gender relations occasionally came up when my informants discussed ethnic difference. Several elderly Kazakhs made the complaint that the Russian girls and women who came in the course of the Virgin Lands opening did not dress or behave properly and that they got married to anybody, regardless of confession or ethnic group. A German woman, on the other hand, described the attitudes of Kazakhs to women as controlling and 'cruel' and she told of how she witnessed beatings of girls and women. The same informant told me about an episode in which she explicitly stood up to two Kazakh boys:

> I was always straightforward, you know, I interrupted people and had to state my opinion. Once, in the village, two of them said that girls can't ride as well as men. Two Kazakhs. I disagreed with them, too. And so we made a bet, let's bet, who'll get to the MTS first. And

then we rode! Through cold water, and snow was still on the ground. I really drove the horse, and they were always behind me! At the MTS a lot of men were standing around, the chairman, and some brigade leader I think, and I got there at full gallop. They said, you crazy girl, what's this? I told them, when those two *dzhigits* [Kazakh boys] get here, write down a centner of wheat for each one of them, and the wheat is mine, that's how it is. You should have seen their expressions! And when those two arrived, they said the devil take it, what kind of girl is that? I mean that was a great gift for me! We used to only get 150 grams of bread a day, so you can imagine, two centners, what that meant for us! And then my thighs hurt for two weeks, *ach ja*. Those two, they had real saddles, and I just had a rope.[42]

This kind of confrontational attitude (whether the incident is idealised or not) was not common, however, either among the German women, or among former Virgin Landers who remained in Kazakhstan, mainly Russian and Ukrainian collective farm women. The documents only occasionally reveal instances of assertiveness or rebelliousness on the part of girls and women, and then they were indeed usually workers or students from the capital. Moscow youth were more likely to know people with some influence, and they were not shy about voicing their complaints. By the time of the third large-scale mobilisation of women to Kazakhstan, in 1959, the Virgin Lands settlers routinely used several collective tactics for attempting to deal with indifferent bosses and intolerable conditions, and women used these methods, too. The primary form of action was the individual complaint letter, sent by the thousands to Soviet leaders, party and Komsomol committees, and newspapers. These letters were monitored and excerpts collected for party leaders in *svodki* (official reports). Komsomol and party bosses paid greater attention to such letters if they were signed by a number of people, and if such letters were 'alarming' and sent as telegrams. When conditions were especially bad and even group letters resulted in no action, some Virgin Landers resorted to dramatic group complaint trips to regional party offices or to Moscow. Such trips became more frequent in the late 1950s, to the point that bosses in Kazakhstan complained that collective trips to the district party and Komsomol investigative committees in search of the 'truth' took up 'the lion's share of the district authorities' time'.[43]

The workers, for their part, learned to use not only collective action but even the threat of it to make their complaints more effective. This is illustrated by a letter from a group of young women working in Kustanai in 1959, which was one of those documents that succeeded in eliciting 'alarm' on the part of the reporting official, and which was cited in its entirety in an update on the course of the 'girls' campaign' in 1959. The women wrote that they had come 'with a clean heart, to work, but found something completely different'. They described unsanitary conditions, poor and expensive food, and low pay. But what angered them most was the neglectful and rude treatment they experienced, and the wild rumours that other state farm workers told about them:

> Every night drunken fellows invade our room. We've repeatedly asked the farm office to stop this hooliganism ... but no one has paid attention. All of the girls get up at 5 to go to work, and all night we have to fight hooligans, and hear only threats: 'We'll cut you, we'll smash in the window'. [...] All kinds of rumors are going around about us at the state farm. They pour dirt on us, saying that we were thrown out of Moscow and that we came with venereal diseases. When we went to the bath house to wash, they screamed at us that we're sick, to go away, and they all ran away from us to the other side of the bath. [...] We've asked them to stop these rumors and to punish the gossips, but without result, even though we all came after a background check, and there's not one among us that is as they say. [...] We are not asking anything impossible, we knew where we were going. We knew it would be hard and that we would have to work. But they have met us so poorly here, insulted us, and they don't try to create even the most elementary conditions for a more or less decent existence. We Moscow girls are not asking but demanding, precisely demanding that you send us a representative from the Komsomol Central Committee as soon as possible, to investigate our letter. We ask you to read our letter very carefully, because we cannot live in these circumstances. If we are all forced to come and see you, it will be very unpleasant. All of the girls have agreed to wait until 20 June. If no representative shows up by 20 June, all fifty of us will come to Moscow, to the Komsomol Central Committee, directly, with all of our things. And we girls are close friends, the girls are decisive, they will do what they promised. We have included only twenty signatures, because the rest of us are working in the outlying farm sections. Those girls have it even worse. Out there they have no baths, the men drink a lot, and start fights. If you don't help us, by 1 July we will all pay you a visit.[44]

Obviously, short-term visits by outside representatives, however powerful, could do little to effect lasting change in the Virgin Lands regions. This frustrated not only the settlers. Party bosses in Moscow tried a number of expedients and administrative reorganisations to improve their control of the situation, including, ultimately, the creation of a entirely new party organisation in the north of Kazakhstan, in the form of the so-called 'Virgin Lands *krai*', run directly from Moscow (1961–65).[45]

'The best things in life were family and friends'

Why did settlers stay, considering the dire circumstances that they described over and over in their letters and testimonies? Antonina Azeeva, who describes her construction work above, exclaimed:

> Oh, how we cried! Oh! Where did we end up? Why did they tell us it was so great here [*sil'no khorosho*]? On the radio it said how in Kazakhstan, how it couldn't be better than that! Well, afterwards, after we opened the new lands, we really did have a great life. Only the surroundings remained strange, but we had all the goods we needed.[46]

Two important concerns kept women in the Virgin Lands. First, the overall economic situation in the region began to change dramatically about a decade after the project started, in part as a result of the formation of the Virgin Lands *krai*. The party once again made enormous investments in housing, infrastructure and consumer goods. In 1962 Akmolinsk was transformed into 'Tselinograd' (Virgin Lands City) and the city offered employment and 'shops full of foreign goods' and it became 'more cultured', acquiring sports and entertainment complexes and a new radio and television station. In my interviews and conversations, it was often women who came to Kazakhstan in the mid-1960s who spoke most fondly of the entire Virgin Lands undertaking. They spontaneously and enthusiastically recounted how their material lives improved when they came to Akmolinsk in the mid- or late 1960s, saying 'they shipped everything'; 'they had shops full of everything'; 'in the stores here they had goods from East Germany, Poland, Czechoslovakia, they had shoes'.[47]

Second, many of the women settlers wanted to get married and to start a household. The Virgin Lands regions were a Mecca for the marriage-minded, and many of those who found a husband or wife ended up staying, at least for a while, despite the difficulties. Initially, so many marriages took place between settlers, some short-lived, that Komsomol instructors became worried about the 'moral laxity' of the volunteers. Numerous documents mention 'light-hearted weddings'. 'Frivolous weddings have become a widespread practice. Some settlers marry each other after two or three days of acquaintance, and after a few weeks they get divorced.'[48] For this reason, some farm directors refused to make transport available to have weddings registered in the district or oblast' centre. Even though some weddings were thus never registered, or with some delay, the number of newly founded families grew significantly, as the figures in Table 3.1 from Akmolinsk show.

The party was especially proud of the fact that the number of multi-national or 'mixed' weddings grew (and along with them, presumably, a spirit of 'internationalism') as the collection and presentation of statistics such as the above indicate. Of course, the majority of these 'mixed' weddings were Slavs marrying each other (Ukrainian–Russian, Russian–Belorussian), or Slavs marrying Europeans (Germans, Poles, Balts), while marriages of non-Muslims to Muslims were less common. Virgin Landers who courted and married women from among the deportees (Germans, Poles) sometimes encountered obstacles and resistance on the part of male relatives or the special settler police, but such marriages nevertheless grew more frequent over the years.[49] None of my interview questions generated as much enthusiasm among the settlers as the simple request to describe courtship and weddings. Rima Rodionova fondly recalled her 'brigade wedding' and the sense of community it created, even as she remembered 'how poor we were at the beginning':

> We had a brigade wedding! The whole brigade had a party! How many people in the brigade, let's see, twenty, or thirty, and our neighbours. We were in this little tiny room, sat down, people

Table 3.1   Registered marriages in Tselinograd (Akmolinsk), 1950–65

Year	Number of marriages	Percentage of smeshannye ('mixed') weddings
1950	1198	20.5
1955	1315	36.5
1960	1623	38.8
1965	1974	44.2

Source: S. S. Shvachko, *Tselina preobrazhennaya, tselina preobrazhayushchaya* (Tselinograd, 1968), p. 116.

everywhere! We never used to look who's friends with whom! We didn't make any distinctions, like, you're up there, you're a boss, you know, we were all the same. Who could, brought something, anything. When we used to gather together the first years, oh! On the days off, 'Here, I've got some potatoes', somebody else has something else, that's it, 'let's go', and we danced, we enjoyed our-selves! That's all gone now. And it was so friendly before, so nice.[...] We were all the same, friends. It was great; we celebrated for three days. No one paid attention, you know, director, worker, tractor driver, or whatever, we were all together. [...] After we got married we lived on a little iron bedstead, there where he lived [her husband], in the dormitory. We had a mattress, and one blanket, and slept there together. Back then nobody gave us presents. [...] We had a small section ... in the middle of the room, the stove stood by us, and that bunk bed, and a table. My sister gave me two cups, spoons, a plate, one cooking pot. That was it! My whole dowry![50]

Richard Stites has remarked that women in the Virgin Lands were 'shunted into housekeeping roles'.[51] Most documents and my conver-sations indicate that it went completely without saying that women would keep house, in addition to these jobs, whether in barracks or family housing. 'Keeping house' in rural Kazakhstan meant daily hard labour and extremely time-consuming chores. Apart from taking care of cows and chickens, it meant tremendous amounts of cooking and preserving (300–600 jars each season, according to my informants, depending on the size of the family). Russian, Ukrainian and Belorussian settlers nearly universally attempted to start up vegetable gardens. In the local climate and on steppe soils, without protection from the wind, this was a difficult task that required hours of digging and carrying water. As the women spontaneously pointed out, this was their unique contribution to Kazakhstan: 'everything you see around you, we planted,' 'there was nothing green here before we planted vegetables'.[52]

Most of the Russian women I spoke to in Kazakhstan expressed no conflicts with the genderings of work and daily life that they encoun-tered. Nor did they resent the fact that it fell to them to struggle for *kul'turnost'* in the new surroundings. They clearly embraced the one consistent mission in the Virgin Lands that was created for 'girls' by propagandists and they endlessly strove to make life more 'cultured'. This was also their main role in terms of 'ethnic contact routines' as

defined by Natalya Kosmarskaya above. By 'more cultured' my interviewees meant the introduction of Russian or Soviet culture. So, too,
did the mechanisers cited above who were concerned about the song
repertoire. Kazakh culture remained largely invisible to them, with the
important exception of the concept of hospitality.[53] The Komsomol
archive contains dozens of similarly worded earnest reports from
female activists who, exactly like exemplary 'girl settlers' described in
stories in newspapers and magazines such as *Krest'yanka* (*Peasant
Woman*), tried to 'improve the cultural level' by organising formal
dances and singing, regardless of everyone's exhaustion, or of the superior attractions of drinking.[54] But where, in fiction, the girls nearly
always managed to draw reluctant young men away from their drink
and their cards, in real life they were less successful. However, by a
widely shared consensus events where 'everyone put on their best
clothes and were on their best behaviour' (Komsomol activist, 1954)
or where 'everyone! everyone came dressed in their black suits'
(Rodionova, 1996) were something to aspire to. Moreover, women's
role in the kind of socialising that was ostensibly and officially frowned
upon by the party – with alcohol (while the party bosses themselves
drank to excess) – was also enormously important. My informants told
me again and again what a satisfying social life they had in the *tselina*,
and what a central role drinking and having fun together played in
this. When I asked them what Soviet holidays 'were really like', they lit
up with great enthusiasm and described nostalgically '*kak my gulyali
vmeste*' (loosely: how we partied together) and they spent hours singing
songs and *chastushki* into my microphone. Most of their repertoire
derived straight from their home regions,[55] but they also sang a few
'official' Soviet Virgin Lands songs that became truly popular, such as
'*Edut novosely*' (The Settlers are Coming) and '*Zemlya tselinnaya*' (Virgin
Land),[56] illustrating a little of how closely their lives intersected with
officially engineered identity and prescribed activities.

Although Soviet models of 'internationalism' were discredited in
Kazakhstan after 1991, locally the idea that the *tselina* was a place that
fostered a special kind of mutual aid and friendship among different
people remains a strong component of people's self-identification, and
women are proud of the role they played in creating this special atmosphere. Rima Rodionova served as a member of the rural council (*sel'sovet*)
in Manshuk for a few years during the 1970s, and while she laughed at
my notion that this might have 'empowered' her, she nevertheless
recounted, not without satisfaction, what she contributed to her community. According to her, the women on the council worked to make the

village look 'neat': they ensured that streets were swept and cleaned, that the few existing lights and the public loudspeakers worked, and that farm workers painted their fences white once a year and planted some flowers and bushes. The achievement of which she was most proud was that she and her husband were known as an orderly and, most important, hospitable couple, and that over the years they put up a steady stream of outside visitors to Manshuk in their house, including geologists, party bosses, journalists and finally myself, a foreign researcher. This Rodionova clearly considered one of the more successful and exciting visits of recent memory (and an unexpected and hilarious occasion, with a bit of 'lubrication', to tell a flood of old Soviet jokes about American spies). She was clearly unaware of most aspects of Kazakh culture and even of how her own stories of previous visitors and the 'great parties' they had sounded similar to stories told in Kazakh families about feasts and celebrations.[57] But she also felt comfortable in Kazakhstan despite some concerns about the future and about Kazakh intentions; the white fences and holidays, the drinking and the jokes and the hospitality added up to genuine pride in her achievements. In a more serious moment, she stated: 'And so we put our modest little labour into this undertaking [the Virgin Lands opening]. And we consider that for the people this was one of the greatest and smartest decisions of the government.'[58]

Conclusion

Women's voices from the *tselina* do not only add to our knowledge of women's history of the Khrushchev period. They also represent a key piece of evidence on the outcome of the Virgin Lands project, along with recently more visible Kazakh regrets about the loss of steppe wetlands, the closing of Kazakh schools and the decline of Kazakh villages. Successive 'invasions of brides' but also of headstrong activists from Moscow were initially upsetting both to rural bosses and isolated villagers in Kazakhstan. Letters from the settlers testify to the darker sides of the Virgin Lands experience for women: hunger and shortages, disease and high accident rates, ubiquitous violence, consistently lower pay and less satisfying jobs than men. In addition, those of the female youth who developed a subculture, especially teenagers from Moscow, were frequently denounced as 'amoral' and 'loose'. However, the *tselina* also offered opportunities and material benefits, especially to those who stuck it out a few years. The women I interviewed usually avoided grand statements, focusing instead on personal achievements or making slightly apologetic observations such as the following: 'Maybe this is too light-spirited, but the best things in life were family and friends.'[59] All their testimonies underline that the *tselina* ended up being attractive to many different people who sought to start a new life, and that it brought material benefits to those who lived here before it started as well. Kazakh women pointed out that all the housing was built during the opening of the Virgin Lands and that 'we all slept on the floor before, whereas now we sleep in beds'.[60] Most older Kazakhs in the Virgin Lands emphatically reject the notion that the project brought them harm. The Moldovan wife of a former deportee, herself born in a remote *aul* some 200 kilometres from Akmolinsk, told me that a 'second life' began with the Virgin Lands.[61] Many women from different backgrounds, including 'special' settlers and former prisoners, came to embrace similar notions of Soviet *kul'turnost'* and the new regional identity that was encouraged by the growth of prosperity. According to women, the initial years of shortages and adjustments were terribly difficult ones for nearly every family, but ultimately the *tselina* satisfied dreams of marriage, a home and modest prosperity for thousands of people.

Notes

1 See, for example, D. M. Crowe, Zh. Dzhunusova and S. O. Sabol (guest eds), *Focus on Kazakhstan: History, Ethnicity, and Society*, Special Topic Issue, *Nationalities Papers*, vol. 26, no. 3, September 1998, pp. 405–6, 428.

2 M. Pohl, '"It Cannot Be that Our Graves Will Be Here": the Survival of Chechen and Ingush Deportees in Kazakhstan, 1944–1957', *Journal of Genocide Research*, vol. 4, no. 3, September 2002, pp. 401–30.

3 The interviews were carried out with a Human Subjects Clearance for my project from Indiana University, and the interviewees cited by name signed a Human Subjects Clearance, agreeing to an 'authorial' (*avtorskii*) interview, while all others cited agreed in writing or verbally to be cited anonymously in my publications.

4 Especially important for this chapter were the records of the 'Rural Youth Sector' of the Komsomol Central Committee, TsKhDMO, f. 1, op. 9, and reports and settlers' letters in the former party archive of the Akmola region, OPDAO, f. 1, op. 1.

5 N. Kosmarskaya, 'Russian Women in Kyrgyzstan: Coping with New Realities', *Women's Studies International Forum*, vol. 19, nos 1–2, 1996, p. 126.

6 See Pohl, op. cit., pp. 418–23, and M. Pohl, 'The Virgin Lands between Memory and Forgetting: People and Transformation in the Soviet Union, 1954–1960', unpublished PhD dissertation, Indiana University, 1999, Ch. 6, 'Collective Violence', pp. 321–68.

7 C. Simmons, 'Lifting the Siege: Women's Voices on Leningrad (1941–1944)', *Canadian Slavonic Papers/Revue canadienne des slavistes*, vol. XL, nos 1–2, March–June 1998, pp. 43–65.

8 See for instance, M. Buckley, 'The Untold Story of *Obshchestvennitsa* in the 1930s', *Europe–Asia Studies*, vol. 47, no. 4, 1996, pp. 569–86; T. G. Schrand,

'Soviet "Civic-Minded Women" in the 1930s: Gender, Class, and Industrialisation in a Socialist Society', *Journal of Women's History*, vol. 11, no. 3, Autumn 1999, pp. 126–48; M. Ilič, '*Traktoristka*: Representations and Realities', in M. Ilič (ed.), *Women in the Stalin Era* (Basingstoke, 2001), pp. 110–30; and M. F. Oja, 'From Krestianka to Udarnitsa: Rural Women in the Vydvizhenie Campaign, 1933–41', *Carl Beck Papers in Russian and East European Studies*, no. 1203 (1996).

9 *Akmolinskaya pravda*, 21 July 1954, p. 1.

10 N. S. Khrushchev, *Khrushchev Remembers: the Last Testament* (Boston, 1974), pp. 123–4; L. I. Brezhnev, *Tselina* (Moscow, 1978), p. 35.

11 L. I. Brezhnev, *The Virgin Lands*, tr. Robert Daglish (Moscow, 1978), p. 43.

12 Interview with D. A. Esipenko, Moscow, 3 April 1996, Tape No. 96–33.

13 'Priezzhaite, devushki, k nam, na tselinnye zemli!', *pravda* (Moscow), 17 July 1954; and see also the document collections by V. K. Savosko (ed.), *Narodnoe dvizhenie za osvoenie tselinykh zemel' v Kazakhstane* (Moscow, 1959), pp. 150–3, 672; I. M. Volkov (ed.), *Velikii podvig partii i naroda. Massovoe osvoenie tselinnykh i zalezhnykh zemel': Sbornik dokumentov i materialov* (Moscow, 1979), pp. 138–9.

14 *Akmolinskaya pravda*, 21 July 1954, p. 1.

15 I was not able to find these letters. They are mentioned in Nikolai Zhurin, *Trudnye i schastlivye gody: Zapiski partiinogo rabotnika* (Moscow, 1982), p. 198, and Brezhnev, *Tselina*, pp. 35–6. However, it is clear from oral testimonies that this appeal made an impression on potential settlers (quite a few remembered it by name). Ironically, I found dozens of letters written by *men* in 1954 and 1955 (by demobilised soldiers) in the local party archive, which mention Marinovskii state farm and the 'girls' initiative' in their letters asking about the conditions of employment in the Virgin Lands. OPDAO, f. 1, op. 1, d. 1983, ll. 19–21, 28, 47, 58, 71–4, 81, 86.

16 TsKhDMO, f. 1, op. 9, d. 297, l. 18, 'O potrebnosti iz chisla devushek v MTS i sovkhozakh Kazakhskoi SSR, osvaivayushchie novye zemli, po sostoyaniyu na 20.8.1954.'

17 Ibid., d. 297, ll. 59–60.

18 TsKhDMO, f. 1, op. 9, d. 470, ll. 1–11.

19 TsKhDMO, f. 1, op. 9, d. 297, l. 59, 31 July 1954, Veselov/Shelepin; and see Savosko, op. cit., p. 672, n. 37.

20 Interviews with Rima Konstantinovna Rodionova, b. 1938, Manshuk (Akmola region), Kazakhstan, August 1996, fieldnotes and Tape No. 96-41.

21 B. Urazakova, 'Ne khochu sidet' slozha ruki,' *Akmolinskaya pravda*, 25 February 1994, p. 2.

22 APRK, f. 708, op. 32, d. 525, ll. 54–6, 1 August 1959, 'O trudoustroistve i razmeshchenii devushek, pribyvshykh po komsomol'skim putevkam na postoyannuyu rabotu v oblast''.

23 Anonymous interview, Tape No. 96-51.

24 OPDAO, f. 1, op. 9, d. 295, ll. 19–23.

25 TsKhDMO, f. 1, op. 9, d. 327, l. 67.

26 OPDAO, f 1, d 2821, ll. 32–6, 16 September 1959, 'O nedostatkakh v trudovom, bytovom ustroistve devushek, pribyvshykh v sovkhozy oblasti.'

27 TsKhDMO, f. 1, op. 9, d. 295, ll.19–23, 20 August 1954, Shelepin/Kozlov.

28 Interview with Antonina Nikolaevna Azeeva, 19 August 1996, Manshuk, Tape No. 96-45.

29   TsKhDMO, f.1, op. 9, d. 339, l.16.
30   TsKhDMO, f.1, op. 3, d. 906, ll. 93–4.
31   TsKhDMO, f.1, op. 9, d. 364, ll. 27–8ob.
32   TsKhDMO, f.1, op. 9, d. 566, l. 67, 17 August 1960, letter from brigade No. 3, Priishimskii state farm.
33   Ibid.
34   Anonymous interview, Manshuk, Tape No. 96-43.
35   TsKhDMO, f.1, op. 2, d. 353, ll. 266–7, 27 December 1956, 'Stenogramma VI Plenuma TsK VLKSM, utrenee zasedanie 27/XII-56g.'.
36   Pohl, *Virgin Lands*, pp. 321–68.
37   This may also reflect my use of party documentation rather than court records.
38   Fieldnotes July 1996; Tape No. 96-33; and see TsKhDMO, f. 1, op. 9, d. 327, ll. 61–74.
39   OPDAO, f.1, op. 1, d. 2336, ll. 128–31, 25 June 1956, 'Dokladnaya zapiska o nastroeniyakh i povedenii spetsposelentsev'.
40   OPDAO, f.1, op. 1, d. 1915, l. 151.
41   OPDAO, f.1, op. 1, d. 1915, l. 153.
42   Testimony in German. Anonymous interview, Akmola, 14 July 1996, Tape No. 96-60.
43   TsKhDMO, f. 1, op. 9, d. 566, ll. 65–6, October 1960, Selivant'ev/ *Komsomol'skaya pravda*, TsK VLKSM.
44   TsKhDMO, f. 1, op. 9, d. 470, ll. 23–31.
45   Pohl, *Virgin Lands*, pp. 429–35.
46   Tape No. 96-45.
47   Fieldnotes, June–July 1996.
48   TsKhDMO, f. 1, op. 9, d. 326, ll. 41–54, 29 August 1955, Novoplyanskii/Goryunov, see also ibid., d. 327, ll. 61–74, 20 July 1955, Buryak et al./TsK VLKSM.
49   Fieldnotes; Tapes No. 94-01, 96-51.
50   Tape No. 96-41.
51   R. Stites, *Russian Popular Culture: Entertainment and Society since 1900* (Cambridge, 1992), p. 144.
52   Fieldnotes, August 1996.
53   See Kosmarskaya, op. cit..
54   Compare, for instance, M. Balykin, 'Vesennyaya kolonna. Rasskaz', in F. Morgun (ed.), *Na zemlyakh tselinnykh* (Alma-Ata, 1955), pp. 3–21, with TsKhDMO, f. 1, op. 9, d. 299, ll. 92–100.
55   The couples from Ivanovo in Manshuk knew the same cycles of *chastushki* and identified them as 'Ivanovskie'. Fieldnotes, August 1996.
56   See the lyrics for these and other songs published on the back covers of *Krest'yanka*, no. 2, 1955, and other issues 1954–59.
57   See C. A. Werner, 'The Dynamics of Feasting and Gift Exchange in Rural Kazakhstan', in I. Svanberg (ed.), *Contemporary Kazaks: Cultural and Social Perspectives* (New York, 1999), pp. 47–72.
58   Tape No. 96-41.
59   Fieldnotes, October 1996; Tape No. 96-30.
60   Fieldnotes, 7 July 1994.
61   Tape No. 96-53.

4

'Loose Girls' on the Loose?: Sex, Propaganda and the 1957 Youth Festival

Kristin Roth-Ey

In the summer of 1957, the Soviet Union invited tens of thousands of foreigners to Moscow for a grand fête known as the Sixth International Festival of Youth and Students. Today, the 1957 Youth Festival is commonly referred to as a turning point in post-war Soviet history: the first major break in the 'iron curtain' and as such, the beginning of the end for an autarkic Soviet cultural system.[1] Commentators recall the festival as a moment when not only the Soviet state, but also the Soviet people opened up to and embraced the world community. More often than not, there is a romantic or sexual tinge to these visions of a new Soviet openness. And more often than not, it is young Soviet women who feature most prominently. Mention the 1957 Youth Festival to Russians today, and you are likely to be met with a wry smile and comments about the so-called *deti festivalya* – the alleged cohort of biracial children born to Soviet women after the festival. This chapter examines the relationship between this representation of the festival – its distinctively risqué historical mystique – and 1950s mass media culture and popular sensibilities. Romance and sex prove critical not only to how the festival has been remembered, but also to how it was represented and interpreted by its contemporaries. Moreover, conflicts over adolescent female sexuality and femininity constitute the heart of festival stories, then and now. The figure in the eye of a shameful storm at the festival – or on the barricades of its 'sexual revolution', depending upon your perspective – is the 'loose girl' (*devushka legkogo povedeniya*) who failed to guard her 'maidenly honour' with the foreign guests. This image of a sexually active Soviet girl can be understood, irony in hand, as a distorted reflection of Soviet propaganda – the directive to

75

embrace foreigners at the festival run amok. At the same time, it is a vision that conveys many contemporaries' hopes and fears about foreign cultural influence and the consequences of opening up to the outside world. While certainly not new to Soviet society, these issues were crystallised in controversy and celebration in the summer of 1957, and so helped establish for the festival its potent historical mystique.

The 1957 Youth Festival brought more than 30,000 foreigners from 131 countries to Moscow in late July and early August. As the largest, most expensive and most ambitious in a series of post-war international festivals sponsored by the communist-dominated World Federation of Democratic Youth, the Moscow festival was a blowout – a two-week cultural, political and athletic extravaganza the likes of which no Soviet city had ever seen. There were multiple mass rallies and group excursions, carnivals and parades, and performances and meetings too numerous to count. More than 2 million people flooded the streets for the opening day festivities.[2] Yet the Moscow festival was distinguished not only by its size and scope, but also by its freewheeling, informal spirit. Soviet authorities in charge of the festival did attempt to organise their guests by national delegations, to bus them from event to event, and generally to fill up their days with official activities. However, the festival invitation had gone out to individuals, not to nationalities, and many guests chose to ignore their delegations and schedules and, instead, to plunge into Moscow on their own.[3] By all accounts, delegates who struck out independently had no trouble meeting Soviets. With the weather particularly fine that summer, foreign guests and their hosts thronged Moscow's recently refurbished streets and spruced up parks. Tverskaya – then Gorky Street or, in the argot of stylish Muscovite youth, 'Brodvei' – located in the heart of Moscow and brilliantly illuminated for the festival, was transformed every night into a mass street party and informal dance hall, as was Red Square. According to Soviet and foreign press accounts, many delegates found themselves literally surrounded by crowds of Soviets, some with questions, some looking for an autograph or to exchange a pin or shake hands, and some, perhaps many, just looking.[4]

In 1957, after all, the sight of foreigners on the streets was itself a visceral shock for many people. International tourism inside the USSR had only just begun, and most young Soviets' experience of foreigners was entirely limited to Soviet and foreign mass media sources. Soviet screen star Lyudmila Gurchenko, then a teenager, recalled her amazement in the mid-1950s when she spotted her young director freely associating with a group of French visitors on the set of a film. 'Personally, I knew foreigners from the movies. And not just me. They lived by themselves in their countries, and we lived in ours. There was no [live?] contact with them. ...'[5] Another teenager, jazz saxophonist Aleksei Kozlov, recalls how surprised he was at the festival to see that foreign delegates were young and often casually dressed; they were neither the bourgeois fat cats and racist thugs of *Krokodil* cartoons nor glamorous movie stars. They were, instead, thrillingly ordinary. Exotic, and yet familiar, and, suddenly, present and approachable.

The openness of ordinary Soviets to contacts with ordinary foreigners is one of the most remarkable features of the Moscow youth festival. Although a Gurchenko or a Kozlov may have been too young to have experienced it personally, the virulent xenophobia of late Stalinism was, in historical terms, only a heartbeat away. Just ten years prior to the festival, marriage to foreigners had been a criminal offence; in 1947, another Soviet screen star, Zoya Fedorova, was arrested and sentenced to 25 years in prison for her marriage to an American naval captain.[6] And Fedorova was not alone: in the context of late Stalinism, people with even the most tenuous of ties to foreigners and foreign culture were open to persecution in the USSR.[7]

The atmosphere of the 1957 festival – and, indeed, the mere fact of its having taken place – testifies to the tremendous changes under way in the Soviet Union after Stalin's death. Fedorova and others like her were amnestied in 1954 and 1955; marriage to foreigners was relegalised. And on a broader scale, the USSR embarked in 1955 on an extensive campaign to promote cultural exchanges with the non-socialist world.[8] Certainly, events in Hungary, Poland and at home in the wake of Khrushchev's 1956 secret speech gave Soviet leaders pause.[9] The year 1957 was marked overall by a tightening of ideological controls on literature and the arts and increased surveillance of youth – a partial rollback of the previous year's liberalisation.[10] Yet despite their concerns about the ideological stability of some segments of Soviet society, and particularly the young, when it came to Moscow's youth festival, the Soviet authorities went ahead full throttle. In the world arena, the festival was seen as a terrific opportunity to showcase the achievements of the USSR, including its vibrant, forward-looking and high-minded populace. With any luck, images of young people in Moscow making friends, talking peace and marvelling at Soviet successes would blot out those of Soviet tanks in the streets of Budapest that had so tarnished the USSR's reputation abroad.

One component of Moscow's gambit on the festival was, therefore, international media attention: to ensure widespread coverage, the Soviets welcomed a record number of foreign correspondents – nearly 1000, with roughly half from capitalist countries – and relaxed censorship restrictions for the duration of the festival.[11] No less important, however, was the interpersonal dimension of the event. Although the festival programme itself was structured on collective lines (delegations, interest groups, teams) and featured many mass events (parades, meetings, competitions), festival organisers believed their success depended in large part on personal interactions and actively encouraged the kind of one-to-one contacts that would become the hallmark of the event. Komsomol head A. N. Shelepin spelled out the strategy to Moscow-based activists succinctly: '... we must run the festival in such a way that the overwhelming majority of participants who come, and preferably all festival participants, leave Moscow as our friends. That's our main task, that's our general line.'[12] In the months leading up to the festival, Soviet domestic propaganda waged an extensive campaign to prepare Soviet citizens, psychologically and culturally, for their contacts with foreign guests. In effect, Soviet propaganda cast ordinary people in a starring role: they were to be the hosts and informal ambassadors of the Soviet Union and the Soviet way of life. And it is precisely this model of interaction – horizontal or peer-based rather than hierarchical, individual rather than mass, and (relatively) freewheeling and unpredictable rather than controlled – that so distinguished the Moscow youth festival from the earlier, Stalinist model of public celebrations, as described most recently by Karen Petrone.[13]

Contemporary accounts of the festival frequently emphasised not just the personal and the informal nature of people's interactions, but also their emotional expressiveness and physicality. American writer Kim Chernin, then a 17-year-old unofficial delegate from California, provides a prototypical description of the festival experience:

> Day and night people thronged the boulevards in national costumes, with instruments, with flowers, with arms full of gifts. The Russians threw themselves into this festival as if every stranger were a kinsman, returning home. They flocked around our buses, they forced the buses to stop, they rushed to the windows, took our hands, pressed them and shouted out to us: MIR I DRUZHBA, 'Peace and Friendship', that ritual call no one who attended the festival has ever been able to forget.[14]

In Soviet and foreign press accounts, every bus is always thronged by crowds reaching out to *touch* foreign guests through the windows.[15] Contemporary reports also describe non-stop handshaking, hugging, kissing and dancing. Tears of joy were apparently quite common as well. *Le Monde* reported with some amusement that young people were playing what they called the 'French kissing game' on Red Square, in which girls hid their handkerchiefs, and the boys who found them won the right to a kiss.[16] Soviet newspapers published countless photographs of people embracing or posing with their arms around each other. On 27 July, for example, a *Komsomol'skaya pravda* photo of a young woman who had thrown her arms around a beaming delegate bore the caption: 'Common scenes these days'. Typically, as in this example, the images were of single-sex and comradely in spirit, very much in keeping with the festival's official themes of 'peace' and 'friendship'. Yet not all images were single-sex. Khrushchev himself was photographed in the arms of a young female delegate from England.

The Soviet press, in particular, delighted in hints of romance between delegates. The youth magazine *Yunost'* featured a photo of a Russian girl standing on tiptoe to kiss a foreign athlete sitting with his teammates on the back of a truck: the caption reads 'These French guys are ready to kiss all Muscovites (*rastselovat' vsekh moskvichei*)'[17] (Figure 4.1). *Komsomol'skaya pravda* published a playful '*Festival'naya azbuka*' ('ABC of the festival') in which every letter of the alphabet was assigned a word. 'F' for '*festival*'', of course, and 'm' for '*mir*' (peace), but also 's' for '*svad'ba*' (wedding), 'l' for '*lyubov*'' (love), and 'zh' for '*zhenit'ba*'' (engagement). As for actual weddings at the festival, *Komsomol'skaya pravda* reported two, and hinted broadly that others were to follow.[18]

In general, although friendship was the official slogan of the day, *love* was a surprisingly prominent theme in festival planning and propaganda. The city of Moscow temporarily renamed one of its byways 'Street of Love' in honour of the festival and erected statues there of Romeo and Juliet.[19] Press accounts featured swooning foreigners. In their testimonials (a staple of festival coverage), delegates often declared that they had 'fallen in love' – with Moscow, with their Soviet hosts and with the festival experience. *Komsomol'skaya pravda*'s feature article on opening day answered, 'We feel your love' ('*My chuvstvuem vashu lyubov*''):

We often heard that people in different corners of the globe were dreaming of Moscow. We felt it in the letters we got, in the sound of

На пути в Лужники. Эти француз-
ские парни готовы расцеловать
всех москвичей.

Figure 4.1 'These French guys are ready to kiss all Muscovites', *Yunost'*,
September 1957, p. 66

Russian songs sung by strangers thousands of kilometres from the USSR, and in the warm words of welcome addressed to our emissaries everywhere. ... But only now, when the festival flag has risen and thousands of young guests have filled the streets of Moscow, when buses with terse signs – 'Sweden', 'France', 'Ceylon' – move about, and all of Moscow has broken out in smiles and people's songs in many languages, only now does each and every one of us feel the love of the world for Moscow so fully and clearly.[20]

Love was not a new theme in Soviet mass media culture. The people's relationship to Lenin and, especially, Stalin was often cast in terms of love.[21] Love of labour and of one's work collective, factory or even furnace were critical categories, too, as was love of the motherland.[22] Romantic love between individuals was also a common theme in Soviet culture, and frequently a problematic one: in romance lay the potential for conflict between self and loved one – that is, the romantic couple – and the collective. Stalinist culture played out and resolved this struggle repeatedly, as in, for example, the popular 1953 film *Lyubov' Yarovaya*, in which a wife overcomes her personal affections for her kulak husband in order to denounce him.[23] Propaganda for the 1957 Youth Festival sounded these traditional notes, representing love as purposeful, responsible and essentially civic or collective in nature. It also reverberated with new tones of playfulness and emotion. Love, hinted festival propaganda, was not a mere extension of the official slogan 'friendship', but something new, physical and unpredictable.

In retrospect, the most striking thing about editorial lines such as 'We feel your love' is how powerfully they resonate with the festival's historical mystique. Russian journalists writing in 1997 to commemorate the fiftieth anniversary of the festival echoed contemporary Western accounts in their celebration of the event as a watershed in post-war Soviet history – the first, long-awaited 'injection of freedom' into Soviet veins.[24] They also invariably mentioned love and sex at the festival, most often in ironic tones. For many people today, the 1957 Youth Festival is associated with these themes far more than with culture or politics. When poet Yevgenii Yevtushenko was asked about the festival (for the CNN documentary series *The Cold War*), the first thing that came to his mind was kissing:

How could I forget Moscow Youth Festival? For the first time in my life, my socialist lips touched so-called 'capitalist lip(s)' because I kissed one American girl, breaking any Cold War rules. Not only me, many of my friends, too, they're doing the same too on the streets of Moscow, in all the parks.[25]

Other commentators have argued that what happened in Moscow that summer was nothing less than a spontaneous sexual revolution. For Aleksei Kozlov, the festival was a moment when young people, especially young women, 'broke the chains' of puritanical Soviet morality. Here is how he has described the revolutionary front line:

> At night, as it was getting dark, crowds of young ladies from all over Moscow converged on the places where foreign delegates were staying – various student dorms and hotels on the outskirts of the city. ... Events developed with maximum speed. No wooing, no fake coquettishness. Couples who had just met quickly distanced themselves from the buildings, in the dark, in the fields, in the bushes, knowing perfectly well what they would soon be doing. [26]

Kozlov mentions (with a hint of regret) that he did not personally take part in the revolutionary struggle. Like most other accounts, his is drawn from festival lore dating back to summer 1957, when rumours of widespread sexual contact between Soviets and foreign delegates first coursed through Moscow.[27] One popular story has it that young women caught with foreigners had their heads shaved on the spot by roving Komsomol patrols.[28] A 1993 feature film set at the festival, *The Road to Paradise* (*Doroga v rai*), offers a highly stylised version of this popular tale. In an opening scene of the film – a love story, as befits a festival film – Komsomol patrollers on motorcycles chase several teenage girls down a flight of stairs, along a river embankment and corner them against a wall. As the girls cower and sob, protesting that they are high school students, not prostitutes, the patrollers insult them and shave their heads. In another version of the popular head-shaving story, dozens (or hundreds) of unfortunate girls were not only shaved, but deported from Moscow. It is also said that 'loose girls' were shipped off to the Virgin Lands projects – as in the version told to Sally Belfrage, a young American living in Moscow in 1958.[29] Finally, rumour has it that there was widespread interracial sex at the festival, resulting in a large number of biracial babies born to Russian mothers in 1958 – the so-called '*deti festivalya*' (children of the festival).[30]

Some of these rumours are far easier to substantiate than others. There is no doubt that Komsomol brigades patrolled public spaces at the festival. Komsomol patrols and other civic policing groups were a familiar sight on the Soviet urban landscape of the mid-late 1950s and 1960s. With Khrushchev's enthusiastic and vocal backing, Soviet officials in this period promoted civic policing as a progressive form of popular participation in governance and an essential step on the road to communism. Tens of thousands of civic groups, most loosely connected to the police and the Komsomol, were charged with patrolling public areas to maintain 'order'. In practice, 'order' proved a flexible concept; civic groups detained people for public drunkenness, hooliganism, black marketeering and prostitution, but also for dressing or dancing in a supposedly flashy and demonstrably non-Soviet manner – that is, for being a *'stilyaga'*.[31]

In the months leading up to the festival, civic police groups were mobilised to conduct anti-*stilyaga* dance raids and to rid Moscow of 'criminal elements' and 'loose women'.[32] Nearly 20,000 Komsomol members joined a massive contingent of professional and volunteer law enforcement forces to maintain order during the festival itself.[33] In their daily reports to the Moscow Party Committee, Komsomol leaders repeatedly voiced their concerns about the large number of 'random' (*sluchainye*) people flocking to the foreigners' hotels in the evenings, including 'loose girls', *stilyagi* and black marketeers, and called for reinforcements. Evidently, 'comrades' from fellow socialist countries 'were offended' by the hotel crowds – 'not the sort of people who should represent and personify Soviet youth' – and were pressing the local authorities 'in a friendly way' to remedy the matter.[34] For their part, Komsomol activists claimed to be actively patrolling and expelling 'unworthy conversational partners' (*nedostoinye sobesedniki*) from areas where foreigners congregated.[35]

Tales of Komsomol activists rounding up 'loose'-looking young Soviet women, shaving heads and hounding couples are not altogether far-fetched. Dissident Boris Vail' reported meeting a group of women in a remote Siberian village who had been exiled during the festival.[36] In recent years, the Russian daily *Moskovskii komsomolets* published an interview with a woman who was accused (accurately, as it turns out) of selling sex for cash to a Yugoslav delegate in the first days of the festival and exiled immediately to a village on the 101st kilometre rim outside Moscow.[37] There was also a clear cultural context for the head-shaving stories: shaving or cutting the hair very short was a common procedure in the Komsomol anti-*stilyaga* raids of the day, although in these cases, the victims were more typically male than female. As for hounding couples, there were reports in the foreign press after the festival about Soviet interference in romantic contacts between foreign men and Soviet women.[38] Couples of the opposite mix – foreign woman, Soviet man – were also prey to prying eyes, as American visitor Kim Chernin found late one night, half-undressed with a young Russian 'Tolya' on the banks of the Moscow River. Chernin recalled that the patrollers who spied them checked their documents (and her American sandals) with bright flashlights, 'laughed suggestively' and then left them alone. As Tolya explained to her, there was 'no problem' because she was the foreigner. 'If Soviet girl, American boy, big trouble,' he said, without further elaboration.[39]

Big trouble for some Soviet young women also figures in the archival record for the festival. Police (MVD) reports to the party's Central Committee mention 107 girls detained for 'dishonourable behaviour' (*nedostoinoe povedenie*) during the festival, and at least two girls who had their heads shaved by 'a group of Soviet young men'.[40] The police also reported taking about 50 girls into custody at a Shcherbakovskii raion hotel for 'entering into intimate relations with foreigners'.[41] The majority of the accused were Komsomol members and students, and there is no indication of their fate in the police reports. Sex also made its way into the final report from festival organisers to the Central Committee, albeit in typically bloodless bureaucratic terms. In their words, 'individuals among our girls (*otdel'nye nashi devushki*) did not value their own reputations highly at the festival and behaved frivolously'. On the basis of the festival experience, the organisers recommended that Komsomol organisations 'raise the question of maidenly honour and the dignity of girls' at their meetings and establish special clubs, celebrations and activities for girls.[42]

It is impossible to pin down just how much sex there was and how sex was punished at the 1957 Youth Festival. That there was something out of the ordinary about young people's interactions at the festival is clear and not terribly surprising. What could be ordinary about life in a Soviet city in 1957 when there were tens of thousands of foreign guests in town, essentially uncontrolled, and when the Soviet government itself had encouraged its people to embrace foreigners and befriend them? One of the reasons for the 'romantic' mystique of the festival experience, then as now, is that Soviet coverage of the event was itself shot through with love, romance and at times, even slyly sexualised references. The idea of the 1957 Youth Festival as a great, glamorous international 'mixer' – easy acquaintances, dancing in the street, hugs and kisses with strangers, 'falling in love' with Moscow and Muscovites – all of this was part of the *official* propaganda for the festival. Consider, for example, the similarity between Kozlov's description of how couples paired up cited above, and this depiction of socialising at the International Student Club from a *Yunost'* article called 'Outstretched arms'. (Note, too, that the couple consists of the archetypal Russian woman and non-white, foreign man.)

- What's your name? (The question is asked in gestures, with a handshake and a smile)
- Galya. And yours?
- Ali. Egypt. You?
- Moscow. Chemistry? Agronomy? Law?
- Biology. Shall we dance?

The article continued: 'They didn't try to find out a lot about each other right away; there were practically no groups that stayed talking for a long time, even among those who spoke the same language. But everyone rushed to exchange simple words and be arm-in-arm, to be near each other for a time – to be with as many countries as possible.'[43]

The quotation feels heavy with the weight of double entendre to us now, thanks, in no small measure, to the historical reputation of the festival itself. In 1957, passages such as these may not have raised eyebrows. Nevertheless, they surely contributed to a sense of the festival as an exciting and exotic social experience, and they do hint at romance, if not sex. If people have remembered the festival in terms of romance and sex, it is at least in part because Soviet mass media represented the festival in those very terms.

The influence of official media culture is particularly significant in this instance because interpretations of the 1957 Youth Festival tend to cut in the opposite direction: the festival is celebrated as that moment when Soviet young people first *escaped* the claustrophobic world of Soviet culture and, inspired by foreign youth, took their initial steps towards freedom. The 'sexual revolution' narrative, of course, fits nicely into this overall interpretation; as one journalist put it in 1997: 'Thanks to the 1957 festival, the older generation discovered not only the free world, but the world of sex. ... Free people put pressure on the local population (in both a literal and a figurative sense) and brought about a revolution.'[44] I am not proposing that Soviet mass media replace foreign influence as the single causal spark for Soviet passions at the festival. What official media culture did do was establish a context for festival romance – an atmosphere, if you will – and launch a mode of interpretation already in the summer of 1957 (and, in fact, somewhat earlier, with their extensive pre-festival propaganda). This context cannot be ignored if we are to understand either the festival's meaning for contemporaries or its historical mystique.

With official propaganda setting the tone, romantic and sexual readings of the festival experience flourished in wholly unofficial quarters: the realm of rumour. Already at the time of the festival, Komsomol leaders fretted that Muscovites were 'gossiping a lot, especially about girls' and blowing the problem of 'loose girls' out of proportion.[45] Festival organisers made similar observations in their summary report, complaining that Moscow residents had 'excessively exaggerated' a few cases and drawn invidious conclusions about Soviet youth as a whole.[46] These were predictable complaints; the conception of deviants as exceptions to the rule of excellence – the 'few' in the midst of an overwhelmingly healthy majority – was nothing if not a trope of Soviet discourse. Moreover, as we have seen, some aspects of the festival rumours did have a basis in existing social practices.

Yet while round-ups, head shaving and even deportations were not, in and of themselves, fantastical, the stories about sex and punishment at the festival do veer into the excessive and the spectacular. What the rumour mill purveyed were tales of mass couplings and mass consequences: not a few trysts, but parklands paved with amorous couples, not one biracial child, but a cohort, the *'deti festivalya'*.[47] Fundamentally visual in nature, festival rumours played on notions of what should (and should not) be publicly exposed. In the Soviet context, the idea of biracial children immediately calls to mind *Tsirk* (*Circus*), a classic 1930s musical melodrama that also plays on themes of visibility. In *Tsirk,* the heroine is a white American circus star who had been forced to hide her biracial baby in the racist United States. In the USSR, in the light of the radiant future, the child is publicly embraced (he can, at last, be seen); the circus star finds true happiness, and it is American racism that is exposed and shamed. Rumours about interracial sex at the festival also construed the biracial baby as a form of public exposure – and, notably, as something rather more negative and shameful than the celebratory vision in *Tsirk*. In festival rumours, a biracial baby stands as a mark not of racial tolerance, but of sexual 'looseness'.

Tales of head shaving, too, can be read as fables of exposure and public shaming. In the anti-*stilyaga* raids of the day, forcible hair cutting (or, less often, shaving) was used to rid young people of offending hairstyles such as the *kok* ('DA' or pompadour). Ostensibly, the goal was less to brand people as miscreants than to remake *stilyagi* in the image of 'healthy' Soviet youth. (In reality, the common practice of posting or publishing photographs of *stilyagi* undermined the idea of raids as simple 'correction'.) The head-shaving stories from the festival, however, are indisputably tales of public exposure, shaming and retribution. The bald women of festival gossip recall *les tondues* of liberated France who suffered shaving as punishment for their relationships with Germans. The Soviets' tales of large-scale deportations after the festival take the notion of retribution one step further by narrating not just a moral, but also a physical expulsion from the community.

With their distinctly didactic and spectacular sensibility, festival rumours bear the marks of a Soviet 'moral panic'; the festival rumour mill expressed widespread anxieties in the majority culture about perceived threats to its values and norms.[48] Much has been written about the 'sexophobic' nature of Soviet public life, and festival rumours certainly confirm this general assessment.[49] At the same time, they also betray the extent to which it was not merely sex, but adolescent female sexuality that pushed the panic button. Common to all the rumours is a vision of young women who actively pursue sexual contact; 'loose girls' are the central figures of festival gossip.

The 'loose girl' image was, needless to say, utterly at odds with Soviet values and norms in the 1950s and 1960s. Much like her counterparts in the US and Europe, the ideal Soviet young woman was 'modest'; she did not pursue.[50] Contemporary etiquette manuals and advice literature promoted these ideals in a chivalric vision of gender polarity, invoking, in Catriona Kelly's apt formulation, 'a world in which politeness was enacted by men as a tribute to women'.[51] The perfect metaphor for this idealised gender behaviour was the dance – and in the 1950s, dancing was also the most widespread (often, the only) form of organised youth recreation in the Soviet Union. As portrayed in countless period films, dancing was understood to be a female passion; women loved to dance, and a woman without a partner had two choices: wait for a man's invitation 'Shall we dance?' or take a spin with another woman.[52] Etiquette manuals pointedly reminded readers of their proper roles and the importance of politesse: 'a girl may decline without giving a reason', conceded one, 'but she must say thank you for the invitation'.[53]

Given its central role in Soviet chivalry and youth culture, it is no surprise that the centrepiece of the festival's 'Holiday of Girls' was a grand ball for 17,000 participants at the Central House of the Soviet Army. During the day (the festival's ninth), female delegates were escorted to visit local factories, offices, schools and maternity wards. 'The evening was even more interesting', reported *Komsomol'skaya pravda* breathlessly; the House of the Soviet Army was transformed into 'a female kingdom [*zhenskoe tsarstvo*] in the full sense of the word'.[54] In one room, composers performed songs in honour of women, while in another, poets read their verse. There was a fashion show with advice to delegates 'on what they are wearing this season and what flatters the face'. There was also a restaurant area called 'My favourite dish' where delegates might sample and learn to prepare regional cuisines of the USSR.[55]'And, of course, the evening was filled with music and dancing.

The 'Holiday of Girls' was an extremely popular event – so popular, in fact, that it was thronged by thousands of people without tickets, prompting the authorities to call in more than 1500 additional police and military troops to guard the entrances to the House of the Soviet Army.[56] With its focus on beauty and domesticity, the official topography of the festival's 'female kingdom' is a telling reflection of Soviet ideals for young womanhood in the 1950s. Moreover, the presence of armed forces protecting Soviet women and their foreign guests resonates symbolically with contemporary chivalric ideals.

Yet the 'Holiday of Girls' was, like all dances, a kingdom apart. In the everyday world of Soviet schools and workplaces, young women were expected to work hard at guarding their 'maidenly honour'. Soviet mass media culture promoted this concept unstintingly, as in the Leningrad Radio programme *Beregi chest' smolodu!* (Guard your honour in your youth!), which, despite its name, addressed itself exclusively to girls.[57] In this sense, while generically sexophobic, Soviet culture did tacitly acknowledge male (hetero) sexual desire. The idea that young women might themselves be interested in sex was off the table. Seven years after the festival, an official with the Ministry of Health declared that there was, in fact, no such thing as adolescent female sexuality: it had been 'scientifically established' that women did not develop any interest in sex until their early twenties (22–24). Since physical need (*potrebnost'*) was impossible for younger women, adolescent sex was unnatural and 'incited only by dissipation and curiosity'.[58]

Ironically, this negation of adolescent female sexuality was made at a high-level meeting to discuss rising teen pregnancy and abortion rates. Given the absence of sociological surveys in this period, it is extremely difficult to track the evolution of sexual mores among young Soviets. Some anecdotal evidence suggests that the most significant liberalisation in attitudes took place in the mid- to late 1960s, and it was also around this time that Soviet schools took a few cautious and ineffectual steps towards sex education.[59] Yet already in the mid-1950s, officials in charge of the mass agricultural and construction projects in

Siberia were registering their concerns about widespread 'debauchery' among young volunteers.[60] In the early 1960s, the Soviet Union's top venereologist sounded the alarm to his colleagues about the high rates of syphilis among Soviet youth.[61]

At no point in the 1950s and 1960s did Soviet official culture address these issues comprehensively as social problems. (There were no published statistics on teen pregnancy or VD, for example.) Still, beginning in the mid-1950s, Soviet media did make space for stories of troubled youth as personal dramas – in radio programmes, such as *Beregi chest' smolodu!*, and on the pages of youth-oriented publications, such as *Yunost'*, *Komsomol'skaya pravda* and even the rather official monthly for young activists, *Molodoi kommunist*, which launched a regular column about family and love, 'Very personal'. There was nothing revolutionary about these programmes and publications per se; in editorial line, they were the standard bearers for 'maidenly honour' and other Soviet gender ideals. Yet by introducing a forum for discussing, however obliquely, sexuality, gender and generational conflict, they helped Soviet audiences see themselves and their society in a new light. Not only did these stories reflect actual changes in social practices and the many conflicts they generated, they also contributed to a new and often alarming vision of Soviet youth in crisis.

Festival gossip was far more extreme in its depiction of sexual anarchy than Soviet official culture and perhaps more explicitly focused on female sexual behaviour as well. Yet on the whole, the rumour mill resonates strongly with the surrounding contemporary culture and its concerns about Soviet youth. What is more, festival rumours suggest an earlier moment in Soviet cultural history: the 'moral panic' of the NEP period as recently described by Eric Naiman and Anne Gorsuch.[62] In both cases, fears about uncontrollable youth sexuality came wrapped up with anxieties about Western cultural influences. Soviet critiques of Western popular culture did not substantially change from the NEP era to the 1950s (although there were periods of greater and lesser tolerance); leaders of both eras condemned the popular music and dance of the West as lascivious and seductive – an incitement to immoral behaviour.[63] By the time of the 1957 Youth Festival, Soviet officials had come to a kind of rapprochement with big-band-style jazz; boogie-woogie and rock 'n' roll were the new cultural tricksters.[64] Yet these were the fine points. In the long run, the idea of Soviet youth as vulnerable to seduction by nefarious outside influences was a perennial facet of the official Soviet worldview.[65]

In some respects, the rumours about sex and punishment at the 1957 Youth Festival mesh well with this way of imagining Soviet youth. Festival rumours are about not just sex, but sex with foreigners; these are stories about what happens when outsiders are introduced into Soviet space. In this schema, Soviet young people are construed as receptive and fundamentally vulnerable. In the months leading up to the festival, Soviet officials betrayed considerable concern about how people would react to the presence of foreigners in their midst and interpret their role as personal ambassadors of the 'Soviet way of life'. Pre-festival propaganda encouraged ordinary Soviets to eschew passivity in their dealing with foreigners and go on the offensive to protect 'our Soviet honour'. Komsomol and party activists were also exhorted repeatedly to stand their ground against anticipated foreign criticism. 'Comrades, we have reason to be proud of ourselves', declared Komsomol chief Shelepin to a June meeting of activists in Moscow. 'We don't have to bow down before anyone.'[66]

That Shelepin found it expedient to promote Soviet pride before even an audience of young activists is one indication of the uncertainty in many quarters about Soviet youth at this time. In their fixation with foreigners and with the notion of honour, popular rumours about the festival echoed these concerns in striking fashion. However, their echo is interpretive rather than strictly mimetic: in festival gossip, unlike festival propaganda, Soviet honour is linked almost exclusively with young women. The 'loose girl' emerges as the leading lady and, importantly, she is cast in the role of an active agent rather than victim. As official culture struggled to counteract the passivity and vulnerability of Soviet youth faced with foreign influence, self-assured Soviet girls flocked to hotels in order to seduce the foreign guests – or so the rumour mill had it.

In both official and non-official space, the *idée fixe* is that the presence of foreigners in Soviet space upsets the balance of the social and moral order: 'Sovietness' is threatened by 'foreignness'. Rumours about sex at the festival evince a level of anxiety among the population about the consequences of Soviets' opening up to the world culturally – including an obvious uncertainty about whether Soviet officialdom would take a punitive tack in response (that is, would there be head shaving, or worse?) At the same time, they also acknowledge enthusiasm for greater interaction with the outside world (the girls themselves) and betray hints of sympathy for it. Even in the late 1950s, rumours about sex at the festival could have a positive valence. Certainly Aleksei Kozlov and his friends were impressed and delighted, if not a bit intimidated, by the girls they thought led a Soviet 'sexual revolution'. Yet either way, negative or positive, it is images of young women, and of female sexuality, which carry the most meaningful symbolic freight. At the heart of gossip about 'loose girls' at the 1957 Youth Festival is the very meaning of Sovietness, and of the Soviets' evolving and conflicted relationship to the non-Soviet world.

The festival rumour mill is a vivid manifestation of the cultural turbulence brewing in post-war Soviet society. By listening to rumours, we can hear the rumblings of change, and of the anxieties and the exhilaration that accompanied it. Propaganda, too, offers evidence of new thinking. The 'romantic' or 'sexual' version of the festival got its first footing in the dusty precincts of Soviet mass media culture, as did the heart of the festival's historical mystique – the notion of Moscow 1957 as a watershed event in Soviet history and a challenge to 'Sovietness'. In this sense, to tell the story of the 1957 Youth Festival is not only to speak of the Soviets' opening up to the outside world, but also to consider new, embattled openings within Soviet society itself.

Notes

1 See, for example, A. Adzhubei, *Te desyat' let* (Moscow, 1989); Y. Brudny, *Reinventing Russia* (Cambridge, 1998); R. Stites, *Russian Popular Culture* (Cambridge, 1992); A. Troitsky, *Back in the USSR* (Boston, 1988); W. Taubman, *Khrushchev: the Man and His Era* (New York, 2003), pp. 382–3; E. Zubkova, trans. H. Ragsdale, *Russia after the War* (Armonk, NY, 1998).

2 According to official statistics, there were 791 concerts at the festival (excluding 63 'mass concerts'), 67 performances of dramatic, opera and puppet theatres, and 99 circus performances. Festival organisers claimed an audience of around 10 million for these events. RGASPI–m, f. 3, op. 15, d. 84, l. 3.

3 *Courtship of Young Minds: a Case Study of the Moscow Youth Festival* (New York, 1959), p. 19. While some delegates clearly came to Moscow intending to explore on their own, others may well have been prompted by the Soviets' numerous organisational problems (missing buses and interpreters, postponed and cancelled events, etc.).

4 For examples of foreign coverage, see '"B" et "K" n'oublient pas la politique', *Le Monde*, 31 July 1957; 'La jeunesse muscovite s'émancipe de plus en plus', *Le Monde*, 1 August 1957; 'Youngsters Fill Moscow for Fête', *New York Times*, 28 July 1957; 'Youth from 102 Lands Swarms over Moscow', *Life*, 12 August 1957; 'Leaven of Western Youth in Russia'', *Manchester Guardian*, 16 August 1957; 'The Red Cue-Softer', *Newsweek*, 12 August 1957; 'I Baited the Reds in Red Square', *New York Mirror*, 9 September 1957; 'Free Speech in Moscow', *Manchester Guardian*, 1 August 1957.

5 L. Gurchenko, *Aplodismenty* (Moscow, 1994), p. 299.

6 M. Popovskii, *Tretii lishnyi* (London, 1985), pp. 346–53. One of Fedorova's sisters was sentenced to ten years in a labour colony, while another was

exiled to Kazakhstan with Fedorova's Soviet-American baby daughter, born in 1946. See also F. Razzakov, *Seks-simvoly Rossii* (Moscow, 2000), pp. 30–47.

7   The widespread promotion of foreign language study in the weeks and months preceding the festival (including on radio and television) is one indication of how much the cultural climate had changed by 1957. In Stalin's waning years, an interest in foreign languages was regarded with great suspicion. See V. Shlapentokh, *Soviet Intellectuals and Political Power: the Post-Stalin Era* (Princeton, 1990), pp. 70–1.

8   M. R. Zezina, *Sovetskaya khudozhestvennaya intelligentsiya i vlast' v 1950-e–60-e gody* (Moscow, 1999), pp. 236–42.

9   Soviet leaders had special reason to be wary of the youth festival format as the last World Federation of Democratic Youth (WFDY) festival, held in Warsaw in 1955, was considered by some to have helped trigger unrest in Poland. See the comments of a Polish delegate to this effect in 'Youth from 102 Lands Swarms over Moscow', *Life,* 12 August 1957, p. 23. See also Radio Liberation's analysis of the festival, 'Radio Liberation and the Moscow Youth Festival' (Open Society Archives, Box 300-81-1-1 /Analysis Reports 1957–68), p. 6. The Soviets were predictably inclined to attribute unrest to 'ideological subversion' by outsiders, and in this case, their suspicion that Western governments, the US in particular, would use the relative openness of the festival format to their advantage was not altogether wrong. According to a long-time CIA operative, the US government sponsored students (via its covert funding of the National Students Association) to do propaganda work at international youth festivals. The CIA established its first contacts with dissidents in the USSR during the 1957 Youth Festival. See H. Rositzke, *The CIA's Secret Operations: Espionage, Counterespionage, and Covert Action* (New York, 1977), pp. 159–63.

10   Zezina, op. cit., pp. 242–60.

11   For figures on journalists, see RGASPI–m, f. 3, op. 15, d. 2, l. 105. According to the *Manchester Guardian,* 1 August 1957, dispatches on the festival were transmitted abroad uncensored. The US State Department reported a temporary lifting of the ban on bringing undeveloped film out of the USSR. See *State Department Intelligence Reports,* 'The Soviet Bloc Exchange Program in 1957' (February 1958).

12   RGASPI–m, f. 4, op. 104, d. 7, l. 126.

13   K. Petrone, *Life Has Become More Joyous, Comrades: Celebrations in the Time of Stalin* (Bloomington, 2000).

14   K. Chernin, *In My Mother's House* (New Haven, 1983), p. 267.

15   Although this essay refers primarily to the Soviet press, the festival was a major topic for broadcast media as well. The festival was the first event in Soviet history to receive extended live television coverage. Central Television in Moscow was given over entirely to the festival for 15 days and broadcast 221 hours and 30 minutes of coverage, including live reports on all the major meetings such as the opening ceremony, the Kremlin ball, and the Holiday of Girls. TsAODM, f. 4, op. 104, d. 30, l. 172. Central TV also worked feverishly to distribute footage to foreign and domestic stations (via train and airplane). On 4 August, *Komsomol'skaya pravda* reported that filmed segments of the festival were already being shown on local TV in Kiev, Minsk, Tblisi, Riga, Tallin, Kharkov, Omsk, Sverdlosk, Barnaul and

Vladivostok. There were also several full-length films made about the festival. What I have seen of Soviet footage suggests that print and broadcast media were, unsurprisingly, very similar in their tone and approach. The camera loved hugged and dancing couples as much as the page.

16 'La jeunesse muscovite s'émancipe de plus en plus', *Le Monde*, 1 August 1957, p. 12.

17 *Yunost'* (September 1957), p. 66.

18 *Komsomol'skaya pravda*, 28 July 1957, p. 4.

19 J. Gunther, *Inside Russia Today* (New York, 1957), p. 36. *Komsomol'skaya pravda* printed a poem entitled 'Street of Love' on 4 August.

20 'My chuvstvuem vashu lyubov'', *Komsomol'skaya pravda*, 28 July 1957, p. 1.

21 For a discussion of eroticism in the mythology of Stalin, see I. C. Kon, *Seksual'naya kul'tura v Rossii: klubnichka na berezke* (Moscow, 1997), p. 161, and T. Cherednichenko, *Tipologiya sovetskogo massovoi kul'tury* (Moscow, 1994), pp. 34–43.

22 See S. Buck-Morss, *Dreamworld and Catastrophe* (Cambridge, Mass., 2000), pp. 180–2, 195–7. Buck-Morss draws heavily on S. Kotkin's *Magnetic Mountain* (Berkeley, 1995).

23 *Lyubov' Yarovaya*, a filmed theatrical performance, was the most popular Soviet picture at the box office in 1953. For an interesting discussion of love in Soviet cinema, see the interview with Naum Kleiman in *Lignes d'ombre* (Paris, 2000), p. 25.

24 'Povorot', *Itogi*, 27 May 1997; 'Ot korki do korki', *Novaya gazeta – Ponedel'nik*, 9 August 1997.

25 Interview with Yevtushenko for CNN's *Cold War* series published online at http://www.gwu.edu/~nsarchive/coldwar/interviews/episode-14/yevtushenko1.html.

26 A. Kozlov, *Kozel na sakse* (Moscow, 1998), pp. 106–7.

27 TsAODM, f. 4, op. 104, d. 31, ll. 161–2; RGASPI-m, f. 3, op. 15, d. 2, l. 133.

28 A. Rubinov, *Intimnaya zhizn' Moskvy* (Moscow, 1991), p. 224.

29 S. Belfrage, *A Room in Moscow* (New York, 1958), p. 40. M. Popovskii reports that women punished for their relations with foreigners during the festival were forced outside a 100 kilometre radius from Moscow. Popovskii, op. cit., p. 310.

30 Rubinov attributes interracial sex to 'ordinary female curiosity' about 'the anatomy and physiology of healthy men with unusual skin tones and strangely shaped eyes' and claims that patrols were particularly harsh with the Soviet women involved. Rubinov, op. cit., p. 224.

31 By 1960 there were over 80,000 squads in the Soviet Union with more than 2.5 million participants. See H. Ritvo, 'Totalitarianism without Coercion?', *Problems of Communism*, no. 6, 1960, p. 24, citing *Kommunist*, no. 10, 1960. For a description of a dance raid in Moscow in 1956, see TsAODM, f. 4, op. 113, d. 23, ll. 136–7.

32 RGASPI-m, f. 3, op. 15, d. 2, ll. 60–1.

33 The MVD reported it had about 60,000 people on hand to keep public order, including 11,275 police, 4000 police academy students from other cities, 8500 soldiers and MVD officers, 32,000 members of *brigady sodeistviya militsiya*, as well as workers from the firefighting service of the MVD and *dvorniki*. GARF, f. 9401, op. 2, d. 491, l. 427.

34 TsAODM, f. 4, op. 104, d. 31, l. 95.
35 TsAODM, f. 4, op. 104, d. 31, l. 20.
36 Boris Vail' quoted in Popovskii, op. cit., p. 310.
37 'Na bolote, na snegu – ya mogu, mogu, mogu!', *Moskovskii komsomolets*, 14 February 2000. The sentence was three years, and the woman reported she soon had a brisk business (especially among young Komsomol volunteer labourers) in her new residence.
38 See *Courtship of Young Minds*, p. 17.
39 Chernin, op. cit., p. 277.
40 GARF, f. 9401, op. 2, d. 491, l. 433.
41 GARF, f. 9401, op. 2, d. 491, l. 379.
42 RGASPI-m, f. 3, op. 15, d. 2, l. 133.
43 *Yunost'*, September 1957, p. 72
44 *Novaya gazeta – Ponedel'nik*, 28 July 1997.
45 TsAODM, f. 4, op. 104, d. 31, ll. 161–2.
46 RGASPI-m, f. 3, op. 15, d. 2, l. 133.
47 Although I have no way of knowing how many biracial children were born from festival liaisons, it seems safe to say that there was no cohort. Kara Lynch, producer of a 2001 documentary film on people of African descent in the USSR (*Black Russians*), has told me that while many of her subjects are mistaken for '*festival'nye*' by fellow Russians, she herself has never met such a person in her many years of interviewing in Russia. Personal communication, June 2002.
48 The classic work on 'moral panic' is S. Cohen, *Folk Devils and Moral Panics: the Creation of the Mods and the Rockers* (Oxford, 1972; rev. edn 1980).
49 'Sexophobia' is Igor Kon's term.
50 On the post-Stalin ideal of 'the modest girl without makeup', see N. Azhgikhina and H. Goscilo, 'Getting under their Skin: the Beauty Salon in Russian Women's Lives' in H. Goscilo and B. Holmgren (eds), *Russia – Women – Culture* (Bloomington, 1996), p. 99. For an insightful account of the American experience of young womanhood in the 1950s, see S. Belfrage's memoir, *Un-American Activities: a Memoir of the Fifties* (New York, 1994).
51 C. Kelly, *Refining Russia* (Oxford, 2001), p. 347.
52 Young men with a passion for dancing were apt to be labelled *stilyagi*. Like their fashion sensibilities, their 'unnatural' interest in dance operated as a mark of their alienness in Soviet culture.
53 *Estetika povedeniya i byta: metodicheskie rekomendatsii* (Moscow, 1963), p. 10.
54 *Komsomol'skaya pravda*, 6 August 1957.
55 S. Vladimirova, 'Prazdnik devushek', *Rabotnitsa*, no. 7, 1957, p. 3.
56 GARF, f. 9401, op. 2, d. 491, l. 329. *Le Monde* reported that 'an entire neighbourhood in Moscow was cordoned off' and 'thousands of police and soldiers ... had to hold back several thousand people who were trying to penetrate the immense block of buildings and gardens ...' 'Le festival de Moscou suscite toujours une incroyable animation', *Le Monde*, 8 August 1957, p. 3.
57 S. I. Golod, *XX vek i tendentsii seksual'nykh otnoshenii v Rossii* (Moscow, 1996), p. 40.
58 RGASPI-m, f. 1, op. 5, d. 1009, l. 100.

59 Popovskii, op. cit., p. 217.
60 For a report on Bratskaya GES and other mass construction sites in 1957, see RGANI, f. 5, op. 34, d. 24, ll. 1–17.
61 Golod, op. cit., p. 106.
62 E. Naiman, *Sex in Public: the Incarnation of Early Soviet Ideology* (Princeton, 1997); A. Gorsuch, *Youth in Revolutionary Russia* (Bloomington, 2000).
63 Soviet leaders were, of course, far from alone in their anxieties about commercial popular culture. For a recent work on the problem in the Germanies of the 1950s, see U. G. Poiger, *Jazz, Rock, and Rebels: Cold War Politics and American Culture in a Divided Germany* (Berkeley, 2000). For a study of the Italian communists' approach, see S. Gundle, *Between Hollywood and Moscow* (Durham, Nc, 2000).
64 According to S. Frederick Starr, by the mid-1950s, there were jazz bands in every little town in the Soviet Union, and 'the jazz evening was firmly established as a community rite of the younger generation'. S. Frederick Starr, *Red and Hot: the Fate of Jazz in the Soviet Union* (New York, 1983), p. 251.
65 On the notion of youth vulnerability, see H. Pilkington, *Russia's Youth and Its Culture: a Nation's Constructors and Constructed* (London, 1994), pp. 66–71.
66 TsAODM, f. 4, op. 104, d. 7, l. 129.

5
Mothers and Fathers and the Problem of Selfishness in the Khrushchev Period

Deborah A. Field

By the 1950s, utopian visions of completely socialised child rearing had mostly withered away and it was widely assumed that parents were necessary for raising children.[1] Radical proposals for reorganising the family did arise from time to time, but they were never seriously implemented. For example, the state-run boarding schools introduced in 1958 proved quite controversial and unpopular, and by the early 1960s experts were hastening to explain that they were meant not to replace parents, but merely to help families, especially those headed by single mothers.[2] Yet pedagogues and officials worried that while parental love and care were vital, mothers and fathers did not always understand that because they were raising future citizens, they had a social obligation to mould their children into hard-working communists. In order to convince parents of the social importance of their role, the pre-eminent Stalinist pedagogue, Anton Makarenko, among others, had spent the 1930s producing materials delineating the correct methods of *vospitanie* (upbringing) and in 1946 the journal *Sem'ya i shkola* (Family and School) was established in order to propagandise these principles more thoroughly.[3] This barrage of advice for parents continued under Khrushchev and took on new importance in the changed political climate.

Khrushchev's goal was to repudiate Stalinism and establish a reformed Soviet polity on the basis of activism rather than coercion.[4] This populist approach to government depended for its success on citizens who had internalised communist morality, a code of conduct that required a conscientious attitude towards family, diligent work, activism and the willingness to sacrifice individual interests for the social good.[5] Officials, professionals and the activists in new and newly revived voluntary organisations, such as comrades' courts and house committees, were all supposed to help to inculcate communist morality. Mothers and fathers, each taking on the distinct responsibilities deemed appropriate to their gender, had to play a major role in this process as well. Mothers were responsible for physical and emotional nurturing and for instilling manners and morals; fathers were in charge of discipline and intellectual stimulation. Armed with pedagogical information and reinforced by community volunteers, every family was to raise 'a true patriot, an honest labourer, a good collectivist, a worthy successor and continuer of our great revolutionary task'.[6] In the event that parents failed to achieve this lofty goal incipient welfare organisations were empowered to reprimand or fine them.[7]

An examination of efforts to impart proper parenting methods can cast light on the diverse ways in which ideology was put into practice during the Khrushchev period. Oleg Kharkhordin has argued that under Khrushchev, Soviet citizens experienced less individual freedom and more social control than they had under Stalin.[8] This provocative assertion certainly captures some of the aspirations of the state. It is true that as part of its emphasis on instilling communist morality, the Khrushchev government did initiate new attempts to monitor and regulate everyday life and personal behaviour. Theorists and experts determined what attitudes and behaviours constituted a correct communist private life, and trade union, party, Komsomol and voluntary organisations were supposed to enforce these standards by shaming and punishing the people who did not live up to them. However, because Kharkhordin relies mainly on official documents, such as party policy statements and Khrushchev's speeches, he ignores the extremely variable ways in which people implemented and responded to official visions. To gain a more multivocal understanding of this process we must turn to sources of a different kind.

In examining what happened when pedagogues and welfare officials attempted to discipline parents, I shall draw here on two sets of materials that allow us to hear, however fleetingly, the distinct and diverse voices of individuals. First there are the records from one of the new interventionist welfare institutions of this period, the Moscow city *raion* (district) Commissions on the Establishment of Children and Adolescents, which were later called Commissions on the Affairs of Minors. These organisations were responsible for enforcing the payment of child support, petitioning courts to deprive neglectful or abusive parents of their parental rights, working with badly behaved and delinquent children and adolescents, and punishing them by sending them to 'Children's Educational Colonies'.[9] The second set of sources consists of a series of informal interviews I conducted in Russia during the 1993–94 academic year with a diverse group of people, ranging from retired scientists to custodians. Both interviews and archival records are from Moscow and are not necessarily representative of the entire Soviet Union. However, focusing on one area allowed me access to concrete cases and individual viewpoints, so that while my sources provide particular perspectives, rather than a complete picture, they do make clear the wide spectrum of parental reactions. Some parents resisted official intervention. Others adopted those bits and pieces of expert advice that suited them, and even elicited the help of public and state organisations, without necessarily accepting the ultimate goals and overall philosophy of official Soviet family pedagogy. Specifically, many parents seemed to ignore the call to raise the unselfish young collectivists whom government leaders considered both vitally important and alarmingly scarce during the Khrushchev period.

Selfish youth

Many Soviet officials perceived a youth problem during the thaw period, and their anxiety about the putative apathy and selfishness of young adults added urgency to their concern with proper communist child rearing. The Komsomol leadership, for example, held many worried discussions about youthful *bezdelnichestvo*, a concept that encompassed materialism, disdain of physical labour, and reluctance to leave cities to work in areas of greater need.[10] Moscow State University Komsomol activists frequently complained about students, and even Komsomol members, drinking, playing cards, fighting, and engaging in premarital sex; young people seemed more intent on immediate self-gratification than on building a new society.[11] During a 1961 conference of Komsomol activists from various Moscow universities and colleges, a representative from the Moscow Steel Institute reported an incident that exemplified this threat: a student had written on a blackboard in English 'Communism – is women and wine.'[12] Socially irresponsible behaviour was not limited to the future elites; a 1962 Komsomol Central Committee report expressed grave worry about widespread drinking, violence, political and social indifference, apathy, and crime among young people in general and high rates of abortion among young women.[13]

The figure of the *stilyaga* (the word comes from *stil'*, Russian for style) became a symbol for all that was wrong with the younger generation. During the late 1940s, *stilyagi* were drawn from the children of the country's top leadership, but by the time the press started to discuss them in the mid-1950s, *stilyagism* had spread beyond the upper echelons of Soviet society.[14] The *stilyagi* made themselves conspicuous by their flamboyant pursuit of Western fashions: the men wore zoot suits and signet rings, the women lipstick and slit skirts. They dropped French and English phrases into their speech, admired the popular culture of the West and tried to avoid working.[15] Although even alarmed critics admitted that *stilyagism* was not a widespread phenomenon, they saw the *stilyaga* as dangerous nonetheless because, as one lecturer put it, 'by his behaviour he makes a challenge to public opinion'.[16] *Stilyagi* personified consumerism, frivolity, licentiousness, and most of all a deplorable lack of social responsibility. At a 1956 meeting of the Komsomol committee of the Geography and Geology Department at Moscow State University, a speaker complained about the desire of many students to 'stand apart from societal life, to not participate in societal life'. He tied this trend to the '"*stilyagi*", who, unfortunately, have started to appear more and more in the geography department'.[17]

Such attitudes were problematic because the future of communism depended upon the willingness of citizens to sacrifice their individual needs and desires for the social good. Under communism, party theorists predicted, such delayed gratification would become second nature: 'In communist society, there will be such harmony of personal and social interests, such high consciousness, that when "conflicts" arise between the personal and the social, people will, without special difficulty, by habit subordinate their desires to social interests.'[18] In the mean time, during the transition from socialism to communism, any clashes between public and private interests had to be resolved in favour of the public, because 'the interests of society are higher than the interests of the family, the interests of the family are higher than the interests of the individual'.[19]

Selfishness represented a real threat to Khrushchev's populist vision of communism. Parents were the country's first line of defence against this danger, and they could ensure that their children grew up to become self-sacrificing activists by following the advice of pedagogical experts.

Official family pedagogy

In the late 1950s, educational experts began to assume a slightly more flexible approach than their Stalinist predecessors. Researchers paid more attention to the distinct stages of child development and the concept of personality, and these new concerns were reflected in materials for parents that detailed distinct stages of development and specific temperaments.[20] However, for the most part the goals and methods experts recommended were derived from Makarenko's work and so, as in previous decades, they emphasised self-discipline and order. Accordingly, parents were supposed to establish strict daily schedules so that their children rose, dressed, ate, studied, played, and did chores at the same time every day in order to impart regular habits and 'discipline, conscientiousness, neatness, persistence'.[21] Household chores were a necessary component of this daily routine because they taught children independence and respect for labour.[22] Pedagogical writers sternly cautioned parents against spoiling their children, which they held to be dangerous not only because overindulged children are unpleasant to be around, but also because they would not develop the sense of idealism and collectivism that communism required. After describing a pampered daughter, a writer reflected, 'what kind of life has this mother raised her daughter for? Social interests cannot affect her tightly closed soul. Lofty ideals, the noble impulse of the human soul, unselfish aid to comrades, all of these feelings are ... alien to her.'[23]

In addition to structure and discipline, experts also stressed the importance of *kul'turnost'*, a concept encompassing hygiene, etiquette, taste and some knowledge of high culture. One professor explained to parents, 'The new person of socialist society must be ahead of the people of the old society in all respects; more cultured (*kul'turnyi*) and organised, more sensitive and attentive to people, more polite and tactful.'[24] From the start, *kul'turnost'* had been part of the Soviet Union's modernising project. Because officials associated what they saw as bad taste and bad manners with peasants, disorder and backwardness, instilling *kul'turnost'* was a way to impose 'modern', urban standards of behaviour on the population; promoting *kul'turnost'* also allowed the state to acknowledge and justify people's aspirations for status and possessions.[25] Different aspects of *kul'turnost'* were emphasised in various times and contexts. Scholars have recently asserted that, with the Khrushchev government's increased production of consumer goods, good taste in clothing and home décor replaced hygiene and self-education as the main emphases of advice literature.[26] Certainly, the 1950s witnessed a dramatic increase in books about home decorating, housework and cooking.[27] However, materials that focused on child rearing in particular still stressed education and etiquette in their discussions of *kul'turnost'*. Pedagogues directed parents to impart good manners and to involve themselves in their children's education, which required staying in close contact with school, supervising homework, and providing a place for children to study, which was no easy task given contemporary housing conditions.[28] Formal education was not enough to produce *kul'turnost'*, however, and so experts advised parents to take their children to museums, on walks, to nourish an interest in technology, to read to them and to encourage them to read themselves.[29]

Pedagogues never cast mothers and fathers as interchangeable parents; their belief in essential gender differences was too profound for this to be a possibility. As a prominent sociologist put it in a 1960 work, 'Never will any kind of equality of the sexes erase those differences between men and women that are an expression of their natural essence.'[30] Rather, as in Stalinist times, they assigned different aspects of child rearing to each parent. Maternal care was considered especially vital for young children, so that in divorce cases custody was automatically granted to the mother unless she was shown to be unfit.[31] Mothers were responsible for feeding and nurturing and most of the everyday care in the early years. Thus a popular health magazine ran a series of articles providing advice on such topics as nutrition and speech development under the rubric 'Letters to Mother' rather than letters to parents.[32]

What was left for fathers to do? Sergei Kukhterin argues that as the Soviet state took over traditional patriarchal functions, the role that fathers were supposed to play within the family shrank (in principle, if not always in practice).[33] This was evident in pedagogical literature: while vividly describing the negative behaviours fathers were to avoid, it was much vaguer about the positive actions they were supposed to take. Hence the ideal father was defined mainly in opposition to the harsh disciplinarian, the drunkard and the neglectful careerist. Following Makarenko, pedagogues criticised corporal punishment and bullying.[34] Heavy drinkers were obviously a disruptive influence on family life, but pedagogues also condemned men who pursued success at work while ignoring their families. A satiric piece in *Sem'ya i shkola* denounced a man who was so out of touch with his son's life that he showed up at the wrong school for a meeting with the director.[35]

In a rare article that specifically delineated fathers' duties, one pedagogue, N. Levitov, explained, 'The tone in the family is set by the father ... he is responsible to society, his wife and children for "order" in the family.'[36] Fathers were supposed to oversee discipline. Mothers, stereotyped as naturally caring, were not always capable of chastising and controlling their children; in pedagogical literature, cautionary tales about overindulgent parents most often featured mothers, or perniciously old-fashioned, coddling grandmothers.[37]

In addition to their disciplinary responsibilities, fathers also had an obligation to inculcate *kul'turnost'* and this had emotional as well as intellectual importance. *Kul'turnost'*, like other aspects of child rearing, was divided into male and female components. While mother was supposed to teach etiquette, father had to provide intellectual stimulation and cultural enlightenment: 'The question of intellectual upbringing is more often decided by the father, and the traits of cultured behaviour are taught by the mother.'[38] A good father helped his children with homework, took them on interesting excursions and taught them hobbies. As well as being educational, these activities were also a way for fathers to demonstrate concern and affection. In one description, an inattentive father was faulted not because he failed to feed or clothe his child but rather because although he knew 'that his son was interested in football, he never took him with him to the stadium, there were no occasions on which the father invited Volodya to the theatre or devoted a day off to his son'.[39] By contrast, a description of an ideal family featured a father who worked hard, was active in societal affairs, shared household responsibilities with the rest of the family, and still found time to teach his son woodworking.[40] As feminist scholars have noted, from at least the mid-1930s onward, Soviet discourse glorified the joys and importance of motherhood. In a society in which mothers' responsibility for feeding, clothing and cherishing children was assumed, and maternal love exalted, prescriptions about *kul'turnost'* provided one of the only terms in which pedagogues and officials could imagine paternal nurturing.

Fulfilling the normative roles I have described required a certain amount of education, space and time. Parents had to be literate in order to read to their children, to help them with their homework and to understand pedagogical advice appearing in magazines and books. They had to have enough room to set up a desk or workspace for their children, and they had to have enough time and energy to establish a strict daily routine and to supervise play, chores, excursions and hobbies. The underlying assumption of official pedagogy was that the Soviet government had fulfilled its promises to provide education, culture, decent housing and sufficient leisure to all of its citizens and that parents experiencing difficulties had only themselves to blame. One expert proclaimed, for example, 'There can be no "difficult children" in families where the parents take the upbringing of their children seriously, visit the school often, and constantly watch over the success and accomplishments of their child.'[41]

Disciplining parents

Some parents were unwilling or unable to meet the demanding standards that pedagogues established. Because, in the words of one pamphlet, 'the upbringing of children ... is not only a personal, but also a great societal affair', it was 'the duty of the collective to help a family in this if it needs it... '.[42] During the Khrushchev era, this helping collective took various forms. It consisted in part of local party and trade union organisations as well as voluntary groups, such as parent-teacher organisations, house committees and comrades' courts, which dispensed pedagogical advice and tried to pressurise 'inadequate' parents into improving their relationships with their children.[43] These activists could attempt to shame parents into changing, but serious cases came under the jurisdiction of the courts and the Commissions on the Affairs of Minors.

Minors' commissions consisted of volunteers, usually teachers, party, trade union and Komsomol leaders, local government officials and representatives from the police and local education departments. During their hearings, police or members of the commission presented reports. Then commissioners asked the parents and children questions and ended by issuing their decisions. Official pedagogy provided commissions with specific terms in which to express blame so that during hearings, commission members often echoed expert opinion in attributing children's problems to parental neglect or indulgence. For example, in a 1964 session, one district commission reprimanded a mother for spoiling her son, a fault she compounded by trying to suggest that her son had been wrongly accused of vandalism. A commission member summed up the case: 'Misha is a badly raised adolescent, because of the strong love of the mother for her son, he has turned into a hooligan.'[44] Drawing the opposite conclusion in 1956, another commission blamed parental neglect for the problems of a 12-year-old girl who stole money from her parents, misbehaved in school, came home as late as two or three in the morning, and had repeated several grades in school. The commission concluded: 'The mother did not pay the necessary attention to her daughter, she did not watch over her behaviour or her studies in school, and was ... completely preoccupied with herself.'[45]

Pedagogues, as was discussed above, stressed the importance of *kul'turnost'*, advising parents to take their children on excursions and to encourage educational hobbies. Because these pastimes were supposed to be both a means of instilling culture and demonstrating love, reprimanding fathers for failing to take their children to the cinema or museum became a way to charge them with emotional neglect. In a 1964 session, a district commission member prodded a father: 'Did you go with your son to the theatre, to the cinema, did you discuss readings with him? How did you help him gain an understanding of life?'[46] The widowed and recently remarried father of two troubled sons was similarly interrogated in a 1961 case. The commission started by asking the father, 'What has happened to your children since the death of your wife?' When the father could not provide an explanation for their behaviour, the commission tried to ascertain if he had tried to build a relationship with his sons by asking what activities he had initiated. The father admitted, 'It wasn't possible to get the older one to read literature, but the younger is interested in it. I wanted to teach them carpentry, but they did not want to.' A commission member persisted: 'Did you go anywhere with the children, take them on excursions, to exhibits, and such like?' The father said, 'We did not, there was no time.' Upon this admission, the commissioner launched into a full-scale reproach, 'So you see, comrade K., you are a communist, but could not find an approach to your children's heart.' Another commission member added, 'Your mistake is that the children did not see parental warmth.'[47]

The elastic concept of *kul'turnost'* was a useful one for commission members; they could stretch its meaning in order to discuss a subject not otherwise easily described in the available pedagogical clichés: paternal love. But official pedagogy was not always so valuable and in fact in many instances it was irrelevant to the situation commissions faced. In cases of parental neglect and abuse, the question was not whether parents established a strict daily routine or took their children to the cinema, but whether they managed to feed and clothe them. For example, in 1964 a district commission initiated action to deprive a woman of parental rights over her 14-year-old son and 2-year-old daughter because, according to their report, she 'does not educate her children and takes no interest in them. She does not make supper for them. The room is in disorder, dirty. She does not clean the floor; the children have no bedding – blankets, sheets, pillows. The bed has a grey, dirty, torn mattress.' The mother stays out late, the report continued, and in December of the previous year, she had left home with the baby girl, leaving her son alone, without any source of support. As a result the boy, not surprisingly, had become a 'lying and nervous child'.[48]

Even in less extreme instances, commissioners confronted parents who, though not gruesomely negligent, simply lacked the time or the resources to meet the ideals of Soviet family pedagogy. For example, a 1963 case involved a teenage boy who had been loitering in the doorways to apartment buildings where he played cards and got drunk. A commission member, implicitly scolding the father for failing to arrange more wholesome activities for the son, asked him: 'how much living space do you have? Why could you not organise chess or checkers games?' The father replied, 'We have 22 metres, and there are five people in the family.' This evidence of overcrowding seems to have confounded the commission (the legal minimum was 9 square metres of space per person, and the actual norm for Moscow was 5.7 square metres as of 1959).[49] A commission member concluded the session by telling the father, somewhat ineffectually, 'we cannot give you advice here. We want to protect you and your son from unpleasantness. Playing cards for money is a matter of even greater concern than drinking vodka. You are obligated, as a father, to draw the conclusion and establish control.'[50]

Parents, especially single ones, were often unable to provide the supervision that was a basic component of ideal family upbringing. In a 1964 case a commission investigated a 17-year-old boy who had quit work and been caught stealing a radio and a bicycle. When asked to account for his behaviour, his mother replied, 'I work day and night. I have no time to supervise the children.'[51] The same year, another mother explained to a different district commission, 'I want to raise my child well, but it is hard for me to do this alone. No one does any work with children where we live.'[52]

Officially approved child-rearing methods were predicated upon a certain standard of living, which, despite government promises, was not yet available to all Soviet citizens, even in the capital. The officials, teachers and police officers who served on the commissions could not acknowledge the material constraints facing parents: the cramped living conditions, the long work hours, the shortages of childcare and leisure activities for older children, although all these problems were the object of public criticism from at least 1954. To do so would have sounded dangerously anti-Soviet. Instead, they simply continued to blame and punish individual parents. This is not to deny that some parents may have been truly abusive or neglectful, but to observe that official discourse placed limits on the ways in which commissions could represent problems and propose solutions.

While official discourse and its silences constrained minors' commissions, parental attitudes presented another set of problems. Some parents were either unaware of, or were resistant to, the parenting methods commissions tried to instil. Commission hearings make it evident that, despite decades of pedagogical propaganda, people retained ideas about child rearing that expert opinion deemed retrograde or dangerous. For example, some parents matter-of-factly mentioned beating their children, seemingly unaware that pedagogues had been condemning physical punishment for the previous 20 years. One father explained, 'I thought a lot about the upbringing of my son, I talked to him and beat him, for the better, I thought, to scare him.'[53]

Another group of parents assumed that relations between parents and children were 'private' and therefore beyond the legitimate purview of the state. They protested not the methods and precepts of official pedagogy, but the general principle of interference. They defied the commissions' reprimands and asserted that raising their children was their own business. In a 1963 hearing, a father responded to questioning from the commission about his daughter's living conditions by insisting, 'Lyuba has her own bed. I am her father and ask you not to interfere in the upbringing of my daughter.'[54] In a 1964 case a representative from the police department reported that when he tried to make a home visit, the mother under investigation yelled at him, 'he's my son, and none of your business' and 'I myself am raising him, it is not your affair'.[55]

The defence of privacy was by no means universal, however. Other people, especially abused children and desperate parents, sought the intervention of voluntary and state organisations.[56] In 1959 a widower with two adolescent children told the Leningrad district minors' commission, 'I am busy at work a great deal of time and get home late ... I can't do anything with them, especially with my daughter ... I punished her physically, but this did not help'. When a commission member asked, 'Can you guarantee the normal upbringing of your children?', he replied, 'No, I cannot, they do not listen to me.'[57]A hopeless mother told the Kalinin district commission in 1963 that her son 'does not listen to me, does not study ... I ask you to send him to the children's colony'.[58]

Some parents expected assistance, and objected when it was not forthcoming, thus making clear their assumption that the state was obliged to help them.[59] A mother, whose son had started stealing, grumbled that since she had returned to work, the boy 'is left by himself, does not listen to us, and we cannot cope with him. At work they know that the boy is badly behaved but they do not help us.'[60] Explaining that his adolescent daughter refused to work or enrol in school, one father complained, 'I went to the police department and the executive committee [of the district soviet] on the question of my daughter, but nobody took any measures with her. I need help.'[61]

These diverse reactions to official intervention demonstrate the lack of consensus among parents concerning the boundary between public and private. Resistant parents cast child rearing as a purely private matter. Those who sought the help of state and voluntary organisations accepted the authority of social institutions to mediate relations between parents and children. In doing so, however, they were not necessarily endorsing the relationship between public and private required by official pedagogy. The whole purpose of intervention in family relations was to guarantee that parents raised disciplined, unselfish, future communists. The desperate, overwhelmed parents and abused children who appealed for help to minors' commissions and comrades' courts, however, had more short-term and personal goals in mind. Unlike the most defiant parents, they did not deny the authority of societal and state organisations; they assumed that such groups were legitimate and had the right to involve themselves in family relations, which is after all one of the basic premises of any modern welfare state. However, they saw public involvement in private life as a way to solve personal problems and family crises, not as a means of communist construction. In official pedagogy, parents were to raise good citizens because private life was supposed to serve public goals, but in the conception of some citizens, the reverse was true: public power was meant to promote private aspirations.

In contrast to the families described above, several of the people I spoke with who were raising children in the 1950s and 1960s recalled that they enjoyed pedagogical articles and radio programmes. They described taking their children to museums and theatres, assigning chores and supervising homework, although they did not use the term *kul'turnost'* in describing these activities.[62] While parents' recollections should not be conflated with their actual practices, their narratives do indicate what they valued in principle, at the very least. One man in particular seemed to embody the ideal, cultured, responsible Soviet father. His reflections reproduced the pedagogues' emphasis on *kul'turnost'* and its division into maternal and paternal components:

I was involved in my daughter's upbringing. I should say, I didn't just supervise her homework and who she made friends with, or go to parents' meetings. No, I wanted to broaden her horizons, show her something interesting. ... Once, in secret from her mother, we agreed to leave early in the morning and walk around Moscow while everyone slept. It was summer, it got light early, the weather was good. ... We got up at four and left ... and walked to Red Square ... we walked for two hours. [My daughter] was twelve, it was something unusual for her, very pleasant, interesting ... I wanted her to see it all ... that's what my child rearing, my role as a father consisted of. I must say, intimate subjects ... her character – this, her mother took charge of. ... From me she got a social foundation, and from her mother, a psychological and moral one.[63]

In some cases parents shared the experts' assumptions about parental gender roles and, according to their self-representations, complied with pedagogical recommendations. However, this does not mean that they accepted official values completely. Even though they seem to have implemented some of the advice, they may have ignored other aspects of it. Indeed, one sociologist has found evidence to indicate that Soviet parents disregarded in particular the exhortations to teach their children collectivism and self-sacrifice.[64] This tendency was certainly made clear to me during several conversations. In one, a woman recalled that her mother, though a 'convinced communist', would not allow her daughter to join the Komsomol during the 1950s. The reason for this seemingly anomalous decision was that during this period, urban Komsomol members could be sent away to work in distant regions, where their skills were needed, but this mother wanted to keep her daughter in Moscow, presumably to enjoy the emotional, cultural and material comforts of life in the capital.[65]

Similarly, Nina T. presented herself to me as an exemplary Soviet mother in many ways. She paid close attention to her son's studies, but, as popular pedagogy recommended, did not excuse him from household chores. She told me:

It was clear, when he became a little more independent, that there were things around the house that nobody would do if he didn't do them. For example, he had to fetch bread, he had to get the milk, he had to put the garbage out, he had to get the newspaper. If he didn't buy milk, then there would be no milk at home. ... It was his responsibility.[66]

Her ultimate aim was to make her son not a communist, but an outstanding individual. She recalled:

> After my son was born, I was still in the hospital in a fairly serious condition and I thought: at last I have my long-awaited child, a son ... and I thought, how do I want him to turn out? And here is what I did, took this scrap of paper, that I have kept even now ... and I wrote down how I wanted him to be: for him to have warm heart, to be open to nature and art, be educated, know foreign languages, be athletic, know how to do everything – to be a real man.[67]

On the basis of such anecdotal evidence, I am not trying to make claims about all Soviet parents. My point is simply that, like parents in other modern contexts, they had the possibility of choosing which aspects of expert advice they implemented and so could deconstruct official pedagogy to stress, for example, culture, responsibility or self-discipline without collectivism.[68]

Didacticism was a permanent feature of Soviet policy, but scholarly discussions of prescriptive literature do not always delineate its impact. In this essay, I have described official ideas about child rearing and uncovered some of their ramifications for everyday life. For child welfare workers, official pedagogy provided standards by which to judge all parents, regardless of their material circumstances and education; and it set the terms in which they explained family crises and formulated responses. Parents had more diverse and sometimes subversive ways of dealing with official ideology. Pedagogues promised that by employing the recommended practices, mothers and fathers, each fulfilling their complementary responsibilities, could raise children to become socially active, self-denying, cultured and hard-working citizens, in short, ideal communists. Yet parents could, and sometimes did, uncouple ends from means. They adopted certain child-rearing methods, accepted gendered parenting roles or welcomed the intervention of public institutions, without endorsing the final aim pedagogues envisioned. Parents ignored the very virtue Soviet leaders deemed most important to the success of communism: the willing sacrifice of individual, private aspirations in favour of public goals.

Notes

1 On early Soviet plans for socialised child rearing, see L. Attwood, *Creating the New Soviet Woman: Women's Magazines as Engineers of Female Identity, 1922–1953* (Basingstoke, 1999), pp. 7–8; W. Goldman, *Women, the State and Revolution* (Cambridge, 1993), pp. 60–7; A. Kollontai, 'Communism and the Family', in A. Holt (ed. and trans.), *Selected Writings of Alexandra Kollontai* (New York, 1977), pp. 250–60.

2 J. Dunstan, 'Soviet Boarding Education: Its Rise and Progress', in J. Brine et al. (eds), *Home, School and Leisure in the Soviet Union* (London, 1980), pp. 124–5; A. G. Kharchev, *Sem'ya v sovetskom obshchestve* (Leningrad, 1960), p. 105; M. I. Lifanov, *Za kommunisticheskii byt* (Leningrad, 1963), p. 74.

3 L. Liegle, *The Family's Role in Soviet Education* (New York, 1975), p. 22.

4 G. Breslauer, 'Khrushchev Reconsidered', in S. Cohen et al. (eds), *The Soviet Union since Stalin* (Bloomington, 1980), pp. 51–2.

5 For scholarly treatment of communist morality, see R. De George, *Soviet Ethics and Morality* (Ann Arbor, 1969); D. Field, 'Communist Morality and Meanings of Private Life in Post-Stalinist Russia, 1953–1964', unpublished PhD dissertation, University of Michigan, 1996; P. Juviler, 'Communist Morality and Soviet Youth', *Problems of Communism*, vol. 10, no. 3, 1961, pp. 16–24. For contemporary works, see, for example, Akademiya nauk SSSR, *Nvravstvennye printsipy stroitel'ya kommunizma* (Moscow, 1965); S. M. Kosolapov and O. N. Krutova, *Voprosy vospitaniya trudyashchiekhsya v dukhe kommunisticheskoi nravstvennosti* (Moscow, 1961); A. F. Shishkin, *Osnovy kommunisticheskoi morali* (Moscow, 1955).

6 A. Bardyan, 'Samyi blizkii, rodnoi chelovek', *Sem'ya i shkola*, no. 3, 1961, p. 7.

7 During this period, the Soviet government greatly expanded social welfare programmes, reforming the social insurance system in 1956 and creating new institutions aimed at helping families, such as the minors' commissions, discussed below. See B. Madison, *Social Welfare in the Soviet Union* (Stanford, 1968).

8 O. Kharkhordin, *The Collective and the Individual in Russia: a Study of Practices* (Berkeley, Calif., 1999), pp. 279–80, 302–3.

9 These commissions operated under a 1957 Russian Republic Law. See 'Polozhenie o komissiyakh po ustroistvu detei i podrostkov', *Sovetskaya yustitsiya*, no. 10, 1957, p. 67. I have found little information about these colonies or the conditions inside them. They were first established in 1943, and by 1958 they numbered 66. The colonies were subdivided into 2–5 groups of 25–30 young people, who lived, studied and worked together. TsKhDMO, f. 1, op. 32, d. 951, l. 77.

10 D. Burg, *Oppozitsionnye nastroeniya molodezhi v gody posle 'Ottepeli'* (Munich, 1962), p. 30; A. Kassof, *The Soviet Youth Program* (Cambridge, Mass., 1965), p. 149.

11 For Komsomol complaints, see for example, TsAODM, f. 6083 op. 1, d. 5, l. 142; TsKhDMO, f. 1, op. 46, d. 318, ll. 106–8.

12 TsAODM, f . 6083, op. 1, d. 37a, l. 20.

13 TsKhDMO, f. 1, op. 32, d. 1101, ll. 12, 48. For a 1953 complaint about drinking, card playing, poor work discipline, and hooliganism among young workers living in dorms, see also f. 1, op. 3, d. 786, l. 88.

14 Burg, op. cit., p. 35. For a description of *stilyagi* in the 1940s, see V. Aksenov, *In Search of Melancholy Baby* (New York, 1987), pp. 12–14. Juliane Fürst draws a distinction between *stilyagi* and overtly political youth opposition groups. See J. Fürst, 'Prisoners of the Soviet Self? – Political Youth Opposition in Late Stalinism', *Europe–Asia Studies*, vol. 54, no. 3, 2002, p. 369.

15 E. Crankshaw, *Russia without Stalin* (New York, 1956), pp. 242–3; B. Grushin and V. Chikin, *Ispoved' pokoleniya* (Moscow, 1962), p. 200; S. F. Starr, *Red and Hot: the Fate of Jazz in the Soviet Union, 1917–1980* (Oxford, 1983), pp. 239–40; R. Stites, *Russian Popular Culture* (Cambridge, 1992), pp. 124–8; E. Zubkova, *Russia after the War: Hopes, Illusions, and Disappointments, 1945–1956* (Armonk, 1998), pp. 192–3.

16 Public lecture delivered in Moscow and published as I. F. Svadkovskii, *O kul'ture povedeniya sovetskoi molodezhi* (Moscow, 1958), pp. 16–17.

17 TsAODM, f. 6083, op. 1, d. 3, l. 30.

18 *Printsipy tvoei zhizni* (Moscow, 1963), p. 49.

19 M. Chalin, *Moral' stroitel'ya kommunizma* (Moscow, 1963), p. 54.

20 Liegle, op. cit., pp. 25, 28, 57. On the particular developmental needs of preschool children and adolescents, see for example: Z. Boguslavsksaya, 'Malysh igraet', *Sovetskaya zhenshchina*, no. 5, 1961, p. 34; R. Brustnichkina, 'Put' k serdtsu podrostka', *Rabotnitsa*, no. 1, 1958, pp. 44–5. On personality types, see for example A. Il'ina, 'Vpechatlitel'nye deti', *Sem'ya i shkola*, no. 3, 1960, pp. 7–9.

21 O. S. Bogdanova, *Zdorovyi byt sem'i* (Moscow, 1956), p. 19. See also, for example, S. Grombakh, 'Shkol'niku – tverdyi rezhim dnya', *Sem'ya i shkola*, no. 8, 1957, pp. 9–10.

22 M. Gel'fan, 'Trud i igra', *Sem'ya i shkola*, no. 11, 1960, p. 8; K. Lapin, *Slovo o materi* (Moscow, 1961), p. 54.

23 A. Sergeeva, 'Ty vsegda so mnoyu, Mama!...', *Sem'ya i shkola*, no. 3, 1962, p. 11.

24 E. Medynskii, 'Vezhlivost', prilichiya, takt', *Sem'ya i shkola*, no. 1, 1957, p. 10.

25 S. Boym, *Common Places: Mythologies of Everyday Life in Russia* (Cambridge, Mass., 1994), p. 105; V. Dunham, *In Stalin's Time: Middle-Class Values in Soviet Fiction* (Cambridge, 1976), p. 22; S. Fitzpatrick, *Everyday Stalinism: Ordinary Life in Extraordinary Times: Soviet Russia in the 1930s* (New York, 1999), pp. 79–83; V. Volkov, 'The Concept of kul'turnost': Notes on the Stalinist Civilizing Process', in S. Fitzpatrick (ed.), *Stalinism: New Directions* (London, 2000), p. 216.

26 C. Kelly, *Refining Russia: Advice Literature, Polite Culture and Gender from Catherine to Yeltsin* (Oxford, 2001), pp. 317–21; S. Reid, 'Destalinization and Taste', 1953–1963', *Journal of Design History*, vol. 10, no. 2, 1997, pp. 177–202.

27 Field, op. cit., pp. 41–2.

28 On good manners, see, for example, G. Puzis, 'Kak vesti sebya v obshchestve', *Sem'ya i shkola*, no. 7, 1956, pp. 9–11. On homework and study space, see I. Solov'ev, 'Khozyain rabochego mesta', *Sem'ya i shkola*, no. 9, 1961, p. 32; E. Nikol'skaya et al., *Besedy o domashnem khozyaistve* (np., 1959), p. 42.

29   Bogdanova, op. cit., p. 22.
30   Kharchev, op. cit., p. 58.
31   G. M. Sverdlov, *Sovetskoe zakonodatel'stvo o brake i sem'e* (Moscow, 1961), pp. 54–5.
32   See for example *Zdorov'e*, no. 3, 1960, p. 12. See also O. Kitaigorodskaya, 'Kakaya pishcha nuzhna rebenku', *Sem'ya i shkola*, no. 5, 1960, p. 42.
33   S. Kukhterin, 'Fathers and Patriarchs in Communist and Post-communist Russia', in S. Ashwin (ed.), *Gender, State and Society in Soviet and Post-Soviet Russia* (London, 2000), p. 80.
34   See, for example, Z. Efimova, 'Sekret nashego avtoriteta', *Sem'ya i shkola*, no. 6, 1963, p. 17; T. Panfilov, 'Put' k myslyam i serdtsu yunosti', *Sem'ya i shkola*, no. 4, 1963, p. 2.
35   V. Yarchuk, 'Rodnoi otets', *Sem'ya i shkola*, no. 1, 1957, p. 31. For condemnations of drunken dads, see, for example, a letter from N. Zhuravleva, a teacher, in *Sem'ya i shkola*, no. 8, 1961, pp. 36–7.
36   N. Levitov, 'Otets – vospitatel'', *Sem'ya i shkola*, no. 8, 1961, p. 7.
37   For stories about spoiling mothers and grandmothers, see, for example, 'Anechka i ei mat'', *Rabotnitsa*, no. 10, 1954, p. 25; A. V. Kosareva, 'Pedagogicheskaya propaganda – vazhnaya chast' raboty s roditelyami', *Sovetskaya pedagogika*, no. 7, 1953, p. 45.
38   Levitov, op. cit., p. 8.
39   A. Demina, 'O blizosti k detyam', *Sovetskaya zhenshchina*, no. 3, 1956, p. 46.
40   Bogdanova, op. cit., p. 12.
41   L. Kletenik, '"Trudnye" deti i trudnye roditeli', *Rabotnitsa*, no. 1, 1955, p. 25. See also Efimova, op. cit., p. 18.
42   *Printsipy tvoei zhizni*, p. 82.
43   Leigle, op. cit., p. 94, reports that in 1963, 80,000 parent activists worked in voluntary committees at schools, housing complexes and workplaces throughout the city of Moscow.
44   TsMAM, f. 122, op. 1, d. 1165, ll. 94–5.
45   TsMAM, f. 257, op. 1, d. 265, l. 24.
46   TsMAM, f. 257, op. 1, d. 944, l. 147.
47   TsMAM, f. 197, op. 1, d. 883, ll. 182–4.
48   TsMAM, f. 273, op. 4, d. 1113, l. 7. See also TsMAM, f. 1078, op. 2, d. 147, l. 3.
49   T. Sosnovy, 'The Soviet Housing Situation Today', *Soviet Studies*, vol. 11, no. 1, 1959, p. 18.
50   TsMAM, f. 122, op. 1, d. 1055, l. 47.
51   TsMAM, f. 257, op. 1, d. 944, l. 130.
52   TsMAM, f. 197, op. 1, d. 1415, l. 30.
53   TsMAM, f. 494, op. 1, d. 790, l. 61. For other cases involving matter-of-fact attitudes towards corporal punishment, see TsMAM, f. 257, op. 1., d. 433, l. 17; f. 122, op. 1, d. 1055, l. 164; f. 257, op. 1, d. 510, l. 74.
54   TsMAM, f. 310, op. 1, d. 737, l. 87.
55   TsMAM, f. 257, op. 1, d. 944, l. 89. See also TsMAM, f. 257, op. 1, d. 510, l. 8.
56   For an appeal from abused children, see for example TsMAM, f. 257, op. 1, d. 752, l. 37.
57   TsMAM, f. 257, op. 1, d. 510, l. 74.

58 TsMAM, f. 310, op. 1, d. 737, l. 5.
59 Shelia Fitzpatrick finds evidence of this attitude already in the 1930s. See Fitzpatrick, *Everyday Stalinism*, pp. 226–7.
60 TsMAM, f. 310, op. 1, d. 737, l. 25.
61 TsMAM, f. 122, op. 1, d. 1165, l. 13.
62 Field, op. cit., pp. 265–6.
63 Yuri Z., interview by author, Moscow, 4 June 1994.
64 Liegle, op. cit., pp. 142–3.
65 Vera B., interview by author, Moscow, 21 May 1994.
66 Nina T. interview by author, Moscow, 2 June 1994.
67 Ibid.
68 A. Hulbert, *Raising America: Experts, Parents and a Century of Advice about Children* (New York, 2003), pp. 367–70.

6
Reconstruction or Reproduction? Mothers and the Great Soviet Family in Cinema after Stalin

John Haynes

The singling out of cinema for special mention in Khrushchev's so-called 'secret' speech to the closed session of the XX Party Congress in 1956 is more than simply an insider's view of the level of importance attached to cinema by Stalin. In a key passage, Khrushchev evokes the still recent memory of the notorious *lakirovka* of the collective farm musical comedy genre cycle: 'Many films so pictured kolkhoz life that the tables were bending from the weight of turkeys and geese. Evidently Stalin thought that it was actually so.'[1] Whether or not one takes this assessment of Stalin's critical faculties at face value, what is at stake in this assertion is a kind of double debunking of two myths central to Soviet society of the Stalin era: the much vaunted wisdom of the all-knowing leader is reduced to a bad case of 'false consciousness' by his successor, who is further able to see through the myths promulgated by socialist realist cinema at its monumentalising and heroicising peak. That is to say, there is a recognition of the potential of film as a central weapon in the arsenal of the propagandist, which is of course closely related to its (inescapable) potential for distorting and falsfying the 'reality' it so often claims unproblematically to represent.

This chapter begins by examining cinema's position within the broader context of official and publicistic responses to Khrushchev's speech, and addressing the film industry's contribution to debates on the future direction of the 'Great Soviet Family' following the crisis in the imagined Soviet social order provoked by the denunciation of Stalin. The remainder of the chapter will offer a comparative analysis of two key films to emerge from the Mosfil'm studio in the immediate post 'secret' speech era – *The Cranes are Flying* (*Letyat zhuravli*, 1957)

114

and *Ballad of a Soldier* (*Ballada o soldate*, 1959). Both of these films received widespread recognition on an international scale, picking up awards at Cannes and generating a critical and popular discourse that continues to this day: their canonisation in critical histories and on university syllabuses, as well as their relative availability, with subtitles, on video cassette, testify to this abiding currency; and the present analysis – through a refracting lens focusing specifically on the figure of the mother – is intended as a contribution to this ongoing debate.

Cinema's response to the speech was both characteristically slow, for a number of institutional and logistical reasons, and uncharacteristically diverse, if only by comparison with the much more limited fare of the immediate post-war years. Many of the new films were undoubtedly much less static than their predecessors; these certainly incorporated a broader range of thematic material, as well as foreign influences and even conflicting perspectives; and the Soviet film industry of the 'thaw' era did indeed develop to produce a number of films which – especially in terms of their turn from monumental public themes (the heroic con-quest of space) to the private inner realm of psychology and emotion (the complex negotiations at the heart of everyday life in the new Soviet Union) – are still championed today for their 'honesty' and 'authenticity'. On the other hand, appeals to such abstracted values need to be treated with some caution, and it would be misleading to represent Khrushchev's speech as marking a watershed moment in a 'liberation' of Soviet cinema from the shackles of ideology. First of all, the new leader was far from liberal in matters of culture, an attitude that he was prepared to perform quite publicly on the occasion of his notorious visit to the Manezh to confront members of Moscow's fine art avant garde;[2] more fundamentally, cultural productions inevitably betray the hallmarks of *some* informing ideology, and their claims to 'truth' and 'honesty' must be seen as partial, at best.

It would be equally misleading to suggest that Soviet film-makers abandoned wholesale their traditional function of circumscribed social commentary. As Josephine Woll demonstrates, Soviet cinema was still expected to respond, and in fact did so, to specific, identifiable, social imperatives – although with a much greater degree of relative auton-omy with respect to both subject matter and form.[3] This new-found relative flexibility testifies to a very real effect of the 'secret' speech: to broaden the parameters of film discourse and open up a space for debate, within which different films were able to offer their distinctive takes on a limited variety of social themes. Films of the era, then, can be seen to represent contributions to the construction of competing hegemonic nodes, launching specific consensual appeals and attempting to mobilise audiences in support of them.

One such topic for particularly urgent debate was the very organisation of society itself. Culture of the 'thaw' era was concerned not only with a reappraisal of the past in light of Khrushchev's revelations about Stalin, but also with carving out a new future for Soviet society. These revelations, however, had also debunked a third, and perhaps the most highly cherished structuring myth of Soviet society under Stalin, that of its leader as the 'wise father' of a 'Great Family of the Soviet State'.[4] This myth had provided the model for Soviet society for the best part of the past two decades, but, I would argue further, was so tied to its figure of the patriarch as leading and guiding his children in all aspects of their public and private lives that, deprived of this rhetorical focal point by the death of the 'great helmsman', the social order mythologised in socialist realist narratives under Stalin was no longer tenable and *had already failed* by 1956. The myth simply could not accommodate such a loss; the gap between cherished illusion and hard reality had become too glaring; and cinema, which had attempted to bridge that gap for so long, was now co-opted as an apparently objective measure of the illusion itself.

In a sense, then, Khrushchev's attack on the benevolence and wisdom of the patriarch at the head of the Soviet family had to be made so decisively after his death not only in the interests of justice and truth, but precisely because this structuring myth, with its very narrow discursive emphasis on a sole father figure of a nation that could only bring forth 'model sons' – never themselves fathers – organised an imagined society that was *fundamentally incapable of reproducing itself*. In this respect at least, Khrushchev's 'secret' speech was simply a public acknowledgement that the field was now relatively open for competing attempts to reimagine the social order; that the need was there; and he might have added that such attempts were already somewhat overdue.

Such reimaginations, however, were always going to be somewhat constrained, like the cautious reforms of the leader himself, by their continual negotiation with representatives of both innovation and conservatism. The compromise 'third way' of the 'thaw' era resulted in a faith in innovation, technology and a tangible future (with Khrushchev's famous, and perhaps somewhat ill-advised, declaration that communism would be achieved by the year 1980) without any radical commitment to a questioning of the core values informing the organisation of Soviet society. The principles of communism, then, despite their hijacking towards the construction of Stalin's 'personality cult', were still the correct and only imaginable means by which Soviet society, itself consequently still figured in many films as a 'great family', could respond to the demands of 'modernisation' conceived as a process of efficiently streamlined adaptation to an unproblematic present scheduled to last for approximately the next quarter century.

Bloodied, compromised and yet unbowed, the 'great family' was to soldier on – the critic Maiya Turovskaya noted the 'widespread enthusiasm for the theme of "family" life' in the years following the 1956 Party Congress[5] – but still had to negotiate the twin crises of paternal authority and social reproduction outlined above. After decades in which the 'father of the nation' had been portrayed as the one true patriarch, flesh and blood fathers did reappear on the Soviet screen, along with a refreshingly new awareness of their anxieties and internal contradictions. I have argued this point in connection with the hero of *Fate of a Man* (*Sud'ba cheloveka*, 1959) elsewhere, although the research for this chapter indicates that what little optimism I detected in that film's 'honest' approach to the issue of fatherhood may need to be somewhat tempered.[6]

In fact, in the (relatively few) films of the Khrushchev era that tackle this issue, there is a marked degree of confusion regarding the question of who is bringing up whom. First of all, the child very often turns out to be 'father to the man', and this may indeed turn out to be the case with *Fate of a Man*. Such confusion is parodied in a scene from a film that many regard as emblematic of the 'thaw' era, *Il'ich's Gate* (*Zastava Il'icha*, 1961, released in 1965 as *Mne dvadsat' let*). The original version appropriates the figure of Hamlet (more explicitly reworked under Khrushchev both in cinema, by veteran director Grigorii Kozintsev in 1964, and through Boris Pasternak's poetry and translation) when Sergei, one of the film's young heroes, asks the vision of his father's ghost for guidance. The ghost first asks Sergei's age and, on hearing that he is 23, replies that he, the father, is just 21 – and simply vanishes.

Khrushchev's extreme discomfort with this scene prompted a detailed condemnation during a speech to a meeting of artists and intellectuals in the Kremlin in March 1963, which is worth a brief discussion here. The leader was quick to recast the wilfully anarchic confusion into a more simple and resolvable tension between father and son, which he could easily refute: 'In our time, the father-and-son problem is not what it was in Turgenev's day. ... In Soviet socialist society there are no contradictions between generations'; such tensions were in fact long familiar to the Soviet censors, and this example was to be dealt with accordingly; crucially, however, before Khrushchev can effect this recasting, there is a not insignificant slippage between genders: 'No one will ever believe that! It is common knowledge that even animals don't abandon their offspring. If you take a puppy *from its mother* and throw it into the water, she will at once dash in at the risk of *her* own life to save it.'[7] This confusion over gender certainly resonates with Woll's argument that, in a number of films of this period, the man/father threatens to straddle the gender divide – 'the "good mother" is a male figure who displaces the biological mother'.[8]

Off screen, meanwhile, it was the party's own youth organisations that quietly continued to provide the children of the state with the practical and political education and mentoring – the induction to the public sphere – that one might usually have expected from their fathers. The state was not about to hand back the terrain of fatherhood to its male citizens, yet was still uneasy about nominating a replacement for the post of sole repository of patriarchal authority – perhaps not least on account of its associations with obscene excesses and arbitrary abuses. I would argue, rather, that what is crucial here, as in Woll's comment above, is that this thorny issue was, by and large, sidestepped both in cinema – which mobilised, in a number of cases, the already familiar trope of the Soviet orphan – and in the broader arena of official discourse, by an intensification of discursive interventions focusing, instead, on motherhood.

It is vital to note at this point that this shift was effected not only in cinema, and that any break it represented with the immediate past was hardly radical but, rather, a question of degree. Motherhood had not been neglected during Stalin's lifetime: despite changes of name, for example, the specialist journal *Voprosy materinstva i mladenchestva (Questions of Motherhood and Infancy)*, which had declared in its first issue that 'motherhood is the social function of women – this is our watchword', continued its twin function of providing both the latest news on scientific medical enlightenment, and a forum for state policy on the exercise of motherhood in line with the perceived needs of Soviet society.[9] As such, and at the limits where official discourse impacted on the bodies of Soviet women, the journal was not only called upon to justify and rationalise the ban on abortion of 1936 – significantly, the year that also witnessed both the unveiling of the new Soviet constitution and the first rumblings of Stalin's 'terror' – but also to apply, as Issoupova argues, *normative* pressure to women to continue providing the state with at least one or two children following the lifting of that ban in 1955.[10]

Similarly elsewhere, as the coercive apparatus of state terror was replaced by appeals for Soviet citizens to internalise the tenets of the new 'communist morality' first developed in the mid-1950s, an increased emphasis was placed on the specific dynamics of motherhood and the upbringing of children, characteristically enshrining the new duties of Soviet women in this area as 'rights'.[11] Private life, which under Stalin had been unproblematically submerged into the realm of public duty, was now firmly back on the public agenda, and at the top of that agenda lay what is traditionally conceived as the most intimate relationship of the private, domestic, 'feminine' realm, that between mother and infant. While there is every reason to celebrate such a shift to the 'honest' and 'authentic' exploration of people's 'real lives', then, it has to be set in the context of an officially incited problematisation at the level of discourse, which aimed to set the parameters for the debate on normatising self-regulation through the willing and active support of the values of communist morality.

As one might expect, cinema made its own interventions. In the aftermath of the Party Congress of 1956, and against the background of the repealing of the ban on abortion and the drive for communist morality, a number of films tackled the issue of motherhood at least obliquely. A brief round-up courtesy of Woll: following her arrival in Moscow and seduction by a local *poseur*, the heroine of *A Person is Born* (*Chelovek rodilsya*, 1956) gives birth and herself becomes a Soviet person, in the classic guise of a 'worker-mother', thanks to a system that can accommodate her work schedule to a programme of institutionalised childcare; in *Spring on Zarechnaya Street* (*Vesna na Zarechnoi ulitse*, 1956), the cherished 'progressiveness' of the intelligentsia is effectively debunked by the heroine's insensitivity to the wearying effects of pregnancy and childbirth; Lida, the philandering wife of a geologist in *The House I Live In* (*Dom, v kotorom ya zhivu*, 1957) is condemned by the film 'less harshly for her infidelity, a consequence of her discontent, than for her childlessness, a result of her egotism'; even the superhuman Lenin is scaled down to a product of good upbringing by his mother in *The Ul'yanov Family* (*Sem'ya Ul'yanovykh*, 1957) – a trope elaborated by the later diptych, conspicuously entitled *A Mother's Heart* (*Serdtse materi*, 1966) and *A Mother's Loyalty* (*Vernost' materi*, 1967) respectively; and the common threads of unconditional love, loyalty, morality and self-sacrificing service to the state are tied together in *Someone Else's Children* (*Chuzhie deti*, 1958), in which the heroine enters a loveless marriage to a widower for the sake of his children, and then stands by them as he leaves for another woman.[12]

In such representations, however, references to motherhood are characteristically oblique, and motherhood in and of itself is very rarely to be found centre stage. In the present instance, for example, we might note a certain displacement of attention from the mother, in both films and criticism of the 'thaw' era, to the child – as itself a 'natural' metaphor for the major social themes of the day, such as questions of guilt, innocence, hope for the future and social regeneration.[13] It has to be acknowledged from the outset, then, that on the face of it, the figure of the mother is characteristically marginalised in both *Cranes* and *Ballad*. On the other hand, I would like to argue that either film responds in very different ways to this marginalisation. It is also certainly true that neither film comes up with any radically new imagining of the social order to emerge from a time of turmoil figured by the traumatic crucible of the 'Great Patriotic War'. At the end of both films, there is a sense that everything and nothing has changed: in *Cranes* the war has come and gone, and while the film has emphasised the tragedy and sense of loss entailed by the conflict, the reappearance of the cranes in the sky over Moscow indicates some sense of continuity with the heroine Veronika's pre-war idyllic happiness with her now dead fiancé Boris; at the end of *Ballad*, on the other hand, we are returned to the figure of the eponymous Alesha's mother on the country road in exactly the same position as we left her at the beginning – knowing, as she has from the start, that her son will not return from the front. This is not to say, however, that neither film responds to the Khrushchev era imperative to imagine *some* form of social order in the wake of Stalin's death and denunciation; in fact, I would argue that both films fit into the broader arena of Soviet discourse of the period precisely by staking their claims in this regard around the figure of the mother, however marginalised.

To begin with *Cranes*: the overwhelming and heart-rending conclusion of the film, in which Veronika's final acceptance that Boris will not return is first counterposed to, and then subsumed into, the mass celebrations for Victory Day, marks the beginning of a new stage in both her own life, and that of society as a whole. What I aim to make explicit about this conclusion is the extent to which the degree of optimism evinced by the movie for the (nonetheless uncertain) future is underwritten by Veronika's adoption of the orphan, Bor'ka, towards the end of the action; that is to say, the sense of closure effected by the final scene of *Cranes* relies very heavily on its charting of Veronika's progress from her earlier troubled, and troubling, status as 'woman', to her final assumption of a stable identity as 'woman-mother'.

   Up to this point Veronika has passed, more dead than alive, through a
series of tragedies wrought by the traumatic irruption of the Great
Patriotic War into her happy relationship with Boris Borozdin. The
couple's missed encounter at the rallying point, as Boris marches off to
the front never to be heard from again, sets in motion a narrative chain
of events that sees Veronika orphaned and destitute after a direct hit on
her parents' apartment; taken into her fiancé's household only to be
raped by Boris's cousin Mark, a stereotypically narcissistic 'class enemy'
who has dodged conscription and indulges in pleasure to the detriment
of both his relationship and society as a whole; consenting to marry her
assailant, who promptly embarks on an affair after the family has been
evacuated to Siberia; condemned by association as a 'faithless fiancée' by
both patients and staff (including Boris' failing patriarch father, a prominent doctor) at the hospital where she is working as a nurse; pushed to
attempt suicide by throwing herself under a train – an attempt that is
forestalled by her rescue of Bor'ka from under the wheels of a speeding
truck; and finally acquainted with ultimate proof of Boris's death, by an
eyewitness account from his best friend and comrade in arms, Stepan.
Stepan then addresses the Victory Day celebrations, while a tearful
Veronika is encouraged to distribute flowers to the assembled crowd,
before being led away under the arm of Dr Borozdin.
   Stepan's final confirmation provides an almost palpable sense of resolution, for the audience, of an intense and protracted dramatic irony
– we have known about Boris's death, perhaps somewhat pointedly,
since the scene inserted between Veronika's rape and the announcement over the Borozdin's breakfast table that she and Mark are to
marry – and this sense of closure is backed up and appropriated by the
customary socialist realist pronunciation that all is once again in order,
and closing perspective on the future, albeit a far less certain and
shining one than had appeared in Stalin's day. Although Bor'ka is
nowhere to be seen, the climactic Victory Day scene is replete with
implicit signifiers of motherhood – the newborn baby held aloft,
Stepan's privileging of mothers' security and peace of mind as the
primary justification for fighting the war in the first place, and of
course Veronika's own assumption of the role, in its richly symbolic
dimension, as she passes through the crowds handing out flowers –
and yet the extent to which this resolution is propped up by
Veronika's ultimate symbolic identification with the figure of the
mother is noted by very few critics.[14]
   Veronika, it seems, has finally found her place in the social order to
emerge from the ruins of the war. Tat'yana Samoilova's devastating

performance here makes it clear that some coherent sense and meaning have been imparted to her life, which simply cannot be accounted for by the mere facts either that she now knows for sure that her fiancé is dead, or that the war has stopped, apparently as arbitrarily as it started. The fact is that the figure of motherhood, as ultimately appropriated by *Cranes*, is able to resolve a number of structuring tensions within the film's narrative. First of all, according to critical consensus, the movie sets out to defend the private (implicitly encoded 'feminine') realm: Veronika's stubborn and heroic refusal to yield up her 'enigma' (which clearly both fascinates the movie *and* determines its construction of ideal audience positions), coupled with the film's widely celebrated refusal to pass judgement on her, is taken as a powerful assertion of the right to a private life. What such accounts fail to question is the extent to which such a defence actually does Veronika any favours *as a woman*: the narrative of *Cranes*, in its excessive attempts to figure public abuses of its cherished private realm, pushes Veronika into the series of traumatic situations described above, and at each point in the series the conventions of realism are downgraded in favour of a hystericised *mise-en-scène*.

This is most obviously the case with the rather heavy-handed treatment of the rape scene: as the windows of the Borozdin family's nicely appointed apartment are blown in by the explosions of an air raid outside, the film quite sadistically relocates this brutalising public invasion of the private realm on to the body of its heroine. On the one hand, this metaphor is making a point strikingly clear, but on the other, we should note at this stage that such a metaphor also evokes the troubling issue of male and female sexuality. Male sexuality is disposed of, in a stock socialist realist way, *within* the narrative: Mark is ultimately excommunicated from the Soviet family, not on account of his sexual crime, but for his explicit *public* failings as an egotist and draft dodger. *Female* sexuality, however, troubles the remainder of the film, in the course of which the narrative desperately tries to 'tame' the unrepresentable ('enigmatic') difference now embodied in Samoilova's fascinating performance, until her only refuge is provided in a reassuringly desexualised subject position as an *adoptive* mother.[15]

This subject position, however, seems to be of more use as a means to resolve the *film's* hystericisation – manifested in the conversion formations of its *mise-en-scène* and again displaced on to the figure of Veronika who is made to suffer, in the classical Freudian sense, from the repetitions championed in formal analyses of the movie, until she is finally able to draw some degree of hope from the sight of the cranes over the Victory Day celebrations.[16] A psychoanalytical reading of Veronika's character might point to the spatial and temporal discontinuities in the scene of her flight to the station and suicide attempt, and suggest that, in this scene, the heroine is finally 'cured' of her hysteria by a process of 'going through the fantasy' –– a process aided somewhat by the appearance of the orphan Bor'ka as an 'answer of the Real', to which, apparently *instinctively*, she responds.[17] On the other hand, *Cranes* takes great pains to 'naturalise' Veronika's 'decision' to rescue the child (if she is even allowed a choice in the matter, which would certainly go against the grain of the movie as a whole). In the rapid course of this somewhat chaotic scene, for example, there is barely a reaction shot of Veronika registering the danger to the child – the effect of course being a fore-echo of Khrushchev's own 'puppy' analogy cited above; there is also the implication that Veronika instinctively knows exactly *how* to mother, as well as the newborn and the ocean of flowers accompanying the film's closure.

Although the ideological nature of this interpellation is submerged, first in a representation of an instinctual lunge to adopt the orphan Bor'ka, and second, as the 'truth' of a love figured as transcendental (the mnemic echoes represented by the cranes in flight), the articulation of these 'natural' signifiers to Stepan's victory speech indicates that there is plenty in this matter that is far from unideological – quite apart from the final, successful calling of the heroine into a social identity as a mother.[18] Most importantly for this chapter, Veronika's motherhood stands centre stage, for the briefest of moments, and is then whisked away before any sustained inquiry as to the specific dimensions of this role may be undertaken.[19] As Veronika is led from the scene in the care of the (by now fully recuperated) bourgeois patriarch Borozdin, Veronika is finally reintegrated into the Soviet social order by becoming an *agent*, as well as an object of state practices in her assumption of the traditional dual 'woman-mother' role prescribed for women in the Soviet Union since well before Stalin's time.[20] The 'Great Family' of the Soviet state was indeed to soldier on much as before, with the only apparent difference being a relative liberalism in cinema which allows for claims to be staked on the terrain of private life in defiance of the regime's attempts to inculcate values of 'communist morality'. An analysis of the film's treatment of motherhood exposes a purely instrumental appropriation of one of Russian culture's richest symbols as a somewhat one-dimensional metaphor for social regeneration pure and simple, and this conservative economy appears to offer little of value for any development of women's politics in Khrushchev's Soviet Union.

The mother figure in *Ballad of a Soldier* also stands at the margins of the film, bookending the journey of Alesha which Maiya Turovskaya, among others, sees as the action proper of the movie – the scenes of the mother, as well as Alesha's desperate fight with the German tanks, relegated to the position of 'a kind of prologue to his unpretentious story'.[21] It is certainly the case that *Ballad* – unlike *Cranes* – does little to make the figure of the mother attractive either through the use of a strikingly (and unconventionally) beautiful actress, or through any resolution of the tensions inherent to such a subject position. From the very start, the mother is marked out as distinct from, for example, the group of giggling young women (who seem to have walked straight off the set of a kolkhoz comedy, but nervously stop their chatter as the mother passes them by) both by her mourning attire and, more dynamically, her movement towards, rather than away from, the spectator. The only figure to follow the mother in this opening scene is another young woman cradling a baby, although her gaze, as it follows Alesha's mother, registers not hope for the future, but a kind of mute incomprehension at the disturbing fate that awaits, it seems, all mothers.

On the other hand, Alesha's *maternal* trajectory during the course of the narrative, as he struggles to make his way back home to the countryside on a week's leave, is already in stark contrast to the ideological tug towards Moscow and the 'father of fathers' in films of the Stalin era. This point is emphasised not only in words, as Alesha explains he would like leave of absence specifically to see his mother and repair the roof of their home, but also by the increasingly frequent signifiers of motherhood that make their way into the film's *mise-en-scène*, most particularly the scarf he has bought as a gift for her, and which we have already seen her wearing. I would argue, however, that the film goes even further in its rejection of the patriarchal codes and conventions that characterised Stalin era features than a mere emphasis on the purely personal, and by no means heroic, nature of Alesha's initial 'exploit'.[22] For if we turn proper attention once again to the figure of the mother as she stands on the roadside during the 'prologue', and examine the way in which we are drawn into the narrative 'proper', we cannot help but notice that, despite the male voice-over's claim to be telling us, and the mother, things she never knew about her son, the dissolve to Alesha's fight against the tanks is mediated through the gaze of the mother. This is not to suggest that we are instantly identified with the gaze of the mother – we know that she is unaware of what is to follow, and in fact for such an identification cinematic conventions would require that her gaze was turned back upon us. Instead we have an oblique gaze towards the narrative, while the camera closes in on, and into, her eyes. We are invited to identify with the mother *not* in terms of a gaze presumed as mastering events, but with her *experience* specifically as a mother, without which and without whom the film has only a very limited meaning.

The 'meaning' referred to here, however, is not to be taken in the restricted logocentric sense of a direct communication through language, but as the transmitting of a certain *affective* impact, a communication that is *beyond* verbal representation, which exceeds the film's attempts to marginalise that experience and contain it within a voice-over narration privileging a cinema that can tell the objective truth about events (including a suspect ethnocentrism explicit in the closing eulogising of Alesha as a specifically *Russian* soldier). If critics occasionally complain that the 'fairy tale' plot of *Ballad* is oversimplified, then frankly they are missing the point that the movie is simply not concerned either with carefully constructed, riddle-obsessed complexities, or with cinematic 'mastery' (an epithet that itself more than hints at relations of domination and subordination) in the sense in which it is so often applied to Mikhail Kalatozov and Sergei Urusevskii's work on *Cranes*.

Above all, to establish the centrality of the mother (and the figure of motherhood) in *Ballad*, we need only ask what the film would be without that figure bookending the linear narrative? The answer is, indeed, simply another Stalinist *skazka*, albeit one which reverses a few terms in the characteristic binaries of Soviet socialist realism to privilege the individual, the human, the 'natural' (however defined). There is no irony in *Ballad*, and certainly not the kind of dramatic irony at work in *Cranes* to maintain an audience position of superiority over the woman. The affective power of the mother figure in *Ballad* is not saved up to bolster the ideological priorities inherent in a rather pat ending so as to sustain social stability, but is a constant, rhythmical, *structuring* force: it irrupts into the attempted linear narrative, rupturing the modern forms of communication traditionally celebrated as Bolshevik achievements – telegrams remain unsent, trains are blown off their tracks, roads disappear beneath floods.

Such a perspective complicates the readings offered by, among others, Zorkaya, which suggest rather simply that *Ballad* is the story not of a soldier, but of the private citizen Alesha Skvortsov; it is much more than a picture of 'the war ... seen from inside, through a soldier's eyes'.[23] Leaving aside the attempts of the voice-over narrator to recuperate the story, the visual and iconographic text of *Ballad* is unambiguous on this point: it is the story of how the figure of the mother came to be in the condition in which we first encounter her. As such, the mother accepts the marginalised position allotted her by both the narrative and the critics, but uses this position as a strategic starting point in her attempt to overcome such limitations, refusing the priorities of her appropriation by both the Bolsheviks and those who would resist their claims while remaining wholly within their terms. This is more than a return to the pre-war, or even pre-Stalin, era, in which, for example, the eponymous *Mother* of Pudovkin's celebrated 1927 film is relegated to the sidelines by a focus on the son's heroic exploits in the revolutionary struggle which requires, as Judith Mayne has demonstrated quite convincingly, 'the continuation of an oedipal narrative form which can only repeat the very law of the father that this film purports to reject'.[24]

The skill and entrancing quality of the movie rest instead in its success at communicating to the spectator something of the *sheer extra-ordinariness* of the experience of motherhood, and celebrating it specifically as such even in the most abject of circumstances – the intensity of the mother's grief hints at counterbalancing moments of extreme exhilaration, but this is a far cry from the suggestion that motherhood is some kind of solution to the problems of being a woman in Soviet society. This celebration is especially evident in the early framing of Alesha's mother against the sky, marking out her heroism in much the same way as Alesha's battle scene serves to emphasise precisely his lack of it: such framing recalls the heroicising iconography of women in Soviet films made during the 'Great Patriotic War', most specifically *She Defends the Motherland* (*Ona zashchishchaet rodinu*, 1943), in which the heroine's child *is* in fact crushed under the wheels of a Nazi tank, but again this *rodina-mat'* is hardly the willing handmaiden of the Soviet state – bourgeois or proletarian.

There is a danger lurking in this characterisation of the mother, which to an extent already smacks of a certain essentialism, but it should be pointed out that, if not in spite of, then perhaps precisely on account of its attempts to marginalise the mother, and mark her out as separate from the rest of society, *Ballad* manages to effect a disarticulation of the Soviet figure of the woman-mother – and to the immense political advantage of both. Even within the narrative of Alesha's journey home to his mother, we witness women performing valuable, productive and socially useful work: from driving trucks, to operating telegraph services, right down to fetching water supplies, these women have a social role (and a degree of solidarity uncommon in Soviet films of *any* era). Some, like the truck driver or the women sharing Alesha's train journey shortly before their carriage is blown off the rails, also happen to be mothers, although this is hardly their defining achievement; they are by no means underestimated or undervalued, still less figured as a 'problem'. The one exception appears to be the (genuinely) 'faithless fiancée' Liza, to whom Alesha delivers his cargo of soap – entrusted to him at the front by her intended. Although he immediately returns to take back the soap, delivering it instead to her perhaps more deserving family in the town's air raid shelter, any condemnation of her actions is tempered by a certain parallel between her and Alesha: circumstances have forced her into prostitution, as much as they forced our purported hero into military life. The scene in which she moves off camera to have a whispered conversation with her client is a study in sympathetic understatement, especially by comparison with the melodramatic excesses and self-conscious 'artistry' of the analogous rape and breakfast table scenes in *Cranes*.

Ballad of a Soldier's appeals to a pre-modern sensitivity – along with the ethnocentric appeals it attempts to negotiate – can hardly be counted as a particularly radical, innovative contribution to the debate on social organisation outlined at the start of this chapter. However, if we are to draw only one conclusion from this analysis of the movie, it must take into account two factors: firstly, the paradoxical centrality and structuring role of the marginalised mother – who speaks in a language that is beyond direct signification but not without a certain affective *signifiance*;[25] and secondly, the fact that the film's disarticulation of womanhood and motherhood jettisons the age-old conservative argument that biology is destiny (which so informs the resolution of *Cranes*) to reveal a much more politically useful side of essentialism, in terms of the positive valuation of women's experience, whether or not they turn out to be mothers.

Notes

1   See 'Khrushchev's Secret Speech', in *Khrushchev Remembers*, trans. Strobe Talbot (London, 1971), p. 554.

2   The fairly one-sided exchanges are reprinted in translation in P. Johnson and L. Labedz (eds), *Khrushchev and the Arts: the Politics of Soviet Culture, 1962–1964* (Cambridge, Mass., 1965), pp. 101–5.

3   The tugs and pushes of the ongoing dialogue between film-makers, critics and politicians during Khrushchev's spell in office is documented in Josephine Woll's recent broad survey *Real Images: Soviet Cinema and the*

Thaw (London, 2000). The changing contours of the wider public debate engendered by Khrushchev's reforms, meanwhile, are concisely elaborated in D. Filtzer, *The Khrushchev Era: De-Stalinisation and the Limits of Reform in the USSR, 1953–1964* (Basingstoke, 1993).

4 See, for example, H. Günther, 'Wise Father Stalin and his Family in Soviet Cinema', in T. Lahusen and E. Dobrenko (eds), *Socialist Realism without Shores* (London, 1997), pp. 178–90; J. Haynes, *New Soviet Man: Gender and Masculinity in Stalinist Soviet Cinema* (Manchester, 2003), which owes much to Katerina Clark's chapter on the theme's treatment in literature, 'The Stalinist Myth of the "Great Family"', in *The Soviet Novel: History as Ritual*, 3rd edn (Bloomington, 2000), pp. 114–35.

5 Cited in Woll, op. cit., p. 47, with reference to Maya Turovskaya, 'Marlen Khutsiev', in N. R. Mervol'f (ed.), *Molodye rezhissery sovetskogo kino: sbornik statei* (Moscow, 1962), p. 181.

6 See Haynes, op. cit., pp. 176–7.

7 A translation of the full text of Khrushchev's speech is included in Johnson and Labedz, op. cit., pp. 147–86 (for these quotes, see pp. 155, 154, my italics); the film is treated at more length in Woll, op. cit., pp. 142–50 and, under its 1965 title *I Am Twenty* (*Mne dvadtsat' let*), in L. Attwood (ed.), *Red Women on the Silver Screen: Soviet Women and Cinema from the Beginning to the End of the Communist Era* (London, 1993), pp. 75–6.

8 Woll, op. cit., p. 116; Woll identifies such an inversion of traditional gender roles as particularly typical of films dealing with the 'Great Patriotic War' (p. 92).

9 The journal is discussed, and the quotation cited, in O. Issoupova, 'From Duty to Pleasure?: Motherhood in Soviet and post-Soviet Russia', in S. Ashwin (ed.), *Gender, State and Society in Soviet and Post-Soviet Russia* (London, 2000), p. 31.

10 Ibid., p. 39.

11 See, for example, the chapter on 'The Preservation of the Rights of Mothers' in the Profizdat pamphlet on Soviet women's rights by E. Korshunova and M. Rumyantseva, *Prava sovetskikh zhenshchin* (Moscow, 1960), pp. 56–76.

12 See Woll, op. cit., pp. 43–4 (*A Person is Born*); pp. 45–50 (*Spring on Zarechnaya Street*); pp. 79–82 (*The House I Live In* – the quote is on p. 79); p. 85 (*The Ul'yanov Family*); p. 201 (*A Mother's Heart* and *A Mother's Loyalty*); and p. 92 (*Someone Else's Children*).

13 Woll, for example, devotes an entire chapter to the figure of the child in 'thaw' cinema, but refrains from explicit comment on mothering, despite her wonderful cover image which features a prominent enlistment poster in which 'the mother country calls'. ...

14 Not all criticism is silent on this point, however: the Shlapentokhs, for example, do make passing mention of the fact that Veronika's image finally embodies the motherland, although this perceptive comment is then channelled into an argument regarding the film's apparent defence of private life, a point agreed on by Shilova, among others; see D. Shlapentokh and V. Shlapentokh, *Soviet Cinematography, 1918–1991: Ideological Conflict and Social Reality* (New York, 1993), p. 136; I. M. Shilova, 'Pobeda i porazhenie', *Kinovedcheskie zapiski*, vol. 17, 1993, p. 48.

15 To an extent, the spectre of female sexuality also appears to haunt the critical history of the film, which, as mentioned above, almost without exception admires the film for its apparent refusal to pass judgement on its heroine. While it is certainly the case that *Cranes* represents a departure from earlier films, which would have condemned quite explicitly a decision to marry another man while one's partner was fighting at the front, we should once again note *Cranes'* reliance on the conventions of bourgeois melodrama, and the fact that, in her 'decision' to marry Mark (a much more comfortable source for her identification as an 'enigma'), Veronika is merely obeying the laws and codes of the form. In this light, we might perhaps raise the question of why critics feel that Veronika is 'on trial' at all: why *does* the issue of Mark's rape become a question (however ambivalently posed) of Veronika's 'guilt' or 'betrayal'?

16 M. D. Shrayer, 'Why Are the Cranes Still Flying?', *Russian Review*, vol. 56, July 1997, pp. 427–8; for comparative analyses of conversion hysteria and the question of repetitions in Hollywood melodrama (a very clear source for the form of *Cranes*), see G. Nowell-Smith's 'Minnelli and Melodrama', and T. Modleski's 'Time and Desire in the Woman's Film', both anthologised in C. Gledhill (ed.), *Home Is Where the Heart Is: Studies in Melodrama and the Woman's Film* (London, 1987), pp. 70–4 and 326–8 respectively.

17 The fact that 'Bor'ka' is the diminuitive form of 'Boris' does in a sense imply that the appearance of the child marks a return of Veronika's fiancé – although in an infantilised form that bears some comparison with my previous reference to the position of men in films of the Stalin era.

18 Cf. Slavoj Zizek's comment on hysteria, which seems to apply particularly well to the film's treatment of Veronika: 'in the last resort, what is hysteria if not precisely the effect and testimony of a failed interpellation; what is the hysterical question if not an articulation of the incapacity of the subject to fulfil the symbolic identification, to assume fully and without restraint the symbolic mandate?' in his *The Sublime Object of Ideology* (London, 1989), p. 113.

19 In this respect, it is worth noting the words of Tat'yana Samoilova, when asked in an interview about the subsequent life of the heroine; she responded that she had discussed the possibility of a sequel with Viktor Rozov, on whose play *Eternally Alive* (*Vechno zhivye*) *Cranes* had been based, but that he had declined: 'He probably wasn't interested in that.' See 'T. Samoilova, '"Eto bylo moe ... "', interview with I. M. Shilova and L. K. Kozlov', *Kinovedcheskie zapiski*, vol. 17, 1993, p. 43.

20 See Sarah Ashwin's introduction to her edited volume, *Gender, State and Society in Soviet and Post-Soviet Russia* (London, 2000), p. 3.

21 M. Turovskaya, '*Ballada o soldate*', *Novyi mir*, no. 4, 1961, p. 246.

22 The fact that Alesha is defending only himself, and hardly making a heroic stand in the 'fatherland' war, is picked up by most of the critical literature I have read in preparing this chapter. See, for example, Woll, op. cit., p. 96; Shlapentokh and Shlapentokh, op. cit., pp. 138–9; Turovskaya, op. cit., p. 247; R. Stites, *Russian Popular Culture* (Cambridge, 1992), p. 141.

23 N. Zorkaya, *The Illustrated History of Soviet Cinema* (New York, 1989), pp. 217, 219.

24 J. Mayne, '*Mother* and Son', in her *Kino and the Woman Question* (Columbus, Ohio, 1989), p. 109. Mayne's comments could equally well be applied in an

analysis of *Cranes,* which, for reasons of space, must remain beyond the scope of this chapter.

25 Witness, for example, the sheer banality of the only brief conversation between Alesha and his mother, which nonetheless remains the most devastatingly moving exchange in a film that is rarely short on emotional impact.

7
Monitored Selves: Soviet Women's Autobiographical Texts in the Khrushchev Era

Marianne Liljeström

The late 1950s and 1960s saw an extraordinary boom in Soviet memoir and autobiographical writing. In 1967 (the 50th anniversary of Soviet power) more than 5000 titles of memoir books, brochures and articles were published.[1] The Soviet women's autobiographical sketches I am interested in were an important part of this boom. These *vospominaniya* or *ocherki* are collected in anthologies (*sborniki*) consisting of short narratives – each usually five to ten pages long – and referring to specific events. They are stories about heroic women, Russian and of other nationalities, fighting for a 'bright future', compiled as pieces of information (*svedeniya*) about the emancipation of Soviet women by the party/state. Such collections of sketches were published in 1959, 1963, 1968, 1975 and also in 1983. The rapid growth of this literature was considered an effect of social–historical and political circumstances:[2] it was perceived as a vital, indeed revolutionary, new literary–documentary form associated with moral and spiritual renewal. According to N. I. Glushkov, the development of the genre was dictated by the cultural–historical experience of the new society. 'The acknowledgement of the strength of the word', he writes, 'naturally accompanied people's strivings to use it as an ideological weapon to influence their contemporaries' way of thinking. This promoted the growth and rapid development of the topicality of the essayistic [*ocherkovyi*] literature.'[3] Autobiographical narration was regarded as an important means through which lived experience could be passed to new generations, a task which was declared a conscious moral and historic duty.[4] Thus the anthologies were aimed at the widest possible audience and because of their educational task especially at the younger generations.

In promoting memoir literature, and especially the *ocherkovyi* genre,[5] women were also 'called into' autobiographical subject positions. The availability of these positions was made possible within a specific mixture of discourses. Along with the hegemonic ideological discourse, with its rules of self-representation of revolutionary identity, the discourse on gender equality was strengthened during the period. Here, I read the material by looking at how the particular structure and conventions of the autobiographical discourse as a form of moral public argument, firmly based on the 'truthfulness' and 'factuality' of women's activities, enable the texts to become meaningful. On the one hand, I read Soviet women's sketches as acts of monitoring in writing their selves through official history, where the role of eyewitness to the epoch is emphasised. On the other hand, I will explore how women's autobiographical accounts were produced under surveillance, as regulated speaking positions, as a space to remember within defined gendered boundaries of the collective.

The texts I examine here were published in the anthologies *Zhenshchiny v revolyutsii* (Women in the Revolution, 1959) and also *Zhenshchiny goroda Lenina* (Women from the City of Lenin, 1963). The first anthology is entirely dedicated to reminiscences of women who participated in underground work before February 1917, in the October Revolution, and in work among women up to the early 1920s. More than half of the sketches of the second anthology recall the same period and events. I will take a closer look at two sketches written by Aleksandra Grigor'eva-Alekseeva – 'Vpervye v Rossii' (For the First Time in Russia), published in the 1959 anthology, and 'Zhenskoe utro' (The Female Morning), published in 1963; and two texts by Maria Sveshnikova – 'S mandatom delegatki Kronshtadta' (With the Mandate of a Woman-Delegate from Kronstadt) from 1959, and 'V organizatsii – sila!' (The Strength Lies in the Organisation) from 1963. Grigor'eva-Alekseeva's text recalls the first celebration of International Women's Day in 1913, offering in the later volume a shorter version of the account in the earlier anthology. Sveshnikova's texts recall from slightly different perspectives her work as a revolutionary woman-activist in 1917–18 in connection with preparations for the first All-Russian Congress of Working and Peasant Women at the end of 1918. The texts are constructed as a chronology of events listing the writers' successful advancement in their careers as party workers. The texts are short sketches and, as such, they resemble textualised curriculum vitae, audits of correct political activity and behaviour. This is especially noticeable because of the repetition of characteristics and reported events republished in the later volume.

The repetition is of special importance here because it points to certain themes and codes circulated in the majority of the sketches. The revolutionary woman-activist is recorded and refracted by the regulatory mechanism of repeated codes within hegemonic public narratives. The narrated selves are thus mediated and constructed by coercive discursive practices of writing the female revolutionary self, and results of acts of monitoring and surveillance. The prominence of these women writers stems from their direct contact as both eyewitnesses and active participants in revolutionary events and political work among women.

Eyewitness stories about collective activism and political dedication

In his 'secret speech' at the XX Party Congress in 1956, Khrushchev emphasised that the process of de-Stalinisation required that people should be encouraged to take initiatives in handling social matters concerning themselves. In this connection he drew attention to the passivity and low political participation of women. A policy of 'differentiation' was introduced to effect an intensification of women's participation in political work. One specific outcome was the revival of women's councils (*zhensovety*). Their aim was to increase women's political activity and teach them political skills by raising the level of women's overall political consciousness.[6] The *zhensovety* were referred to as the 'spiritual heirs' of the women's departments (*zhenotdely*) and the *delegatki* from the 1920s, organisational forms of work among women warmly supported by Lenin.[7] The primary period of growth of these new women's organisations was from 1958 to 1961. By the beginning of the 1960s they were well established and were to be found at places of work and housing, and operating at all levels of political–organisational structures.[8] Read in this context, the sketches (recalling the heyday of differentiated gender-specific party work) function as calls for more active participation by women in political work. The texts present accounts of the main organisational events in early party work among women.

Grigor'eva-Alekseeva begins her account with a short abstract of the content of the sketch: in 1913 Russian women celebrated International Women's Day for the first time, and in connection with this a 'scientific morning meeting' (*nauchnoe utro*) on the 'woman question' was organised in St Petersburg with the permission of the city mayor. By stating that she was one of the speakers at the meeting, the writer positions herself within this event.[9] Her path to this notable position was filled with study and underground activity, the result of which was a considerable growth in her political consciousness and experience. She constructs this as a precondition for her insights into the correctness of Bolshevik views on the 'woman question'. Thus, she recalls different 'enemies' who, in 1912, when the party initiated work among women, tried to influence women workers and keep them away from the revolutionary movement. These were priests and bourgeois ladies, the 'equal-rightsers' (*ravnopravki*). The latter became especially activated in 1913 when the party started to prepare for the celebration of International Women's Day.[10] In order to emphasise the party's dedication to this work, she notes that a special article was published in *Pravda* exposing the politics of the 'equal-rightsers', *feministki*, 'supporters of a theory about woman's equality in society with the preservation of the capitalist system'.[11] In addition, *Pravda* dedicated six pages to the celebration of International Women's Day.[12]

Sveshnikova's accounts relate episodes in her party work between February 1917 and the First All-Russian Congress of Working and Peasant Women in November 1918. She reports how the magazine *Rabotnitsa* (Woman Worker) and a bureau for party work among women were founded in St Petersburg in March 1917.[13] The first post-revolutionary issue of *Rabotnitsa* appeared in May 1917, and the first St Petersburg working women's conference was held after the October Revolution, in November 1917, with 500 delegates representing around 80,000 women. By declaring that she was a delegate at this conference, Sveshnikova, like Grigor'eva-Alekseeva in her sketch, positions herself as an eyewitness to the event. She concludes her account with the statement that after the First All-Russian Congress in 1918 the party ordered its subordinate organisations to set up committees for propaganda work among women. In 1919 these committees were organised into *zhenotdely* (women's departments), 'which undertook enormous political, organisational and cultural–educational work amongst women, drawing them into social and public activity'.[14]

The published anthologies are presented as historically valuable because they include reminiscences based on empirical data about the dramatic events of the revolution. In her introduction to the anthology *Zhenshchiny goroda Lenina*, T. I. Lyutova emphasises that the authors are not professional writers, but direct participants in the narrated events: 'I know that these pages – simple, honest, without embroidery – will find a place in your heart, and you will fall in love with the real heroines of this book.'[15] In this way she implies that because they lack professional qualities and status as authors, the women write 'more honestly'; they have some sort of 'genuine' interest in remembering and, therefore, they are able to tell only the truth. Hence, the degree of truth-telling is directly connected here to the texts' literary insufficiency.[16]

The 'greater' truth value of the sketches stems from the women writers' role and position as eyewitnesses of, and participants in, the events recalled. This is perhaps the most important characteristic of the literary genre in question: 'The essayistic [*ocherkovyi*] genre is a form of epic (aesthetic, scientific, journalistic) literature, which is based on the reproduction of actual facts, events, and persons that the author himself has witnessed in real life', writes Glushkov. According to Glushkov, it is important 'in connection with reality' to distinguish between two types of sketches: documentary, where 'the reality is reproduced in full authenticity', and fictional, that is 'reflection of the reality in generalised-imaginary forms'.[17] Garanin, in turn, praises the publication of ordinary participants' reminiscences in these great events, the non-professional writers, who contribute to the development of the genre with their 'original evidence of time as such, stories not about what individuals felt, thought and lived through in their lives, but about what they saw, what they witnessed – reality itself'.[18] In contrast to these statements, Lidiya Ginzburg considers the specific quality of 'documentary literature' as 'that setting up of authenticity [*ustanovka na podlinnost'*], the sensation of which does not escape the reader, but which far from always means the same as factual accuracy'.[19] On the one hand, Ginzburg's definition indicates a considerable caution towards the ease with which the authors cited earlier, ignoring the problematic of narration, handle the 'truthfulness' of remembrance as a reflection of reality, and the possibilities of memory to grasp it. Instead, she emphasises the discourse of authenticity as a precondition of the autobiographical genre. On the other hand, she also points to the 'autobiographical pact', the agreement between narrator and reader about the 'truth' of the life history, the arrangement that Michel de Certeau identifies as the institutional determinant of autobiographical credibility.[20]

The women writers correspond to the specificities of the literary genre defined as 'documentalists' testifying here to the 'correctness' of the implementation of specific party politics and work among women. The testimonies relate directly to the present in that they attach specific meanings to the past at the moment of writing – the Soviet 1960s, shaped by specific autobiographical discourses, cultural, historical and political circumstances, and the new attention within party politics to gender specificity.

Compassion for uneducated women

By emphasising the significance of their political work, both authors deliver detailed descriptions of the state and mind of the women workers they met in their activities. Grigor'eva-Alekseeva describes how she, as a weaver at a textile factory, came to know uneducated women who blamed their harsh working conditions on the administration and not the tsarist system.[21] Both writers express a sincere compassion for other women, while at the same time distinguishing themselves from them. Sveshnikova describes in detail the appearances of the women who came to the meeting in Kronstadt in quilted or men's padded jackets and with tired and stern faces.[22] Before she starts to talk, Sveshnikova looks at the women thinking that they have the weight of deepest grief on their shoulders – cold apartments, hungry children, anxiety for husbands and brothers at the front. The women stand silently and wait for her to speak, and her throat is tight with spasms because of their sorrow and need. She urges them to be active and tells them that it is women's duty everywhere to stand in for men so that not one machine or workplace would be left idle. The emphasis of the text is, however, shifted to Sveshnikova and her ability to convince the women of the only right and possible way out of their misery: 'The women's eyes start to shine, and everybody wants to say something', she writes. 'The children starve, Peace, Bread. ... We'll give all we have, we will not give up', the women exclaim.[23] By the end of the meeting, because of her success as an agitator, she is elected as delegate from Kronstadt to the forthcoming congress.

The level of personal feelings in the accounts, the exploration of subjective and emotional experience can, as Susan Reid has suggested, be connected to the return to 'sincerity', which after 1953 was proposed as a panacea to cure Soviet culture of dogmatism, and the impersonal, stock solutions and false embellishment that were retrospectively identified with Stalinism.[24] The 1960s were marked by a certain kind of public, collective emotionality, a romanticising of struggle and hardships, especially about the October revolution and the civil war.[25] This can be easily read in the sketches as the enthusiasm derived from retelling about these glorious days. The emotionality in question extended as individual romanticism, as love, even to the intimate sphere of life, or in Vail's and Genis's words: 'A strong emotion was valuable in itself, even so much that in human life one sphere was differentiated from the cosmic collective romanticism. Love.'[26] However, a certain contradiction between the emotional expressions, the personal style of writing and the object or the content of affection is noticeable in the sketches. Despite the individual feelings expressed in the text, individuality is denied in favour of collectivity. Grigor'eva-Alekseeva writes about her near friend, Emilia Solin, 'a remarkable revolutionary', whom she had come to know in 1912 at a workers' club and whose life ended tragically in 1919.[27] This recollection can be read as a story about Emilia's deep political conviction and decisiveness. Her great sacrifice was to give up living with her mother because of the mother's ignorance and illiteracy, and her inability to understand Emilia's revolutionary activities. On the one hand, it is a story about how the revolutionary collective won over private emotions, personal and family concerns. On the other hand, Emilia's behaviour towards her mother can certainly also be interpreted as highly individualistic and even cruel: she could not, as a revolutionary enlightened person, stand the political 'backwardness' of her mother, and so abandoned her.

Prominent women activists

The texts depict one female party leader of work among women who stands above all others: Konkordia Samoilova.[28] Both writers construct their own achievements through this beloved and honoured leader. In detailed descriptions of the International Women's Day meeting in 1913, the presentations and her own speech, Grigor'eva-Alekseeva recalls how, because of her inexperience, she had received help from Samoilova with the synopsis of her speech. When it was her turn to speak, she was so nervous that she could not make any sense of her notes. She put aside her papers and started spontaneously to talk about women's working conditions, 'which I knew very well from my own experience'.[29] While the audience applauded, she stepped down from the podium, went behind the stage and started to cry. She thought that she had betrayed the party's belief in her and ruined the speech, but Samoilova assured her that she had done very well. In the shorter version, Grigor'eva-Alekseeva recalls the event in even more detail – about her preparations, how she 'endlessly' ran to Anna Elizarova (Lenin's sister) and Samoilova for help, and how Samoilova consoled and praised her afterwards. Thus, especially the latter version concentrates on emphasising the help and support of older and more experienced revolutionary women leaders, underscoring the specific personal qualities that had assured them prominent positions within the party hierarchy.

After a period of political party work at a military factory and in small villages near the front, Sveshnikova recalls how she was sent to Petrograd to work among women, a 'rather tranquil, "secondary" area', she notes.[30] Here, Konkordia Samoilova also became her mentor and teacher: 'Listen carefully, Masha. Women are now equally responsible with men. They leave for the front, and we here must call women to the machines, so that they start producing cartridges and projectiles, sewing uniforms. All of this for the victory. ...'[31] Samoilova entrusted her to talk at women workers' meetings, but in the same way as Grigor'eva-Alekseeva, Sveshnikova felt insecure about her potential to influence women. In spite of Samoilova's encouragement, she hesitated: 'Well, and who do I think I am? ... Where am I to find such words that they, like keys, would unlock human hearts, and that our women, who had centuries lived in grief and slavery, would understand that a bright day had dawned for them?'[32] With these thoughts she participated in the preparations for the First All-Russian Congress of Working and Peasant Women, and later, as already noted, she was elected a delegate to the congress from Kronstadt. Samoilova is praised for her wisdom and ideological commitment, for her skills in motivating and teaching younger women: 'With patience and skill Konkordia Nikolaevna taught us', writes Grigor'eva-Aleekseva.[33] Samoilova took her to meetings in order to teach her how to give speeches on a subject she had been given in advance. Afterwards she corrected her if she had made a mistake.

By identifying prominent Bolshevik women leaders, the writers construct a vanguard representing a collective of dedicated female revolutionaries. These heroines offer a specific, narrowly defined strategy for successful living and for the good cause, for the elimination of suffering and inequality. In their enactment of this strategy, prominent women are depicted as selfless and modest revolutionaries, always prepared and willing to sacrifice personal gain for the collective. This is a common feature in women's sketches: they portray 'galleries of heroines' and emphasise through individual examples the collectivity of revolutionary women's deeds and actions. The autobiographical subjects themselves become simultaneously constituted as prominent individuals, as part of but different from other women of the collective. This means that to write the 'I' includes a negotiation with the 'we', their individuality and 'uniqueness' entail also discord with collectivity. Simultaneously, however, 'their singularity achieves its identity as an extension of the collective'.[34] Both authors write about their success in becoming talented speakers. However, to serve as an *example* of dedication and heroism for the readers, the I-narrators of the sketches employ a modest style of writing. They emphasise the supportive and educative qualities of other revolutionary women in their processes of personal growth. The texts encompass a range of external 'others' whose lives, or rather information about particular aspects of their characters, are in some way made necessary for the justification of writing and publishing the texts.

The Lenin cult

Embarrassed by Stalinism, Khrushchev reverted to a Leninist ideological course with collective leadership, a communist future (communism was to be achieved in 1980 according to the party programme adopted at the 1961 XXII Party Congress), the drive towards economic efficiency, material well-being and international prestige.[35] Under Khrushchev, Lenin's period of office was held up as an example of creative revolutionary and socialist development, a past to be proud of, a time when the Bolsheviks emerged victorious. In the context of Khrushchev's condemnation of Stalin and of substantial parts of the Stalinist system, Lenin's thoughts, Lenin's political practice and Lenin as a human being provided an ideal to be emulated, a rock of faith. The party's pledge to return to the revolution's original 'Leninist principles' implied, among other things, prioritising political consciousness and rationally conceived action over inertia, spontaneity and emotion.[36]

Lenin's presence is time and again reinscribed in the overwhelming majority of the women's sketches. Sveshnikova begins her sketch with a recollection and description of Lenin's appearance in St Petersburg in April 1917, stating that in spite of the fact that he did not have a loud voice and that he said 'even the most ordinary words', everyone was, precisely because of these words, ready to die for the revolution.[37] She was repeatedly an eyewitness to the real-life Lenin at the First All-Russian Congress, where she was elected to the presidium, and 'was extremely lucky to be listening to the speech of Vladimir Ilich'.[38] In her introduction to the anthology *Zhenshchiny goroda Lenina*, Lyutova gushingly emphasises the importance of the pages that are 'dedicated to meetings with Lenin', written by those 'to whose lot fell the enormous happiness to see Lenin, listen to Lenin, to work with Lenin'. Lyutova urges the reader not to be in a hurry: 'Here, every word is dear.

The bright traits of Vladimir Ilich, which are sealed in the memory of the contemporaries, will help you to understand even better the exemplarity of the architect of the new world, our teacher, our leader, personifying for us the future human being.'[39]

By writing about herself as an eyewitness to Lenin's actions, Sveshnikova constructs herself as an extraordinary revolutionary. She rises above ordinary women workers and revolutionaries, and becomes prominent because she has personally seen and heard Lenin. Thus she further contributes to the Lenin cult that peaked during the late 1960s. The cult received an additional impetus from the wave of nostalgia for the 'glorious' revolutionary past and the effort to revive the spirit of that time which swept the country during the three important jubilees of 1967, 1970 and 1972 (55th anniversary of the October Revolution). Outstanding among these was the 100th anniversary of Lenin's birthday in 1970. There was no moderation in the scale of the organised events or in the amount of Leninania produced. Up until the early 1960s the cult of Lenin had consisted of a number of unrelated practices. After that it became incorporated into the system of socialist rituals that were now being instituted.[40]

Hence, the structure, themes and codes of the sketches are linked to the general revival of ideology during the period of Khrushchev's office. The autobiographical subject of the sketches is constructed, on the one hand, through the female revolutionary collective, and on the other through ritualised events. These events are reproduced because of cultural management, but as narrative tropes they give performative force to the female signature of the texts. Through this force, the signature takes up and creates space in the public sphere.[41]

Women – one of many collectives

In his book on the collective and individual in Soviet society, Oleg Kharkhordin states that the post-1953 liberalisation was accompanied by a profound consolidation of the practices identified in the West as 'social control' or 'social pressure'.[42] In the Soviet Union this meant an overall strengthening of the collective in society. According to Kharkhordin, four basic strategies evolved: first, an intensification of the collectivist mechanism in existing collectives (*kollektivy*); second, the development of a mega-collective by means of connecting the collectives through inter-collective surveillance[43]; third, the creation of collectives in those groups that evaded collectivism (prisons, vocational schools and sports teams); fourth, bringing into a collective those rare individuals who still somehow existed on their own in the interstices of the system.[44] According to Kharkhordin, Stalin's regime still allowed for the existence of random patches of individual freedom, it was frequently characterised by chaos and inefficiency, and surveillance and repression were neither omniscient nor omnipresent.[45]

In order to get people to take part in social control, in the people policing itself, persuasion and warning, in addition to collective shaming, were the primary methods of teaching 'correct behaviour'.[46] In 1961 Khrushchev emphasised in his speech at the XXII Party Congress: 'It is necessary to heighten public attention and requirements to people's behaviour. ... We should more actively use the moral weight and authority of the public to fight violators of the norms and rules of common socialist life.' His speech at the November 1962 Central Committee plenum meeting was even more forthright: 'If we could put all these forces into action, if we could use them in the interests of control, then not even a mosquito could pass unnoticed.'[47] Instead of the chaotic and punitive terror of the Stalin years, Khrushchev wanted to see a relentless and rational system of preventative surveillance.[48]

In my reading of Soviet women's autobiographical texts from the late 1950s and early 1960s, the first and second strategies are of particular importance. In adapting Kharkhordin's strategies to the category of women, not only 'revolutionary women', but women as a specific group of gendered citizens is classifiable as both an 'existing' collective and a 'mega-collective', as a target for intensification of 'collectivist mechanisms'. Ideologically and discursively women were expected to follow and internalise a certain set of gendered characteristics of 'emancipated womanhood'. This set included a long list of demands ascribed to women by the 1960s: paid work, higher education, maternity and devoted mothering, political activity and participation in public life, concern about family and relatives, and also about personal appearance, behaviour and looks.[49] Besides the 'inter-collective surveillance', 'people policing itself', the control of women over other women, and especially young girls, in implementing the set of rules for their expected behaviour and 'womanliness', the interpretative advantage of the hegemonic discourse and the control of the party/state through various laws and regulations concerning 'emancipated womanhood' made idealised womanhood (and femininity) an effective tool of collectivist policies.

The boom in the publication of women's autobiographical texts during this period – already in itself a collectivist form of text production and editing – is evidently connected to the strengthening of collectivism. The specificities of the 'collective' autobiographical genre are linked to the collectivism-of-life processes, to gendering of collectivist practices, which anew produced women as one specific collective. The revival of *zhensovety* is but one example of this new emphasis on collectivism. It is, however, important to understand the collectivist politics as programmatic, as idealised aspirations, as evolving around the figure of the Revolutionary Woman.

Acts of monitoring and surveillance

The themes and codes of the texts point to a system of 'internal' monitoring and 'external' surveillance. The autobiographical texts and practices referred to here point to a system of organised remembering for ideological purposes. This is why it is hard to read the texts as expressions of confessional impulses or urges to articulate interiorities. However, if, following Adriana Cavarero, one distinguishes between the self as narratable and as narrated, Soviet women's autobiographical practices become much more complex. By examining the example of Ulysses, Cavarero notes that when his desire to hear his story narrated is realised, he does not only know who he is, but he also knows that it was his narratable identity that allowed him to perform great deeds, because of the desire to hear it *personally* narrated by another. Hence, Cavarero differentiates between the desire to leave one's own identity for posterity in the form of an immortal tale, and the desire to hear one's own story in life.[50] Cavarero argues that the narratable self is not the result of a separated experience or the *product* of our memory. It is not a *fiction* that can distinguish itself from *reality*, a construction of the text, or the effect of performative power of narration. Instead, the narratable self coincides 'with the uncontrollable narrative impulse of memory that produces the text and is captured in the very text itself'.[51] The ontological status of the narratable self is in this way distinguished from the text of her story, even if it is necessarily mixed up with it. Thus, autobiographical accounts result from 'an existence that belongs to the world, in the relational and contextual form of self-exposure to others'.[52] In telling the self, everybody – according to Cavarero – looks for a unity of one's own identity in the story. However, she emphasises that this striving for unity does not have a substantive reality, but belongs only to desire. The desire directs both the expectations of the one who is narrated and the work of the one who narrates.[53]

In view of the way that Soviet women's remembrances are considered solely as an effect and result of mandatory ideological practices, I want to include in my discussion Cavarero's understandings of the difference between the narratable and narrated self, and the strivings or desire for a unified identity in the narration of this self. The ideas put forward by Cavarero offer a possible way to avoid the conclusion that Soviet women's autobiographical writings were only the result of an *ascribed* subject position, irrespective of their own needs and desires of telling their selves. This emphasis on agency and self-representation is, of course, neither acontextual nor ahistorical: the desire for unity of one's identity becomes realised in the process of narration through the figure of the Revolutionary Woman, i.e. it is contextualised and shaped in accordance with a certain set of both available and prescribed, intensively circulated scripts.

Soviet women's autobiographical texts are, nevertheless, first and foremost sites of organisational activities in which women-activists' lives, or rather particular aspects of them, become connected with, and are articulated by means of, permitted, constrained or compelled monitoring and regulatory practices, which was already evident, for example, from the definitions of the genre I referred to earlier. In the Soviet context these regulatory practices are conventionally, and often in a somewhat unproblematic way, connected to the question of censorship. Apart from the conventional view of censorship, which restricts the agency of its operation to an imposition preformed by a pre-given subject on another pre-given subject, a more radical understanding suggests that there are rules that govern the intelligibility of a text. These rules are 'decided' prior to any authorial decision, and simultaneously they form constraining conditions for authorial expressions. This means that censorship precedes the text and, therefore, comes to produce the subjects in question. The rules that regulate the comprehensibility of the text precede and orchestrate the very formation of the subject.[54] It is, however, possible to distinguish between explicit and implicit censorship, where the latter refers to implicit operations of power that rule out in unspoken ways what will remain unspeakable. Here, no explicit regulation is needed. This is the case when the script of the Revolutionary Woman is internalised in such a way that the writing subject completely subscribes to its characteristics. Judith Butler notices in her article on censorship that it may well be that explicit and implicit forms exist not in opposition to each other, but on a continuum, in which the middle region consists of forms of censorship that are not rigorously distinguishable in this way.[55] In an interesting and complex way, then, Soviet women writers, through the production of their autobiographical accounts within the constraining conditions of both explicit (exterior control) and implicit (interior self-regulation) censorship, are generated into subjects with a certain speaking position.

As both a condition for and a reproduction of these regulated speaking positions, the autobiographical texts circulate organisationally created 'personae': the revolutionary women-activists. These personae are constructed by producing aggregations of autobiographical exteriorities, personae, which could be characterised as monitored or audited selves.[56] The relevance of the idea of monitored selves is that it refers to some figures, personae rather than persons, the Revolutionary Soviet Women-Activists. However, the figure being an ideal, and the women writers, therefore, never reaching it in their subscription to it and reproduction of it, the workings of the figure create simultaneously silences and gaps in the application of the normative ideal. Though it is not my task here to trace inconsistencies or disjunctures in the women's texts, I will take but one example. In both of her texts Grigor'eva-Alekseeva is highly exasperated by the 'bourgeois ladies', the 'equal-rightsers', and their cunning methods in trying to get working women to join their ranks: 'The reason for the insecurity of working women's lives does not in the least lie in men's enslavement of women, as the bourgeois ladies explain, but in capitalist exploitation.'[57] In her 1963 text, however, in contrast to this statement, she writes that 'they [*feministki*] enticed working women to their meetings, where the bourgeois ladies endlessly propagandised about women's emancipation from the tyranny of men. ... As if no other tyranny existed!'[58] The interesting contradiction here is, of course, that she actually admits that male tyranny exists. Later in the text, when referring to her speech during the first celebration of International Women's Day, she recalls how she ended her presentation with an appeal to women workers to find their place in the united proletarian family and 'hand in hand with men achieve a better lot'.[59] At the same time as she notes with irritation the overall growth in 'bourgeois ladies'' activities, this concern is contradicted by such phrases as 'working women hardly ever attended the meetings'.[60]

The outcome of the gendered pattern in the form of monitored female selves is that they are accorded and ascribed the status of truths rather than of mere truisms. The women writers shape their self-representation to ideologically informative and discursive needs by providing pieces of information, the form of which is predetermined as relevant or essential for organisational purposes. Thus, the women represent themselves in Sameness, in compliance with the hegemonic male norm, as simulated – and therefore never perfect – versions, where a certain kind of womanhood is foreclosed. By providing the women writers' speaking positions, the autobiographical discourse with its truth-bearing status extends beyond these women and constitutes a regulatory truth also about women as an overall identifiable group: the narrated truths are assembled and deployed as 'knowledge' about the entire group. This means that regulation and monitoring (explicit and implicit censorship) operate simultaneously to make certain kinds of citizen-subjects possible and others impossible. The agency of the autobiographically writing female subjects is an effect of power, but, importantly, never fully determined in advance. The figure of the Revolutionary Woman-Activist must, therefore, be repeated over and over again in order to be effective.

Monitored selves are quintessentially public selves. They are publicly created profiles, which act as measures and prophecies of what 'types' of selves there are and should be. The question in the Soviet context of the 1960s is the new appearance of a public woman, the plethora of public versions of a certain type of politically dedicated woman, and what she 'is like', i.e. a stereotypical version of what 'a Soviet woman' should be. The public woman of monitored selves is associated both with regulation and surveillance, and with enactment and performance.

Notes

1 L. Ya. Garanin, *Memuarnyi zhanr sovetskoi literatury: istoriko-teoreticheskii ocherk* (Moscow, 1986), p. 3.
2 While the print run of the anthology published in 1959 was 100,000 copies, the equivalent figure for the anthology published in 1975 was 200,000 copies.
3 N. I. Glushkov, *Ocherkovaya proza* (Rostov, 1979), p. 204.
4 Ibid., p. 182.
5 On the 'essayistic literary' genre in general, see ibid., and N. I. Glushkov, 'Metodologiya sravnitel'no-istoricheskogo issledovaniya ocherkovoi prozy v sovremennoi teorii zhanra', in *Zhanrovo-stilevye problemy sovetskoi literatury* (Kalinin, 1986), pp. 3–15; on its connections to 'documentary', see S. Zalygin, 'Cherty dokumental'nosti', *Voprosy literatury*, no. 2, 1970, pp. 41–53; to 'documentary literature', see N. Dikushina, 'Nevydumannaya proza (O sovremennoi dokumental'noi literature', in *Zhanrovo-stilevye problemy*, pp. 149–74, and L. Ginzburg, 'O dokumental'noi literature i printsipakh postroeniya kharaktera', *Voprosy literatury*, no. 7, 1970, pp. 62–91; and as sources of Soviet history, see V. S. Golubtsov, *Memuary kak istochnik po*

istorii sovetskogo obshchestva (Moscow, 1970). See also M. Liljeström, 'Regimes of Truth?' Soviet Women's Autobiographical Texts and the Question of Censorship', in M. Kangaspuro (ed.), *Russia: More Different than Most* (Helsinki, 2000), pp. 114–17.

6   G. Browning, *Women and Politics in the USSR: Consciousness Raising and Soviet Women's Groups* (London, 1987), p. 56.

7   N. Tatarinova, *Women in the USSR* (Moscow, 1968), p. 97.

8   M. Liljeström, *Emanciperade till underordning. Det sovjetiska könssystemets uppkomst och diskursiva reproduktion* (Emancipated to Subordination: the Origin and Discursive Reproduction of the Soviet Gender System) (Turku, 1995), pp. 323–4.

9   A. Grigor'eva-Alekseeva, 'V pervye v Rossii', in *Zhenshchiny v revolyutsii* (Moscow, 1959), p. 93.

10   Ibid., p. 96.

11   A. Grigor'eva-Alekseeva, 'Zhenskoe utro', in *Zhenshchiny goroda Lenina* (Leningrad, 1963), p. 65.

12   Grigor'eva-Alekseeva, 'V pervye v Rossii', p. 96.

13   M. Sveshnikova, 'V organizatsii – sila!' in *Zhenshchiny goroda Lenina* (Leningrad, 1963), p. 93.

14   Ibid., p. 98.

15   T. I. Lyutova, 'Slovo k chitatelyu', in *Zhenshchiny goroda Lenina* (Leningrad, 1963), p. 3.

16   S. Smith, 'Constructing Truth in Lying Mouths: Truthtelling in Women's Autobography', in M. W. Brownley and A. B. Kimmich (eds), *Women and Autobiography* (Cornell, 1988), p. 38.

17   Glushkov, *Ocherkovaya proza*, p. 201.

18   Garanin, op. cit., pp. 182–3.

19   Ginzburg, op. cit., p. 63. See also I. Savkina, *'Pishu sebya...' Avtodokumnetal'nye zhenskie teksty v russkoi literature pervoi poloviny XIX veka* (Tampere, 2001), pp. 26–7.

20   See L. Marcus, *Autobiographical Discourses. Theory, Criticism, Practice* (Manchester, 1994), p. 254.

21   Grigor'eva-Alekseeva, 'V pervye v Rossii', p. 93.

22   M. Sveshnikova, 'S mandatom delegatki Kronshtadta', in *Zhenshchiny v revolyutsii* (Moscow, 1959), p. 205.

23   Ibid.

24   Susan E. Reid, 'Masters of the Earth: Gender and Destalinisation in Soviet Reformist Painting of the Khrushchev Thaw', *Gender and History*, vol. 11, no. 2, July 1999, p. 295.

25   P. Vail' and A. Genis, *60-e. Mir sovetskogo cheloveka* (Ann Arbor, 1988), pp. 107, 111.

26   Ibid., p. 112.

27   Grigor'eva-Alekseeva, 'V pervye v Rossii', p. 99.

28   Konkordia Nikolaevna Samoilova (1876–1921) was a party member from 1903 and participated in its work during the years of underground activities. In 1914 she joined the editorial board of *Rabotnitsa* and was, until her death, a leading organiser of party work among women. In the spring of 1920 she was appointed head of the political section of the agitation train 'Red Star', which toured the Volga. During her second trip she fell ill and

died from cholera. See *Zhenshchiny russkoi revolyutsii*, p. 568.
29 Grigor'eva-Alekseeva, 'V pervye v Rossii', p. 97.
30 Sveshnikova, 'S mandatom', pp. 203–4.
31 Ibid., p. 204.
32 Ibid.
33 Grigor'eva-Alekseeva, 'V pervye v Rossii', p. 96.
34 J. Perreault, *Writing Selves. Contemporary Feminist Autobiography* (Minnesota, 1995), p. 7. See also D. Sommer, '"Not Just a Personal Story": Women's *Testimonios* and the Plural Self', in B. Brodzki and C. Schenk (eds), *Life/Lines. Theorizing Women's Autobiography* (Cornell, 1988), p. 108.
35 K-G. Karlsson, *Historia som vapen. Historiebruk och Sovjetunionens upplösning, 1985–1995* (History as a Weapon. The Use of History and the Collapse of the Soviet Union) (Stockholm, 1999), p. 90.
36 R. W. Davies, *Soviet History in the Gorbachev Revolution* (London, 1989), p. 115. See also Reid, op. cit., p. 281.
37 Sveshnikova, 'S mandatom', p. 201.
38 Sveshnikova, 'V organizatsii', p. 97.
39 Lyutova, op. cit., pp. 4–5.
40 Vail' and Glenis, op. cit., pp. 199–200. See also C. Lane, *The Rites of Rulers. Ritual in Industrial Society – the Soviet Case* (Cambridge, 1981), p. 218.
41 M. Liljeström, 'The Remarkable Revolutionary Woman: Rituality and Performativity in Soviet Women's Autobiographical Texts from the 1970s', in M. Liljeström et al. (eds), *Models of Self: Russian Women's Autobiographical Texts* (Helsinki, 2000), pp. 95–8.
42 O. Kharkhordin, *The Collective and the Individual in Russia: a Study of Practices* (Berkeley, 1999), p. 279.
43 In 1962 the Committee of Party-State Control was formed. It unified a number of separate bodies that had existed since 1934 into a single overarching agency. See J. S. Adams, *Citizen Inspectors in the Soviet Union* (New York, 1977), p. 185.
44 Kharkhordin, op. cit., p. 280. As a result of the 'anti-parasite' campaign, the 'law against idlers' was adopted in 1961. According to this law, an individual not legally registered at a job could be sentenced to forced labour. See P. H. Juviler, *Revolutionary Law and Order* (New York, 1976), p. 78.
45 Kharkhordin, op. cit., p. 302.
46 The first victims of conformism as enforced by the masses were the *stilyagi*. By the early 1960s they were apparently all reformed. When they appeared there were still spaces in the grid of mutual surveillance. Under Khrushchev these spaces were successfully eliminated as part of his policies of expanding socialist self-government. See A. Troitsky, *Back in the USSR* (Boston, 1988), p. 10, and Kharkhordin, op. cit., pp. 289–91.
47 Kharkhordin, op. cit., pp. 298–9.
48 In addition, during Khrushchev's period in office, objects of legal concern grew strongly. The codification drive was a major contradiction of Khrushchev's liberalisation. He introduced 'harsher penalties including an unprecedented legal extension of the death penalty for non-political crimes, far outdoing Stalin on that', according to Juviler, op. cit., p. 82. Capital punishment was introduced for 16 crimes, including illegal operations with hard currency, repeated bribery, theft of public property in large

amounts, printing counterfeit money. As a result, Khrushchev's 'liberal' era witnessed an unprecedented growth in the number of criminal sentences: 2.8 million were convicted in 1961–63.

49 Liljeström, *Emanciperade till underordning*, pp. 357–67, and S. E. Reid, 'Cold War in the Kitchen: Gender and the De-Stalinization of Consumer Taste in the Soviet Union under Khrushchev', *Slavic Review*, vol. 61, no. 2, 2002, pp. 232–3.

50 A. Cavarero, *Relating Narratives: Storytelling and Selfhood* (London, 2000), pp. 32–3.

51 Ibid., p. 35.

52 Ibid., p. 36.

53 Ibid., p. 41.

54 J. Butler, 'Ruled Out: Vocabularies of the Censor', in R. C. Post (ed.), *Censorship and Silencing: Practices of Cultural Regulation* (Los Angeles, 1998), pp. 247–9. See also Liljeström, 'Regimes of Truth'.

55 Butler, op. cit., 249–50.

56 I am inspired here by Liz Stanley's thoughts on audit selves, which she develops in another context . See L. Stanley, 'From "Self-made Women" to "Women's Made-selves"? Audit Selves, Simulation and Surveillance in the Rise of Public Woman', in T. Cosslett, C. Lury and P. Summerfield (eds), *Feminism and Autobiography: Texts, Theories, Methods* (London, 2000), pp. 40–60.

57 Grigor'eva-Alekseeva, 'V pervye v Rossii', p. 96.

58 Grigor'eva-Alekseeva, 'Zhenskoe utro', p. 65.

59 Ibid., p. 67.

60 Ibid., p. 65.

8
Women in the Home

Susan E. Reid

Introduction: women and things

In a painting of 1952, Aleksandr Laktionov depicted a 'typical' (that is, exemplary) Soviet family *Moving in to a New Flat* (Figure 8.1). The new occupants are surrounded by their belongings – a radio, a plant, a globe, posters and piles of books – all of which speak of the family's attention to culture and education. Yet before these attributes can be unpacked and put in their places the first question that has to be resolved is where to hang the photo-portrait of Stalin, who, as the personification of the Soviet state, is the provider of this bounty. The flat is large and well appointed, with a high ceiling, double glass doors, quality wallpaper and a parquet floor. The lucky head of household who has received this blessing is a woman. While the absence of a father reflects post-war demographic reality – women outnumbered men by 20 million – it is also symbolic. His rightful place next to mother and son is taken by Stalin's portrait. The composition is structured on the relation between this focal point and the columnar figure of the woman, who occupies the central, vertical axis of the painting. Two diagonals converge on the portrait, one formed by the parquet and reinforced by the piles of things, the other by an imaginary line that joins the three heads, via the top corner of the projecting door, to the unseen corner of the room where the portrait will hang. The female head of household, following this line with her gaze, is placed in direct relationship to the leader-provider. She is the pillar that maintains the family stability and its relation to the state, the firm basis on which the late Stalinist social order is allegedly founded. Most importantly for the purpose of the present essay, the painting situates woman at the heart of an ordered realm of 'cultured'

Figure 8.1   Aleksandr Laktionov, *Moving in to a New Flat*, 1952. State Tret'yakov Gallery

possessions; it is these appartenances, in combination with the fixtures of the flat, which visually structure her relationship with Stalin and state power.[1]

In the early 1950s, genre painting – scenes of everyday life such as Laktionov's – came to the fore at exhibitions of Soviet art. While they ostensibly dealt with the 'private' sphere of the family and domestic life, they carried a moral burden concerning good behaviour, Soviet values and the correct relationship between the individual and the state. In such paintings, the virtue or otherwise of the protagonists is conveyed to the viewer not only by the narrative action and physiognomy of the dramatis personae, but by the material surroundings of their daily lives. As in Laktionov's painting, so in others of the period such as Fedor Reshetnikov's *A Bad Mark Again* (1952), furniture, ornaments and other details of the interior are meticulously inventoried: a rug, a wall clock, a plant on the window sill, a tasselled tablecloth. The idealised image of Soviet domesticity such paintings project is one of cosy, somewhat old-fashioned, indeed bourgeois, respectability: a realm of antimacassars, tablecloths and display cabinets holding the family's treasured ornaments and mementoes.[2] A similar phenomenon was noted in late Stalinist middlebrow fiction by Vera Dunham in her seminal analysis of 'middle-class values' originally published in 1976. As she argued, 'In postwar novels, objects, from real estate to perfume, took on a voice of their own. They provide a material inventory of embourgeoisement.'[3]

The realm of possessions and cosy homemaking was almost universally identified with female virtue in late Stalinist culture. To take another example, in a painting by a prominent woman artist, Serafima Ryangina, *Girlfriends* (1945, Figure 8.2), two young women cadets in a narrow hostel room have taken care to create a cosy home around them. Little curtains and covers, a rug, a fine porcelain tea service and flowers signify their respectability – these are fine Soviet Russian girls – as well as promising the return of peacetime normality. Dunham cites a passage from a story in *Novyi mir* in 1948, where the author similarly characterises a girl student by describing the homely little environment she has carved out for herself from the communal space of a hostel: 'Several brightly embroidered pillows were neatly arranged on her bed. Her small nightstand was covered with pink paper, scalloped at the edge.'[4] To readers versed in the codes of the time, this description identifies the female occupant as 'cultured' (*kul'turnaya*) on account of her homemaking skills.[5]

Socialist realist novels and paintings are not, of course, reflections of actuality, but idealised projections of official values. Visual and verbal representations of things materialise the inner world of the characters and define their worth and status as Soviet citizens. As Dunham notes, 'The clutter of ornate objects was linked with positive personal traits.'[6] Things are neither mute nor innocent of ideology; they articulate ideological positions and project values in the Soviet social hierarchy.

Figure 8.2   Serafima Ryangina, *Girlfriends*, 1945. State Tret'yakov Gallery

A gendered discourse

Women, far more than men, were defined by everyday things, their worth registered by their domestic material environment and the quality of their housekeeping. It was not only in fictional representations of an ideal Soviet order that the nature of the material environment of everyday life (*byt*) was significant. In real life, too, it was a matter of constant and even obsessive discussion and monitoring, beginning in the earliest days of the revolution. According to Marxist materialist political philosophy, on which the revolution was based, the material environment helped shape economic and political relations and the individual social consciousness. In the 1920s, radical artists, architects and theorists extrapolated that in order to bring about a new consciousness it was necessary first to reshape the world of things, to root out the old way of life and create a new one, a *'novyi byt'*.[7]

The discourses of the new and old *byt* were consistently gendered. In the 1920s the old bourgeois *byt*, encumbered by possessions, was firmly identified with women; they were the chief perpetrators of the tendency to accumulate tasteless trash in the home, although men as well as women were exhorted to join battle against petit-bourgeois *byt* and bring some rational order into the world of things.[8] Beginning in the 1930s, and intensifying after the war, genre paintings and fiction continued to constitute the concern for cosiness, possessions and material well-being as feminine, as the examples discussed above demonstrated. Even after 20 years of Soviet rule it remained a commonplace that women's creative instincts consisted primarily in a natural inclination to decorate, to 'beautify *byt'*.[9] By contrast with the First Five-Year Plan, however, official discourse now cast women's 'natural' gift for creating a cosy home in a positive light: as a contribution to the creation of a 'cultured' way of life *(kul'turnyi byt)*.[10]

If the gender of these tendencies was constant then, their valency was not. They oscillated between the negative pole of 'philistinism' *(meshchanstvo)* and the positive pole of *kul'turnost'*. But in the Khrushchev period their evaluation swung back again towards hostility on similar grounds to those of the 1920s. The arrangement of the home continued to be naturalised as a female concern, but the nature of women's role there changed in ways that are the subject of this essay.[11] Women were no longer to be the creators of cosy clutter and minders of mementoes, but to become rationalisers and modernisers of the domestic order. As the Khrushchev regime promoted the 'scientific–technological revolution', it assigned to women the role of introducing a modern, rational, industrial regime into the home.

Socialist paternalism

After Stalin's death in 1953, promises to address the urgent problem of improving the living standards of ordinary Soviet people became an important means to maintain the legitimacy of the regime.[12] Once confirmed in power, Nikita Khrushchev upheld this commitment, although to abandon the Soviet economy's traditional emphasis on heavy industry and defence was more than he could risk. The XX Party Congress, best remembered for Khrushchev's denunciation of Stalin's 'excesses', also saw the adoption of welfare reforms, many of which affected women above all. Western observers at the time debated whether these reforms represented a move towards a 'communist welfare state' and asked what implications they had for the Western, Cold War view of the Soviet Union as a 'totalitarian' state. As French economist Bertrand de Jouvenel observed:

> It is true that after having so long forced upon the people 'what is good for them', the Soviet leaders may now increasingly let the people have what they would like, but even so, they will insist upon forming the people's taste – as a new rash of publications devoted to this purpose indicates. Nevertheless, a tendency toward greater regard for the tastes of Soviet consumers is apparent.[13]

Forty years on, questions concerning the nature of the Khrushchev regime – its continuities and discontinuities with its predecessor, and its relations with the people, especially women – have begun to be reopened. Victor Buchli has argued that the Thaw

> should not be seen as a liberalisation of attitudes towards the domestic realm but quite the contrary. It was the reproblematisation of *byt* and a period of intense state and Party engagement with the terms of domestic life, one that was highly rationalised and disciplined. If the Stalinist state was poised at the threshold of the 'hearth', the Khrushchevist state walked straight in and began to do battle.[14]

A similar assessment of the Khrushchev regime's systematic intrusion into personal life has been put forward by Oleg Kharkhordin, applying Foucauldian theory to Soviet Russia:

> If 1937 can be viewed as a first decisive attempt to install the overarching system of total mutual surveillance, with excessive zeal of comradely control turning to homicide and contributing to the chaotic terror, then 1957 marked the final achievement of the Stalinist goal: a fine-tuned and balanced system of total surveillance, firmly rooted in people's policing each other in an orderly and relatively peaceful manner.[15]

Such categorical and one-dimensional pictures of Khrushchevism require nuance and complication. We should take note of Jouvenel's observation that the state had begun to attend to what people wanted: for this implies a new degree of negotiation with the people and accommodation of their needs and wishes.[16] Furthermore, as Deborah Field notes in this volume, efforts to intervene in the terms of everyday life, in such 'private' matters as child rearing and the arrangement of the home, must also be set against what people made of advice in practice. For the party-state's success in implementing its measures depended on the acquiescence of individuals to act as its agents. To assert, as Kharkhordin does, that Khrushchev set in place a perfectly functioning, ubiquitous disciplinary grid of mutual surveillance is to repeat the old fallacy of the totalitarian school: to take aims for achieved fact, ignoring the elements of chaos, contradictions and dysfunctionality on the ground.[17] Finally, we should not underestimate either the invasiveness of the Stalin regime in the terms of everyday life, as both Kharkhordin and Buchli appear to do,[18] nor the impact on ordinary people's experience of the Khrushchev regime's repudiation of terror. True, it was no liberal democracy, but dissension from norms set by the state was no longer punishable by death or the camps.

With those caveats in mind, it is clear, however, that the Khrushchev regime invested major effort in educating people's habits of consumption, everyday behaviour, leisure pursuits and taste, and that this form of intervention was an essential aspect of the way it sought to maintain its authority and bring about the transition to communism.[19] While relinquishing coercion, it did not relinquish the urge to influence all aspects of life down to the minutiae of *byt*. It attempted to regulate 'private' behaviour and consumption, to establish a code of norms and exclusions, not only through legislation, control over production and universal institutions, such as schools, but also through discursive regimes: that is, norms were promulgated and maintained across a range of texts, both verbal and visual. Voluntary acceptance of both ethical and aesthetic codes was an essential part of the project of preparing the Soviet people for self-government, a precondition for the advent of communism. It was fundamental to the ideology of Khrushchevism, as it developed in the late 1950s and was enshrined in the Third Party Programme adopted in 1961, that coercion was to be replaced by spontaneous action, self-regulation, and voluntary appropriation and internalisation of the party's norms.[20]

In this regard, Khrushchevism may be seen as simply a more thoroughgoing case of a characteristically modern project. In assessing the nature of the Khrushchev regime we may usefully consider critiques of the modern welfare state, for example, in post-war Britain. For all its benefits, an element of control is inherent in the social paternalism of the welfare state, which extends the reach of the state into realms bourgeois society construes as 'private'. As Eric Hobsbawm noted, welfare politics are part of the elaboration of the state that has accompanied the rise of industrial capitalism.[21] The efforts of the welfare state have often entailed attempts to shape the behaviour of women, while its ideology – expressed in the literature of social work and legislation – reinforces women's role in maintaining the family. In Elizabeth Wilson's words, 'Social welfare policies amount to no less [than] the *State organization of domestic life*. Women encounter State repression within the very bosom of the family.'[22] The relation between the Khrushchev state and society was not totalitarian; it was, nevertheless, paternal and patriarchal. And, as in other forms of modern welfare paternalism, the main objects of control and definition were women and children.[23]

The rule of taste

The discursive regime with which we are most concerned here is that of taste in the domestic interior. The reform of the 'aesthetics of everyday life' was established in the press as an essential aspect of de-Stalinisation, beginning with the earliest 'thaw' in 1954, when *Novyi mir* published an article by artist Nikolai Zhukov bemoaning the poor quality of consumer goods, which corrupted popular taste.[24] In the course of the 1950s, as the ideology of Khrushchevism took shape, the cultivation of the people's aesthetic sensibilities and good taste was reaffirmed as an essential aspect of the construction of communism, of no less importance than the development of communist morality. A sense of beauty was to be an attribute of the all-sided, self-possessed, new Soviet person who would live under communism.[25] Yet as long as people were surrounded by tasteless objects in their domestic and working lives, their aesthetic development would be stunted and their mindset trapped in the values of the past – whether Stalinist or bourgeois. To enhance the aesthetic quality of all aspects of Soviet life was, therefore, a precondition for the transition from socialism to communism. For as one aesthetician elaborated, 'communism is not only the abundance of material blessings. It is also the realm of the beautiful.'[26] Since even consumer goods production was controlled by central plans, the state had a responsibility for ensuring that all items of everyday use were produced in accordance with good taste. At the same time, the population had to be persuaded to accept and internalise the new norms of beauty.

The new regime of taste was elaborated and promulgated by a range of specialists, with whom the post-Stalinist party sought a more consultative relationship, including pedagogues, psychologists, and art and design professionals.[27] The latter were particularly concerned to reclaim the intelligentsia's traditional aesthetic authority. Invoking the early Marx, available in a new translation, the founding congress of the Union of Soviet Artists in 1957 embraced the imperative to shape the everyday material environment in accordance with 'the laws of beauty'.[28] Zealously attacking examples of 'philistine' taste in both production and consumption – targeting precisely what only recently had been identified with *kul'turnost'* – they supplanted the taste of the new managerial 'middle class' with their own, more ascetic preferences. The new standard of beauty they prescribed was an austere, simple 'contemporary style' that bore a close affinity to (and was directly informed by) the international Modern Movement, both in its visual characteristics and in such imperatives as 'form follows function' and 'less is more'. Thus the period saw a shift from a middlebrow, historicist conception of taste to a highbrow, modernist one, along with the revival of the intelligentsia's traditional prerogative to 'raise up' the taste of the masses to their own level.[29]

In 1955, just three years after Laktionov painted *Moving in to a New Flat,* a young Moscow painter, Gelii Korzhev, produced a bleak genre painting entitled *They've Gone...* (1955, Figure 8.3), which in many ways inverts the message of Laktionov's celebratory image of Soviet domesticity. It points to the shift of values that had begun to take place. At a conference of architects at the end of 1954, long before Khrushchev denounced Stalin's excesses at the XX Party Congress, he attacked the extravagance of his architecture.[30] The presidential apartment of Laktionov's lucky family, with its generous proportions and deluxe detail, could well have been located in just the kind of late Stalinist building Khrushchev now condemned. Such apartments could not be provided in the vast numbers required to house the Soviet people, but could only be bestowed as a reward and privilege on the few. It was time to house the many; and to do that required economy, efficiency, maximum standardisation of plans and modules, the use of modern materials and of industrial construction methods. Khrushchev called on architects to develop a radical new style for post-Stalinist socialism. A reorientation towards the founding principles of early

Soviet and international modernism was effectively sanctioned by the highest authority, which set the terms for the modernisation, rationalisation and standardisation of all other aspects of the socialist material environment.

Where, in Laktionov's painting, the mother was the central pillar of the home and the place of the absent husband/father was taken by Stalin's image, in Korzhev's painting *They've Gone...* not only has Stalin disappeared, in line with the repudiation of the personality cult (which began in the visual arts in 1954), the wife/mother has also absconded. Where Laktionov depicted a happy family, pinioned to the social order by the mother figure, amidst the paraphernalia of domestic bliss, Korzhev gives us a despondent man, still in his work clothes, seated, alone, on a narrow iron bed in an austere hostel room. The interior is devoid of rugs, curtains, indoor plants or any of the other props of cosy domesticity mandatory in late Stalinist representations of exemplary Soviet citizens. A tea glass perches on a newspaper, in the absence of that essential attribute of Stalinist *kul'turnost'*, a tablecloth. As a female respondent to Zhukov's opening salvo on taste in *Novyi mir* complained, instancing male indifference towards their material environment, a man 'will breakfast at a table covered with yesterday's newspaper'.[31]

Figure 8.3   Gelii Korzhev, *They've Gone...*, 1955. State Tret'yakov Gallery

The painting concerns the break-up of the Soviet family, a cause for growing anxiety in the 1950s.[32] The exposure of contemporary social problems in works of art was a new departure that had only become possible since Stalin's death. A toy duck and a holiday photograph of a woman pinned to the wall provide clues to the events preceding this scene of desolation. The man's wife has abandoned him, taking their child and all but a few unwanted belongings. Compared to late Stalinist genre painting, where every detail reinforced a single message, Korzhev's painting is understated and its moral is ambiguous, for it appeared both at a time of an emerging new aesthetic that repudiated narrative and exhaustive description, and also on the cusp between two antithetical ideologies of homemaking. Two years earlier it might have been read as criticism of the departed wife's failure to make a *kul'turnyi* home even under inauspicious conditions. If the cadets in Ryangina's painting, or the female student in the passage cited by Dunham, could make themselves a cosy nest in their corner of a hostel, surely this absent wife was deficient in the traditional womanly competencies of adorning *byt* and 'making do', in which drapes and embroideries – singularly lacking in Korzhev's interior – featured prominently.[33]

Reviewers in 1955 also read the painting as an indictment of the absconded wife. They did so, however, on antithetical grounds. As they saw it, she bore the blame for selfishly breaking up the Soviet family because she was afraid of the hardship of everyday life. She stood indicted for a petit-bourgeois demand for domestic comfort or even philistine luxury.[34]

Politicising the personal

Beginning in 1956, women's continued responsibility for housework and childcare began to receive much attention from Khrushchev and the party. As part of a commitment to 'broadening socialist democracy' they were concerned to raise women's participation both in production and in politics and social organisations. Women's domestic duties were one factor constraining their presence in the public sphere. As Khrushchev recognised, burdened by jobs, childcare and housework, women could ill afford the commitment of time and energy demanded by political engagement.[35] 'Women's domestic burden' and childcare commitments were to be alleviated through state intervention by taking the servicing of everyday needs out of the family home into the public sphere. The main panacea for women's domestic slavery was

found, in accordance with Lenin's position, in the increase and improvement of communal services such as laundries and communal dining
facilities.[36] Other measures included the introduction of boarding
schools and 24-hour crèches.[37] At the same time, increased mechanisation, not only at work but also in the home, and improved efficiency of
domestic labour also represented part of the solution.

The significance of these efforts to address the causes of women's low
political participation should not be underestimated. They paid scant
attention, however, to gender relations in the home as a source of
inequality. If the question was raised, then it was generally in a
flippant manner, or bracketed out of the normal order of things in carnival features for International Women's Day.[38] Far from challenging
traditional gender roles, Khrushchev's speeches and policies from 1958
actually reconfirmed female responsibility for the home as the natural
order of things. Despite the party's ideological commitment to equality, a number of studies have shown that it and its agents maintained
stereotypical notions of gender difference: they assumed that women's
biological role as mothers determined also their primary responsibility
for *byt*, and attributed to women a lower level of political consciousness and rationality.[39] Thus the 'double burden' continued to be
conceptualised as 'women's problem', and the 'private' domain as
feminine, despite the fact that women were expected also to engage in
productive labour and public activity outside the home. As Donald
Filtzer shows in this volume, the double burden had a direct and
detrimental impact on women's status in society and in the workplace:
it confined them to low-paid, unskilled jobs, and this, in turn, reinforced prejudice about women's ability to do skilled or responsible
work. Far from improving, in the period 1959–65, women's position in
employment worsened, as female labour was deskilled.[40]

Moreover, the gendered dichotomy of public production and private
housework was not symmetrical: Khrushchevism continued to insist
that a person might only become a fully valid individual through
active participation in productive labour in the public sphere.[41] As
Genia Browning has cogently argued, attention to 'women's' issues did
not increase their opportunities for authority or real political power,
for such issues entered the realm of 'low' politics and were retained
primarily as the province of women, while the dichotomy of male and
female, high and low, was further entrenched.[42]

The limitations of the Khrushchev reforms and their failure to challenge either the unequal distribution of labour in the home or the gendered hierarchy of 'public' and 'private' must be acknowledged. Yet

was the public/private dichotomy itself unassailable? The separation of spheres was, after all, a historically contingent phenomenon, associated with the rise of capitalism, and not an immutable absolute. The concept 'private' is problematic in the Soviet Russian context: as Kharkhordin has analysed, the same English term conflates two distinct concepts: *chastnoe*, referring to property, and *lichnoe* connoting the personal. It is more precise to speak not of 'public and private' but, as Kharkhordin does, of 'the collective and the individual', or in our case, to substitute *byt* or 'everyday life' for the lesser term.[43]

The withering away of such oppressive bourgeois institutions as the family, along with the absorption of individual interests into those of the collective, was fundamental to the construction of communism from the start. These aims were reinvigorated in Khrushchevism's most utopian visions, although in practice more compromising and pragmatic approaches were often adopted; concessions were made, for example, in response to hostile public reaction to proposals to remove responsibility for children's upbringing from the family to the collective.[44] It was a key objective of the Khrushchev regime's increased attention to social welfare, consumption and *byt* to break down the traditional divisions between the 'public' and 'private', between the personal and the political. 'Everyday life' – as the title of a brochure for agitators proclaimed – 'is not a private [*chastnoe*] matter.'[45] One analyst of state intervention and state services in the West drew a similar conclusion: 'the organisation of daily life is now intimately related to politics'.[46] If the party-state's intervention in matters bourgeois society considered private was an extension of state power, did this not also imply a transformation and extension of the conception of the political? If the locus of oppression had shifted or extended from the public arena into the 'private' realm of *byt*, then so had the political significance of that realm increased.

The traditionally female domain of good housekeeping had risen to a public and even a state affair.[47] The global context of Cold War, which had entered a more relaxed phase of 'peaceful coexistence' and 'peaceful competition', made living standards and consumption a problem of crucial political importance. Still stereotyping these as women's issues – and having witnessed the potentially regime-toppling effects of women's discontent over consumption matters in East Germany in 1953 – the regime constructed women as a force with which it had to negotiate. Thereby it attributed to them a certain authority and power – if only the power of the powerless to disrupt, drag one's heels, or refuse to cooperate.[48] 'Women's questions' were no longer marginal but central.

The home was not to remain outside the project of forging the citizen of communism but was firmly inscribed in the public domain. No less than the collective realms of work and formal education, the 'private' site of leisure, consumption and reproductive labour was to play a part in forging the new Soviet person. Just as Deborah Field shows how children's upbringing was to be a collaborative venture between the family and state, so public values, communist consciousness, legitimate culture and aesthetic sensibilities were to be acquired not only in the public sphere but in the bosom of the family. Becoming a Soviet citizen began in the 'private' space of the home.[49]

Not that these were settled or consensual matters. State policy in the Khrushchev era was riven with contradiction and compromise, as different agents with competing interests put forward conflicting conceptions of how best to build communism. Whether children should be brought up primarily in the family or in the collective was one such matter of contention. Similarly, the organisation and servicing of *byt* were also subject to contention and contradiction between measures that reinforced a model of home life based on the nuclear family, and a commitment to collectivism. One thing was certain, however: that the status of the home and what went on in it were a matters of public import.

'To each family its own flat'

Perhaps everything would have turned out fine for Korzhev's abandoned husband if he had only been able to get a decent flat for his family, where his wife could create a 'real home' instead of shacking out in a bare hostel room. The effects of substandard living conditions and overcrowding, and the lengths to which people were driven to get their own living space provided the theme for many a drama in the Soviet period, from Abram Room's 1927 film *Bed and Sofa* to Yurii Trifonov's novella of 1969 *Obmen* (The Exchange).[50] In a story set in a hostel, *Seasons of the Year*, published in *Novyi mir* at the end of 1953, novelist Vera Panova also proposed that material things and decent living conditions mattered and affected man's ability to advance ideologically.[51]

To provide homes for all was the most urgent improvement in living standards in the 1950s, as Khrushchev recognised. Housing conditions were worse in 1956 than in 1926 in nearly every large city. Even a prominent artist such as Laktionov had only received a flat shortly before painting his celebration of housewarming in 1952. The 1958–65 Seven-Year Plan made economical mass housing construction a priority. As the party proclaimed in its Third Programme in 1961, within two decades 'every family, including newly-weds, will have a comfortable flat conforming to the requirements of hygiene and cultural living'.[52] The press was full of images of construction and of people moving into new homes, representing this as the great, joyous collective experience of the age. True, cartoons sometimes poked fun at the shortcomings of the new flats – their monotonous standardisation and unfamiliar panel construction, or the fact that the new inhabitants sometimes had to cook on campfires outside because the services were not yet installed (Figure 8.4). Yet the rapidly rising new housing blocks transforming the urban landscape provided a highly visible demonstration of the ways in which, at last under Khrushchev, 'life is getting happier, life is getting jollier', as Stalin had long ago avowed.

The housing programme gave many the physical privacy of their own apartment for the first time. Thus it afforded *fewer* opportunities for surveillance than the old way of life in communal apartments. It is one of the limitations of Kharkhordin's model of a 'faultless and ubiquitous grid of mutual surveillance' that it cannot accommodate such contradictory measures, but paradox was as fundamental a characteristic of Khrushchevism as it was of the project of modernity in general.[53] As Vigdariya Khazanova notes, the *novostroiki*, like other twentieth-century mass housing schemes, were 'an instrument of regimentation of life'.[54] For anthropologists, the material arrangements of the house represent a primary element of socialisation and homogenisation: it is 'one of the most invasive agents of western hegemony'.[55] The role of the Soviet state in the ownership of housing was steadily increasing. By the 1950s it had a virtual monopoly over urban housing construction.[56] Moreover, the physical segregation of the family behind its own front door did not exclude it from the realm of public discourse; it was counterbalanced by vigorous efforts to intervene in the terms of domestic life, to counter the individualistic tendencies it might foster, to rationalise and discipline domesticity, and to propagate a new regime of austere, 'contemporary' taste in home furnishing.

The provision of flats 'even for newly-weds' meant that young couples would no longer slot into an established household run by their mother or mother-in-law, or work side by side with neighbours in a communal kitchen, but would have to learn to fend for

Figure 8.4 G. Ogorodnikov, 'Happy Housewarming!' *Krokodil*, 1966

themselves. Nor, since most women worked outside the home, had their mothers necessarily had time to pass down to them the basic household skills and customs. Generating a need for advice, this rupture created an opportunity for authorised specialists to step in and reshape housekeeping practices: to take the mother-in-law's place as the source of exacting norms of domestic hygiene, thrift, efficiency and taste. 'It is necessary', Khrushchev asserted, 'not only to provide people with good homes, but also to teach them ... to live correctly, and to observe the rules of socialist communality. This will not come about of its own accord, but must be achieved through protracted, stubborn struggle for the triumph of the new communist way of life.'[57]

Disciplining domesticity

It was up to women to teach their families how to live correctly in their new apartments, or to adapt their way of life in older apartments to modern standards. Particular effort was required to wean women off the aspiration to the kind of atavistic ideal of comfort which, under Stalin, had been a legitimate (if rarely attainable) aspiration for good citizens. The potentially corrupting effect of increased availability of consumer goods had, likewise, to be counteracted through ideological work, lest it foster any tendency towards acquisitiveness, complacency or irrational consumption. Women's potential demand for furnishings for the new home had to be shaped to fit state-defined 'rational consumption norms'.[58] There were two related aspects to this campaign: the aesthetic reform of everyday life, introducing new conceptions of taste and beauty; and the rationalisation of housework (recalling the ideology of scientific home management in the West since the late nineteenth century).[59] These two aspects, separated here for the purpose of analysis, were in fact closely related. For, according to the modernist aesthetic espoused by Khrushchevist ideologues and visual arts specialists, rationality, efficiency and appropriateness to function were the foundation of beauty.

The battle for the new material culture of daily life was waged both on the level of production – including the way housing was built and the manufacture of new types of furniture – and at the level of discourse, addressed to consumption. A number of institutions were set up between 1956 and 1962 to establish, disseminate and monitor standards for production and consumption. Voluntary acceptance of new norms in domestic life was encouraged by a proliferation of articles and manuals on family and everyday life, taste and etiquette, which state publishing houses began to produce in increasing numbers in the late 1950s, allegedly at readers' request.[60] Exhibitions of model interiors (see Figure 8.5) and prototypes of furniture for mass production propagated the new style, most notably the exhibition *Art into Life* (its title consciously invoking the Productivist slogan of the 1920s) held in Moscow's huge Central Exhibition Hall (or Manezh) in 1961.[61] Implementation of these new norms of consumption and domestic arrangements was encouraged and monitored both by informal neighbourly surveillance and by voluntary organisations, such as housing committees, which played an increasingly important role in the Khrushchev era in the move towards self-government.[62]

Figure 8.5 Model interior in the 'contemporary style'. O. Bayar and R. Blashkevich, *Kvartira i ee ubranstvo* (Moscow, 1962)

Women were both the managers and the chief manual labour in the home. While they were responsible for directing and efficiently organising household labour, this did not preclude delegating to other family members. One advice manual of 1959 advised: 'The sooner a girl or young woman gets to grips with keeping her small household the more actively members of her family will help her.'[63] Yet one task that fell firmly within women's domain, the same manual made clear, was the aesthetic one. She was charged with the attractive, comfortable, convenient and 'contemporary' decoration and arrangement of the domestic interior. If the concept of cosiness (*uyut*) continued to be identified with 'the idea of an attentive female hand', it was redefined in austere, modern terms, opposed to those of the bourgeois and Stalinist past. Already in 1955 the *Novyi mir* reader cited above noted the redefinition of *uyut* and was clear about what it repudiated: it was *not* 'rubber plants with dusty leaves, nor a herd of marble elephants put out to pasture on one's dressing table "for good luck"'. But, she moaned, while she and her husband might deliberate together about how to furnish their new marital home, in practice it always came down to her alone.[64] The acceptance of the new, ascetic norms of *uyut* and of a conception of beauty premised on utility, and their introduction into millions of homes around the country, was women's responsibility. It was up to women to rationalise the organisation of domestic space and to introduce into the home the simple, functional, modern aesthetic: the 'contemporary style'.[65]

Women were expected to recognise that the reform of *byt* was in their own best interest. Excessive, useless decorative objects were among the chains that bound them into domestic slavery, since it fell to them to dust and polish them. Women were not only the chief perpetrators of clutter, but also its chief victims. If women were to be liberated, as Lenin had promised, they must renounce such material attachments and relinquish irrational desires.[66] Zealous converts to the new *byt*, liberated from the tyranny of trash, women were to lead the crusade for taste.

Women's aesthetic task to furnish and decorate the interior of the family home in a tasteful way was no trifling, private enterprise. Rather it was a civic mission of educational and ideological import. For, as a contemporary slogan put it, 'the interior shapes life'. Aesthetic education was essential to the formation of the fully rounded, self-regulating Soviet citizen. According to one authoritative text on interior design, the decoration of the apartment must not only 'meet everyday [practical] and aesthetic demands. It ... must also ... raise the culture of the Soviet person, and take part in the upbringing of the constructors of Communist society.'[67]

Female-oriented periodicals and advice manuals prescribed the principles and practical details of tasteful, contemporary furnishing and home decorating. These were based on modernist, rationalist precepts

of simplicity, functionality and 'no excesses!'[68] In the interest of convenience, aesthetics and hygiene, the new, small apartment must not be
overloaded with heavy, cumbersome and ornate furniture. Instead,
low, lightweight, simple, multifunctional and easy-to-clean furniture
was to be preferred. Not coincidentally, such furniture also lent itself to
efficient, economical, industrial mass production.

The contemporary style was defined as modern and democratic by
antithesis to the material culture of the recent, Stalinist past, which
was now disparaged for perpetuating philistine notions of luxury
inappropriate for a modern, socialist society.[69] Advice literature kept
up a barrage of attacks on petit-bourgeois ostentation and *poshlost'*
(vulgar kitsch), as embodied in the profusion of disharmonious,
useless ornaments. The laundry list of bad taste was remarkably consistent across a range of specialist and popular publications, and reiter-
ated quite precisely that of the late 1920s. High in the inventory were
the *sloniki* – the sets of miniature carved white elephants, which
already in 1955 the *Novyi mir* reader had recognised as a no-no.
Meanwhile, 'disrespect for plastic' – for example in inkstands of simulated marble – was castigated, in line with both the contemporary
style's modernist demand for truth to materials and function, and
with the imperative to popularise synthetics.[70]

The presence or absence of embroidered cloths was a particularly
charged symbol of the old and new domesticity, and, correspondingly,
of the redefinition of women's homemaking role. Draped over tables,
domesticating and customising such modern, standardised equipment
as radios or televisions, in the form of antimacassars or luxuriant bed
covers, the profusion of embroidered draperies was deeply imbricated
in traditional notions of comfort, homecraft and female worth. They
had been an essential part of a girl's trousseau in old Russia.[71] Under
Stalin, as Buchli has noted, given the dearth of consumer goods to
choose from, and the state's monopoly over production, embroidering
and arranging such cloths constituted one of the few ways an individual could exercise any control over her physical environment, a means
to appropriate and individualise standard-issue domestic space. These
artefacts represented the exercise of women's personal taste and skill in
their design, production and deployment.[72] Furthermore, both the
objects themselves and the skills they entailed were passed down from
one generation of women to the next. They constituted a material
memory of family history and a testimony of continuity in the face of
political ruptures and social upheavals. The requirement to purge the
home of these signs of female diligence not only denied the home the

status of a site of production, it also created a tension between women's traditional homemaking competencies as preservers of family tradition and keepers of memory, and the new conception of good housekeeping.

The new housekeeping required of women a rationalising, standardising and future-oriented role. For, if, in the past, a good housekeeper was one who devoted all her time and energy to domestic affairs, a 1959 household companion noted, the modern Soviet woman also worked outside the home.[73] Therefore, the housewife must learn to rationalise housework. Good housekeeping began to be represented as a specialist activity requiring training and technique, planning and organisation, and consisting, like industrial labour, of differentiated disciplines or branches of expertise. As indicated by the location and address of publications on this matter, the introduction of an industrial model of efficiency or scientific management into housework was also the responsibility of women.[74] She could do much to reduce the burden of housework and improve hygiene by investing in the new style of furniture with its simple contours, smooth surfaces, and, increasingly, plastic coatings. The minimal dimensions of the new flats also demanded a rational organisation of domestic space. Illustrated albums on home furnishing and decorating included diagrams of recommended arrangements for the interior of the modern apartment, indicating the most efficient movements required for various household routines.[75]

Conclusion

The Soviet Union shared in a process common to much of northern Europe in the twentieth century and intensively pursued in the postwar period, whereby the home and women's labour within it became the object of rationalising interventions by professional experts acting on behalf of the state.[76] The expansion of political and public interest into the traditionally female, 'private' realm of the home deprived women of the autonomy and authority they had once enjoyed in their domain: the intervention of experts tended to delegitimate women's traditional knowledge and skills garnered through experience in favour of science. Moreover, since domestic science training and qualifications were apparently intended for women and girls alone, such interventions confirmed housework, once again, as an essentially female area of expertise, with all the detrimental effects this had on their ability to advance in status outside the home. Finally, so long as such skills were deployed within the home, there was no question of ascribing them economic or social value; the official, Marxist ideology determined that value was ascribed to productive labour but denied to reproductive labour.[77] Wages for housework were not on the agenda.

Yet this modernising project was not simply oppressive, but potentially, at least, also held positive implications for the status of the domestic realm, and the identity of its worker-manager, the housewife. If *byt* remained a female matter, it was no longer a 'private' or trivial one. Even as the Khrushchev regime reproduced received gender stereotypes, its enormous ideological investment in domains traditionally regarded as female dissolved the gendered dichotomy of public and private and rendered the personal political and significant. Good housekeeping, still designated as a female domain, had become a public and even state affair, requiring codification and training. Professionalisation and the application of science to housework raised the prestige of activities undervalued because they were engaged in by women in the home. Although the economic value of women's labour in the home continued to be denied, it was now ascribed an aesthetic and educative value considered vital to the construction of communism. Women, in their capacity as housewives, mothers and consumers, were the party-state's agents, delegated to introduce its 'rational', socialist norms and modern aesthetic into family life, to produce aesthetic value and social meaning in the home. Thus women in the home had an important public role to play in the formation of the new life: by fostering the aesthetic sensibilities of the new Soviet person they facilitated the transition to communist self-government.

As Deborah Field argues in this volume, efforts to intervene in such 'private' matters as child rearing and the arrangement of the home must be set against the ways its prescriptions were implemented – or not – in the actual practice of people's everyday lives. What did real women make of the advice that bombarded them? How successful was the pervasive effort to wean women from their 'natural' acquisitiveness, to reform the aesthetics of daily life, and 'modernise' their conceptions of comfort, taste and good housekeeping? To what extent could and did women resist, adapt or simply ignore the normative regimes? How, in practice, did people arrange their furniture, and customise the standard space of their government-issue flat? The scarcity of systematic data on everyday material practices precludes any firm conclusions at this point.[78] That rational norms of living were resisted, and atavistic, 'philistine' ideals of cosiness prevailed is suggested, however, by contemporary observers' descriptions of Soviet homes in which 'the *pièce de résistance* was the drapery, heavily and garishly embroidered'.[79] Further archaeological work is required to establish what people made of the state-directed effort to modernise *byt*, and whether, as Svetlana Boym concludes from an analysis of 'Aunt Lyuba's' commode, still cluttered with clashing ornaments at the end of the Soviet period: 'The campaign against "domestic trash" did not triumph in the majority of the communal apartments. Instead ... the so-called domestic trash rebelled against the ideological purges and remained as the secret residue of privacy that shielded people from imposed and internalized communality.'[80]

Notes

1 See J. Guldberg, 'Socialist Realism as Institutional Practice: Observations on the Interpretation of the Works of Art of the Stalin Period', in H. Gunther (ed.), *The Culture of the Stalin Period* (Basingstoke, 1990), pp. 169–70; S. Boym, *Common Places: Mythologies of Everyday Life* (Cambridge, Mass., 1994); and V. Dunham, *In Stalin's Time: Middle-Class Values in Soviet Fiction* (Cambridge, 1976), ch. 3.

2 Foreign visitors to the Soviet Union in the 1950s remarked on the incongruous persistence of a bourgeois ideal of comfort in actual Soviet interiors, public and private. See S. R. Rau, *My Russian Journey* (New York, 1959), p. 5.

3 Dunham, op. cit., p. 41.

4 Ibid., p. 42.

5 On *kul'turnost'* – literally 'culturedness' – see ibid.; C. Kelly and D. Volkov, 'Directed Desires: *Kul'turnost'* and Consumption', pp. 22–3, in C. Kelly and D. Shepherd (eds), *Constructing Russian Culture* (Oxford, 1998), pp. 291–313; Boym, op. cit.; S. Fitzpatrick, 'Becoming Cultured: Socialist Realism and the Representation of Privilege and Taste', in *The Cultural Front* (Ithaca, 1992), pp. 216–37, and Fitzpatrick, *Everyday Stalinism* (New York, 1999), ch. 4.

6 Dunham, op. cit., p. 42.

7 See, for example, Henry Art Gallery (Seattle), *Art into Life: Russian Constructivism, 1914–1932*, exh. cat. (Seattle, 1990); N. Lebina, *Povsednevnaya zhizn' sovetskogo goroda: normy i anomalii. 1920/1930 gody* (St Petersburg, 1999); A. Gorsuch, *Youth in Revolutionary Russia: Enthusiasts, Bohemians, Delinquents* (Bloomington, 2000); and O. Matich, 'Remaking the Bed: Utopia in Daily Life', in J. Bowlt and O. Matich (eds), *Laboratory of Dreams* (Stanford, 1996), pp. 59–78.

8 See K. Kettering, '"Ever more Cosy and Comfortable": Stalinism and the Soviet Domestic Interior, 1928–1938', *Journal of Design History*, vol. 10, no. 2, 1997, pp. 119–36; V. Buchli, *An Archaeology of Socialism* (Oxford, 1999), pp. 177–8; and Boym, op. cit., pp. 35–40.

9 RGALI, f. 2943, op. 1, ed. khr. 173, l. 17. See S. Reid, 'All Stalin's Women: Gender and Power in Soviet Art of the 1930s', *Slavic Review*, vol. 57, no. 1, 1998, pp. 133–73.

10 See Fitzpatrick, 'Becoming Cultured', p. 231; and RGALI , f. 2943, op. 1, ed., khr. 75, l. 10: 'Obrashchenie k zhenam sovetskikh khudozhnikov i skul'ptorov' (1936).

11 Magazines such as *Ogonek* and *Sem'ya i shkola* consistently cast the readers of domestic advice as female. See also C. Kelly, *Refining Russia: Advice Literature, Polite Culture, and Gender from Catherine to Yeltsin* (Oxford, 2001), pp. 321–93.

12 The shift in party policy began even before Stalin's death. See A. Nove, *Stalinism and After* (London, 1975), pp. 124–8; J. Hessler, 'A Postwar Perestroika? Towards a History of Private Enterprise in the USSR', *Slavic Review*, vol. 57, no. 3, 1998, pp. 516–42.

13 B. de Jouvenel, 'The Logic of Economics', a commentary on A. Nove, 'Toward a Communist Welfare State?', both first published in *Problems of Communism*, January–February 1960. Reprinted in A. Brumberg (ed.), *Russia under Khrushchev. An Anthology from Problems of Communism* (London, 1962) [Nove, pp. 571–90, Jouvenel, pp. 599–605; this passage, p. 604].

14 Buchli, op. cit., p. 138.

15 O. Kharkhordin, *The Collective and the Individual in Russia: a Study of Practices* (Berkeley, 1999), p. 300.

16 Compare P. Hauslohner, 'Politics before Gorbachev: De-Stalinization and the Roots of Reform', in A. Dallin and G. Lapidus (eds), *The Soviet System in Crisis* (Boulder, Colo., 1991), pp. 53–5; and G. Breslauer, *Khrushchev and Brezhnev as Leaders: Building Authority in Soviet Politics* (London, 1982).

17 Kharkhordin, *Collective*, p. 303.

18 Compare S. Kotkin, *Magnetic Mountain: Stalinism as a Civilization* (Berkeley, 1995), pp. 160, 195.

19 For further discussion see S. Reid, 'Cold War in the Kitchen: Gender and the De-Stalinization of Consumer Taste in the Soviet Union under Khrushchev', *Slavic Review*, vol. 61, no. 2, 2002, pp. 211–52; D. Field, 'Communist Morality and Meanings of Private Life in Post-Stalinist Russia, 1953–1964', unpublished PhD dissertation, University of Michigan, 1996; Kelly, *Refining Russia*, ch. 5; Kharkhordin, *Collective*, pp. 297–328; and J. Gilison, *The Soviet Image of Utopia* (Baltimore, 1975).

20 See R. Hill, 'State and Ideology', in M. McCauley (ed.), *Khrushchev and Khrushchevism* (Basingstoke, 1987), pp. 46–60; J. Scanlan, *Marxism in the USSR: a Critical Survey of Current Soviet Thought* (Ithaca, 1985); G. Hodnett (ed.), *Resolutions and Decisions of the Communist Party of the Soviet Union.* Vol. 4: *The Khrushchev Years 1953–1964* (Toronto, 1974), pp. 167–264; and Field, 'Communist Morality'.

21 E. Hobsbawm, *Industry and Empire* (Harmondsworth, 1969), pp. 263–7. See also D. Hoffmann and Y. Kotsonis (eds), *Russian Modernity: Politics, Knowledges, Practices* (Basingstoke, 2000).

22 E. Wilson, *Women and the Welfare State* (London, 1977), p. 9 (emphasis in original). See also pp. 29, 36.

23 On Khrushchev's image as protector of women and children, see S. Reid, *Khrushchev in Wonderland: the Pioneer Palace in Moscow's Lenin Hills, 1962*, *Carl Beck Papers*, no. 1606 (Pittsburgh, 2002), p. 12.

24 N. Zhukov, 'Vospitanie vkusa', *Novyi mir*, no. 10, 1954, pp. 159–76; 'Tribuna chitatelya. O vospitanii vkusa', *Novyi mir*, no. 2, 1955, pp. 247–54;

A. Saltykov, 'O khudozhestvennom kachestve promyshlennykh tovarov', *Sovetskaya torgovlya*, no. 9, 1954, pp. 22–31.

25 Editorial, 'Aktual'nye voprosy estetiki v svete novoi Programmy KPSS', *Voprosy filosofii*, no. 9, 1962, pp. 3–14; see also S. Reid, 'Destalinization and Taste', *Journal of Design History*, vol. 10, no. 2, 1997, pp. 177–202.

26 S. Rappoport, *Tvorit' mir po zakonam krasoty* (Moscow, 1962), pp. 8, 64–6. See also N. Dmitrieva, *O prekrasnom* (Moscow, 1960).

27 Hauslohner, op. cit., pp. 37–63.

28 'Pervyi vsesoyuznyi s"ezd sovetskikh khudozhnikov', *Iskusstvo*, no. 3, 1957, p. 14; Karl Marks, *Iz rannykh proizvedenii* (Moscow, 1956).

29 Authoritative examples include A. Saltykov, *O khudozhestvennom vkuse v bytu* (Moscow, 1959); the new design journal founded in 1957, *Dekorativnoe iskusstvo SSSR*; RGALI, f. 2943, op. 1, ed. khr. 2979; and *Moskovskii khudozhnik*, nos 10–11, June 1959. For further detail, see Reid, 'Destalinization and Taste'; and Iu. Gerchuk, 'The Aesthetics of Everyday Life in the Khrushchev Thaw in the USSR (1954–64)', in S. Reid and D. Crowley (eds), *Style and Socialism: Modernity and Material Culture in Post-War Eastern Europe* (Oxford, 2000), pp. 81–99. See also V. Buchli, 'Khrushchev, Modernism, and the Fight against Petit-Bourgeois Consciousness in the Soviet Home', *Journal of Design History*, vol. 10, no. 2, 1997, pp. 161–76.

30 N. S. Khrushchev, *O shirokom vnedrenii industrial'nykh metodov, uluchshenii kachestva i snizhenii stoimosti stroitel'stva* (Moscow, 1955).

31 'Tribuna chitatelya', p. 247.

32 V. Dunham, 'The Changing Image of Women in Soviet Literature', in D. Brown (ed.), *The Role and Status of Women in the Soviet Union* (New York, 1968), p. 68; D. Field, 'Irreconcilable Differences: Divorce and Conceptions of Private Life in the Khrushchev Era', *Russian Review*, vol. 57, no. 4, 1998, pp. 599–613.

33 See the account by American visitors in 1956: 'We Saw how Russians Live', *Ladies' Home Journal*, February 1957, p. 176.

34 I. Akimova and O. Roitenberg, 'Vystavka molodykh khudozhnikov Moskvy. Zhivopis'', *Iskusstvo*, no. 4, 1956, p. 42.

35 Nove, *Stalinism and After*, p. 130; M. Field, 'Workers (and Mothers): Soviet Women Today', in Brown, *Role and Status*, pp. 7–56; M. Buckley, *Women and Ideology in the Soviet Union* (New York, 1989), pp. 139–60; G. Browning, 'Soviet Politics: Where are the Women?' in B. Holland (ed.), *Soviet Sisterhood: British Feminists on Women in the USSR* (London, 1985), pp. 207–36; G. Lapidus, *Women in Soviet Society: Equality, Development, and Social Change* (Berkeley, 1979), pp. 225–31.

36 'Rech' tovarishcha N. S. Khrushcheva', *Pravda*, 15 March 1958; W. Tompson, *Khrushchev: a Political Life* (Basingstoke, 1995), p. 201.

37 U. Bronfenbrenner, 'The Changing Soviet Family', in Brown, *Role and Status*, pp. 107–9.

38 For example, G. Kulikovskaya, 'Pronikayushchaya v zvezdy', *Ogonek*, no. 11, 8 March 1959, p. 11.

39 See for example, the Women's Day address from the CC CPSU: 'Rabotnitsam i kolkhoznitsam, deyatelyam nauki, tekhniki, prosveshcheniya, literatury, iskusstva, zdravookhraneniya, vsem sovetskim zhenshchinam!' *Pravda*, 8 March 1958; E. Wood, *The Baba and the Comrade* (Bloomington, 1997);

Gorsuch, *Youth,* ch. 5; L. Edmondson, 'Women's Emancipation and Theories of Sexual Difference in Russia, 1850–1917,' in M. Liljeström, E. Mäntysaari and A. Rosenholm (eds), *Gender Restructuring in Russian Studies* (Tampere, 1993), pp. 39–52; and F. Bernstein, '"The Dictatorship of Sex"', in Hoffmann and Kotsonis, *Russian Modernity,* pp. 138–60.

40 See also D. Filtzer, *Soviet Workers and De-Stalinization* (Cambridge, 1992), p. 178 and *passim.*

41 V. Bil'shai, 'Kto prav: V. I. Nemtsov ili E. Nilova?' *Literaturnaya gazeta,* 10 January 1959.

42 Browning, 'Soviet Politics', p. 232.

43 O. Kharkhordin, 'Reveal and Dissimulate: a Genealogy of Private Life in Soviet Russia', in J. Weintraub and K. Kumar (eds), *Public and Private in Thought and Practice* (Chicago, 1996), pp. 333–63. On the antithesis of *byt* and *bytie* (existence) see Boym, *Common Places,* pp. 29–32.

44 Bronfenbrenner, op. cit., pp. 112–16; and Deborah Field's chapter in this volume.

45 O. Kuprin, *Byt – ne chastnoe delo* (Moscow, 1959).

46 A. Showstack Sassoon, 'Introduction', in Sassoon (ed.), *Women and the State: the Shifting Boundaries of Public and Private* (London, 1992 [1987]), p. 32.

47 A. Vul'f, 'Protiv nedootsenki domovodstva', *Sem'ya i shkola,* no. 8, 1961, p. 47.

48 Reid, 'Cold War', pp. 211–52.

49 D. Koenker in discussion, AAASS annual convention, Pittsburgh 2002. Compare J. Hellbeck's argument that the 'private' space of a diary served as a 'technology of the self', a site where the author worked on himself to produce and articulate a social being. J. Hellbeck, 'Self-Realization in the Stalinist System', in Hoffmann and Kotsonis, *Russian Modernity,* p. 229.

50 Yu. Trifonov, *The Exchange;* transl. E. Proffer, in Yu. Trifonov, *The Long Goodbye: Three Novellas* (Ann Arbor, 1978), pp. 17–19. On the normative concept of *zhil'ploshchad'* (living space) and on housing in general, see essays by V. Papernyi and S. Kotkin in W. Brumfield and B. Ruble (eds), *Russian Housing in the Modern Age* (Cambridge, 1993); and Kotkin, *Magnetic Mountain,* ch. 4.

51 V. Panova, 'Vremena goda', *Novyi mir,* no. 11, November 1953, pp. 3–101, and no. 12, December 1953, pp. 62–158.

52 Hodnett, *Resolutions,* p. 230; S. Strumilin, 'Mysli o gryadushchem', *Oktyabr',* no. 3, 1960, p. 141; T. Sosnovy, 'The Soviet Housing Situation Today', *Soviet Studies,* vol. 11, no. 1, July 1959, pp. 6, 13; G. Andrusz, 'Housing Ideals, Structural Constraints and the Emancipation of Women', in J. Brine, M. Perrie and A. Sutton (eds), *Home, School and Leisure in the Soviet Union* (London, 1980), pp. 3–25; and see S. Harris, 'Recreating Everyday Life: Building, Distributing, Furnishing and Living in the Separate Apartment in Soviet Russia, 1950s–1960s', unpublished PhD dissertation University of Chicago, 2003.

53 See Y. Kotsonis, 'Introduction: a Modern Paradox – Subject and Citizen in Nineteenth- and Twentieth-Century Russia', in Hoffmann and Kotsonis, *Russian Modernity,* pp. 1–16.

54 V. Khazanova, 'Arkhitektura v poru "Ottepeli"', in V. Lebedeva (ed.), *Ot shestidesyatykh k vos'midesyatykh. Voprosy sovremennoi kul'tury* (Moscow, 1991), p. 77.

55 D. Birdwell-Pheasant and D. Lawrence-Zúñiga, *House Life: Space, Place and Family in Europe* (Oxford, 1999), p. 28; and I. Cieraad, *At Home: an Anthropology of Domestic Space* (New York, 1999).

56 Sosnovy, 'Soviet Housing', p. 9.

57 Cited in L. Abramenko and L. Tormozova (eds), *Besedy o domashnem khozyaistve* (Moscow, 1959), pp. 3–4.

58 See 'Summary of XXI (extraordinary) Party Congress', *Soviet Studies*, vol. 11, no. 1, 1959, p. 90; P. Hanson, *Advertising and Socialism: the Nature and Extent of Consumer Advertising in the Soviet Union, Poland, Hungary and Yugoslavia* (Basingstoke, 1974), pp. 7–8, 72.

59 D. Hayden, *The Grand Domestic Revolution: a History of Feminist Designs for American Homes, Neighborhoods, and Cities* (Cambridge, Mass., 1981).

60 Field, 'Communist Morality', p. 41; and Kelly, *Refining Russia*, ch. 5.

61 RGALI, f. 2329, op. 4, ed. khr. 1001, 1002; TsALIM, f. 21, op. 1, dd. 123–130; 'Iskusstvo – v byt. Vystavka novykh obraztsov izdelii khudozhestvennoi promyshlennosti', *Dekorativnoe iskusstvo SSSR*, no. 6, 1961, pp. 1–10.

62 Field, 'Communist Morality', pp. 19, 99–101.

63 Abramenko, *Besedy*, p. 4.

64 'Tribuna chitatelya', p. 247.

65 Abramenko, *Besedy*, p. 4; 'Ob uyute v obstanovke kvartiry', in ibid., pp. 7–56; M. Chereiskaya, 'Zametki o khoroshem vkuse', in R. Saltanova and N. Kolchinskaya (eds), *Podruga* (Moscow, 1959), p. 220; E. Nikol'skaya, 'Uyut i obstanovka v dome', *Sem'ya i shkola*, no. 11, 1958, pp. 46–7; E. Nikol'skaya, 'Blagoustroistvo zhilishcha', *Sem'ya i shkola*, no. 1, 1958, pp. 42–4. See also Buchli, 'Khrushchev, Modernism', pp. 161–76; Reid, 'Destalinization and Taste', pp. 177–202; and Gerchuk, 'Aesthetics of Everyday Life', pp. 81–99.

66 'Youth has Its Say on Love and Marriage', *Soviet Review*, vol. 3, no. 8, August 1962, p. 37.

67 I. Luppov, 'Novym zdaniyam – novyi inter'er', in N. Matveeva (ed.), *Iskusstvo i byt* (Moscow, 1963), p. 14; Field, 'Communist Morality'.

68 See Saltykov, *O khudozhestvennom vkuse v bytu*; Mil'vi Kartna-Alas, 'Iskusstvo i byt', *Ogonek*, no. 25, 19 June 1960, pp. 20–2; Ol'ga Bayar, 'Sdelaem kvartiru udobnoi i uyutnoi', *Sovetskaya zhenshchina*, no. 7, 1956, pp. 47–8; O. Bayar and R. Blashkevich, *Kvartira i ee ubranstvo* (Moscow, 1962); Nikol'skaya, 'Blagoustroistvo zhilishcha', pp. 42–4; Nikol'skaya, 'Uyut', pp. 46–7; Z. Krasnova, 'Khoroshii vkus v ubranstve zhil'ya', *Sem'ya i shkola*, no. 1, 1960, pp. 44–5; and A. Bryuno, 'Vasha kvartira', *Sem'ya i shkola*, no. 10, 1960, pp. 46–7.

69 RGALI, f. 2943, op. 1, ed. khr. 2979, l. 54: 'Problemy formirovaniya sovremennogo stilya v sovetskom izobrazitel'nom iskusstve'.

70 I. Zhvirblis, 'Doma s privideniyami', *Dekorativnoe iskusstvo SSSR*, no. 6, 1962, pp. 43–5; N. Voronov, 'Ob iskusstve, meshchanstve i mode', *Sem'ya i shkola*, no. 3, 1962, pp. 14–16; G. L'vov, 'Osteregaites' poshlosti – borites' za khoroshii vkus!' *Moskovskii khudozhnik*, nos 10–11, June 1959; M. Taraev, 'Pervyi vserossiiskii s"ezd khudozhnikov', *Dekorativnoe iskusstvo SSSR*, no. 9, 1960, p. 3; M. Gordeev, 'Protiv bezvkusitsy. Poshlost' iz anodirovannogo alyuminiya', *Dekorativnoe iskusstvo SSSR*, no. 1, 1962, p. 44; I. Suvorova, 'Na urovne plokhogo rynka', *Dekorativnoe iskusstvo SSSR*, no. 6, 1962, p. 46;

O. Aizenshtat, 'Neuvazhenie k plastmasse', *Dekorativnoe iskusstvo SSSR*, no. 1, 1962, pp. 46–7; Yu. Gerchuk, 'Dostovernost' i pravda', *Tvorchestvo*, no. 10, 1965, p. 3.

71 D. and V. Mace, *The Soviet Family* (London, 1963), p. 161.

72 Buchli, *Archaeology*, pp. 92–3.

73 Abramenko, op. cit., p. 4.

74 Even in magazines with mixed readership such as *Ogonek*, features on domestic arrangements addressed the reader as female: for example, N. Svetlova, 'Tvoi dom', *Ogonek*, no. 3, 11 January 1959, pp. 14–16.

75 Bayar, *Kvartira*, pp. 12–13.

76 Compare E. Carter, *How German is She? Postwar West German Reconstruction and the Consuming Woman* (Ann Arbor, 1997), p. 50; M. Nolan, *Visions of Modernity* (Oxford, 1994), ch. 10.

77 Compare R. Schwartz Cowan, *More Work for Mother*, 2nd edn (London, 1989), pp. 70–101.

78 For some indications see RGALI, f. 2329, op. 4, ed. khr. 1001, 1002; TsALIM, f. 21, op. 1, dd. 123–130; and Buchli, *Archaeology*.

79 Mace and Mace, op. cit., p. 161.

80 Boym, op. cit., p. 150.

9
Housing in the Khrushchev Era

Lynne Attwood

One of the major problems confronting the Soviet Union at the start of the Khrushchev era was how to house its citizens adequately.[1] The situation was particularly bad in areas formerly occupied by the Nazis or that had endured heavy fighting during the war, where thousands of people were virtually camping in dugouts, ruined buildings, basements, barns, bathhouses, train carriages and other places considered unfit for human habitation.[2] Even in the capital, the vast majority of people were crammed into so-called 'communal apartments', where they had to share cooking and washing facilities with other residents, while some still lived in wooden barracks that had originally been intended as temporary post-war accommodation.[3]

To address the crisis, Khrushchev launched a massive housing campaign. The aim was to provide every family with its own self-contained apartment, which would meet 'the requirements of hygiene and cultured living', within the next two decades.[4] The Seven-Year Plan, launched in 1958,[5] pledged to build 15 million city apartments and 7 million rural houses, to be distributed 'on the principle "one family, one flat"'.[6]

This mammoth enterprise could only be achieved by radically cutting building costs.[7] Accordingly, the architectural 'excess' (*izlishestvo*) of the Stalin era, with its fussy 'cornices and turrets', was denounced.[8] Not only was it expensive, but it was also presented as anti-socialist, something that would appeal only to 'outdated, petty-bourgeois tastes'.[9] Opulence was to be replaced by utilitarianism. Urban residential construction would be based on a few standardised models and would eschew brick in favour of cheaper building materials such as concrete, plastic and that wonderful new product, asbestos.[10] The 'industrial method of construction' would be developed: the various elements would be produced in factories and just assembled at the building site. The optimum height would be four or five storeys, which would be just low enough to make expensive elevators unnecessary.[11] Since the new apartments would each house only one family, they could be 'small-dimensioned' (*malometrazhnaya*);[12] and although it was acknowledged that high ceilings were healthier as they allowed more air circulation, they would have to be lowered in the interests of economy.[13] Soviet people, brought up to appreciate 'truth and expediency', would be sure to appreciate the 'simple, logical and elegant form' of the new apartment blocks.[14]

Khrushchev admitted that the apartments would not be luxurious: indeed, before long they would acquire the nickname 'khrushchoby', a cross between Khrushchev's name and the word for slums, *trushchoby*. However, 'ask any housewife', he insisted, and she would tell you that the benefits outweighed the disadvantages. 'You have to decide ... do you build a thousand adequate apartments, or seven hundred very good ones? And would a citizen rather settle for an adequate apartment now, or wait ten or fifteen years for a very good one?'[15]

This chapter is concerned with the implications of Khrushchev's housing programme for women. In particular, it will attempt to determine whether the move to single-family accommodation resulted in a more privatised family life; whether the Soviet woman, an essential part of the workforce since the 1930s, was now being recast as homemaker and consumer; and, since the home was presented as a largely female responsibility, whether the move to single-family accommodation was more important for women than men. I will be exploring the writings on housing in four key publications: the architectural journal *Arkhitektura SSSR*, which was concerned not only with the design and construction but also the furnishing and equipping of the new apartments; the newspaper *Trud* (Labour), the official organ of the trade union movement, which was involved both in the construction and distribution of apartments; and two women's magazines, *Sovetskaya zhenshchina* (Soviet Woman) and *Rabotnitsa* (Woman Worker), which drew attention to some specifically female issues in relation to housing and the new domesticity. To go beyond the official proclamations and find out what Soviet citizens themselves thought about the housing programme and its gendered implications, I will also be drawing on a series of interviews, conducted in Moscow in March–April 2002, with eight people who moved from communal to single-family accommodation in and around the Moscow area during the Khrushchev era.[16]

Communal housing

Communal housing, in the form of the 'house commune', was an important part of the socialist project in the early years of the revolution. Grandiose architectural designs for house communes were produced, and some were actually built, though the reality fell rather short of the dream.[17] The urban housing shortage in the post-revolutionary period did result in many families living together, but out of necessity rather than choice, and generally in overcrowded hostels and barracks.[18] The First Five-Year Plan engendered a new outburst of revolutionary zeal and revived interest in communal living, which focused in particular on the socialist cities springing up during the mammoth industrialisation drive; the residential districts of these new cities were to consist exclusively of house communes, with communal dining and washing facilities housed in separate buildings.[19] Insufficient resources were pledged to the project to make it a success, however; and in any case, official commitment to communal living had already waned by the end of the Five-Year Plan. The massive upheaval in people's lives had resulted in an alarming drop in the birth rate, which, it was now hoped, might be offset by strengthening the family; and this involved a return to the single-family home.[20] Yet even if communal housing was no longer promoted, the continuing housing crisis meant that few families had the luxury of their own apartments. Instead they found themselves trying to establish some kind of private family life in the barracks, hostels or 'communal apartments' which made up the Stalinist urban landscape.

Barracks were a stop-gap measure for dealing with the housing crises resulting from the sudden massive wave of inward peasant migration during Stalin's collectivisation and industrialisation drives, and from the homelessness created by wartime housing destruction. They generally consisted of large rooms shared by a number of families or individuals, with curtains providing the only semblance of privacy. Hostels also provided temporary accommodation for families, but were primarily seen as a housing solution for single people. They generally took the form of long corridors with rooms on either side, as many as 40 in total, with several people sharing each room. One of my respondents, Mariya Efimovna, lived as a child in such a hostel, in which her family of six (two adults and four children) occupied two beds in a room measuring 16 square metres and accommodating 15 people. In both barracks and hostels, cooking and washing facilities (where they existed) were shared by large numbers of people.

Communal apartments, colloquially known as *kommunalki*, were considered preferable to barracks or hostels, since the facilities were shared with fewer people and a family was more likely to have its own room. The room could be extremely small, however. Mariya Efimovna's family moved from the hostel to a room in a communal apartment which measured 9 square metres; there was space for only two beds, so her parents slept in one, she and her sister in the other, and her two brothers slept on the floor. Vladimir Borisovich grew up in similarly cramped conditions; he had to sleep on the floor under the table, while his sister slept in a trunk.

Many *kommunalki* had once been single-family residences, requisitioned after the revolution; in some cases the previous owners now lived in one or more of the rooms.[21] Others had been custom-built as communal apartments, a practice which was common in the Stalin era and continued until, and even for a short time after, Khrushchev's pledge in 1958 to provide every family with its own apartment.[22]

The communal apartment was a parody of the old ideal of communal living. There was little genuine sense of community within its walls. As Svetlana Boym explains: 'The communal neighbors [were] most often complete strangers from different classes and social groups thrown together by the local Housing Committee', and the apartment functioned in part as 'an institution of social control, and the breeding ground of police informants'.[23] This was hardly the basis for good neighbourly relations. Even when they were relatively amicable, families lived as separately as possible. In a 1955 article, *Rabotnitsa* lamented the fact that some neighbours refused to share anything with each other: 'each of the residents has her [*sic*] personal lightbulb and personal switch in the kitchen, the corridor, the bathroom, and other places of general use. ... Everything has to be separate. ... '[24] *Trud*, reviewing a play set in a communal apartment in 1961, noted that one female character insisted on securing her saucepans with chains and locks.[25] Il'ya Utekhin's recent study on communal apartments in post-Soviet St Petersburg suggests that little has changed.[26]

The refusal to live communally in a communal apartment was confirmed by the people I interviewed. Vladimir Borisovich said that a family might invite their neighbours to join them for dinner on a special occasion, such as a birthday, but they would never be invited to share an ordinary meal. Lyudmila Ivanovna's family got on very well with their neighbours, but they never cooked together: 'it was always the case that families in communal flats cooked only for themselves'. In the rural workers' settlement where Emma Aleksandrovna grew up, there were no indoor sanitary facilities and each family had constructed its own outdoor toilet, securely padlocked to prevent use by others.

This determined effort to maintain a sense of privacy inevitably led to tension between neighbours, which could explode into physical fights. According to the press, the protagonists in these battles were generally women. One *Rabotnitsa* commentator, G. Rykin, did concede that: 'Men can also ... kindle rows in apartments', but the examples given were all of women, and the article was illustrated by a sketch of a woman wielding a soup ladle like a weapon.[27] The feminisation of so-called 'apartment hooliganism' is not surprising, given that official concern centred on conflicts over common space, and the most important of these was the kitchen, which was firmly identified as a female domain.[28] This was confirmed by my respondents. One of the men I interviewed, Genrikh Pavlovich, was a keen cook, but complained that he was made to feel uncomfortable using the kitchen by the women in his communal apartment; they resented his presence, and would always interfere and comment on his culinary efforts. Another respondent, Emma Aleksandrovna, joked that every communal apartment had a female tyrant who insisted on trying to keep order in the common areas of the apartment, especially the kitchen. The communal apartment in which brother and sister Vladimir Borisovich and Nina Borisovna grew up accommodated three separate families, and hence three women had to jostle for space in the kitchen. Each insisted on having her own table, despite the lack of room. They made no attempt to establish a rota for using the kitchen, and if they all ended up preparing their family's meal at the same time, conflicts were inevitable.

While maintaining privacy *between* families was vital, there was little chance of enjoying any privacy *within* the family. Mariya Efimovna started married life in a relatively spacious communal apartment which consisted of four rooms housing only two families. She, her husband and their child slept in one room, while her mother-in-law lived in an adjoining room. These rooms were linked by a doorway covered only with a curtain; the mother-in-law refused to let them have a door because she was afraid they would keep it closed and forget about her.

Despite the overcrowding in communal apartments, it was not unknown for a family with small children to add a live-in childminder to the ménage. Emma Aleksandrovna's family had taken in a young peasant girl in the years before the war. Elena Mikhailovna employed a childminder as soon as her first child was born, in the 1960s, somehow squeezing her into the communal apartment in which she, her husband, their child and his parents occupied two rooms. Some apartments actually had a small custom-built 'housekeeper' (*dom rabotnitsa*) room; these were generally in the grander buildings of pre-revolutionary times, but they also featured in some apartments built in the post-war Stalin years, when a Soviet middle class had begun to develop. In most cases, however, there was no obvious place for the childminder to sleep, and her bed was placed in a sectioned-off corner of the kitchen or corridor.

The 'single-family' apartment, and who was entitled to one

When Khrushchev launched the housing programme, he declared that every family, including newly-weds, would be entitled to its own apartment.[29] Soviet planners had a distinct tendency to standardise, and the general perception was that two or three different apartment designs would accommodate all types of families.[30] This was seemingly the result of both ideological factors (an idealised image of 'the Soviet family') and economic requirements (it was cheaper to mass-produce a limited number of designs). Few concessions were made by urban planners and architects to geographical, cultural and demographic differences; architect M. G. Barkhin later noted that: 'The country from Brest to Vladivostok was built in identical districts consisting of identical houses.'[31] While references were made to multi-child families consisting of five or more people and the need to provide appropriate accommodation for them, the 'average family' – which apparently consisted of a married couple with two dependent children – was the main focus of the housing programme.[32]

Yet even a family which started out 'average' would inevitably change over the course of time. As Blair Ruble has pointed out: 'Grandparents die; couples divorce, remarry, grow old; preschool-aged children turn into adolescents, and eventually become adults themselves. Grown children, in turn, may marry and have children, all the while continuing to live with their parents.' This, he points out, presented inevitable problems for 'an immobile housing market with inflexible conceptions of how best to design standardised apartments'.[33]

The problem of changing family size was acknowledged by some Soviet commentators. An article in *Sovetskaya zhenshchina* noted that young people have a tendency to marry, and 'a family of two people very quickly becomes a family of three people. Builders have to take this into consideration.'[34] Yet how were they to do so? *Arkhitektura SSSR* reported approvingly on a new experimental housing project in Moscow which incorporated movable cupboards and sliding partitions so that the apartments could be altered: 'each family will be able to modify the layout of the apartment according to its own judgement', increasing the number of rooms when necessary by reducing their size.[35] The extent to which such flimsy partitions would create genuinely separate rooms is questionable, however. Furthermore, in the 'small dimensioned' Khrushchevian apartment, any reduction in room size would have produced little more than shoeboxes.

Despite Khrushchev's insistence that 'newly-weds' would also be entitled to their own apartments, in reality there was little chance of a young married couple with no children receiving an apartment. Even when they did have children, they were unlikely to have a new apartment to themselves. Many young families continued to live with one or other set of parents, whether through choice or necessity. As their own children grew up, and had children themselves, their 'single-family' apartment, with its microscopic kitchen, could become as cramped and overcrowded as the *kommunalka* from which they had escaped.[36] The Soviet apartment of the Khrushchev era remained in multiple occupancy, even if it was now occupied by several generations of one family.

Sometimes it also contained non-family members. Alexander Werth, visiting Moscow in the Khrushchev era, noted that the newspaper *Vechernyaya Moskva* (Evening Moscow) regularly carried advertisements for rooms to let, most of which were in new, supposedly single-family apartments: 'if a fairly large family had a three-room flat, and had only a small income, they were content to cram into two rooms, and let the third one for good money. A lifetime spent in "communal flat" conditions had largely conditioned them to sharing a flat with a stranger.'[37]

Some of my own respondents had been happy to share their new apartments with one or other grandmother, who was able to assist them with housework and childcare. Indeed, in one case an extraordinarily complicated process had been undertaken so that a young couple and the husband's parents could exchange their separate living quarters for one apartment large enough to house the entire multi-generational family. For others it was not such a welcome arrangement. Mariya Efimovna had a particularly difficult relationship with her mother-in-law, who insisted on moving into their new apartment. She refused to do any housework on professional grounds, since she was a dentist and so had to look after her hands; and since she had a full-time job, she was unable to mind the children while Mariya Efimovna was at work. Nor did she do much cooking, though this did not stop her from interfering with Mariya Efimovna's efforts. Her oppressive presence meant that Mariya Efimovna never enjoyed the sense of being in charge of her own kitchen, something which gave other women much pleasure when they moved into self-contained apartments. When her mother-in-law finally died, she still did not enjoy sole occupancy of her kitchen, since one of her sons got married and moved his new wife into the apartment; the two women cooked separately, like unrelated occupants of a *kommunalka*.

Since most Soviet women worked, and there were not enough crèches and kindergartens, many families with young children continued to rely on private childcare. Young girls from the countryside still provided the main pool of childminders, and since they had no other accommodation in the city, space had somehow to be made for them in the new apartment. Mariya Efimovna took on a 16-year-old girl who had recently come to Moscow from the countryside. She was given a windowless storage cupboard to sleep in. When she proved unsatisfactory they had no problems finding another girl, despite the inadequacy of the accommodation on offer.

If a young couple was unlikely to have an apartment to itself, a single person had virtually no chance. Despite predictions in the 1920s that the family would just 'wither away' under socialism, by the Khrushchev era it was firmly back in the centre of social life; being single was considered either a temporary phenomenon, or a sad consequence of the post-war demographic crisis. There was no acknowledgement that some people may want to live alone, and no provision for them to do so. *Arkhitektura SSSR* put this in a positive light, insisting that single people did not need the same type of accommodation as families since they 'do not undertake housekeeping'[38] and that it would be more appropriate for them to live 'in specially constructed, improved hostels, with rooms for one to two people, and a semi-hotel type system: that is, their rooms will be cleaned, their sheets washed for them. There will be a canteen and some form of cultural service (reading room, room for rest and games, etc.).'[39] Living alone was not an option in a socialist society.

If apartment design was overstandardised, there was little standardisation in distribution. City councils had some housing at their disposal, which they assigned to people whose existing accommodation was so poor that it was to be demolished.[40] Most of the new housing, however, was under the control of factories and enterprises,[41] and was in theory assigned to workers according to two main criteria: how productive they were in their jobs, and how acute was their housing need.[42] Length of service at the factory or enterprise was also a consideration. Yet confused letters to the press make it clear that in reality these norms were constantly flouted.[43] Journalists investigating complaints about apartment distribution found that decisions were often made on the whim of an individual, and that this provided much scope for corruption; for example, it was not uncommon for apartments to be given to important officials in return for political favours.[44] Nor were apartments always assigned to appropriately sized families. One journalist reported in *Trud* that 80 families were moved into a new apartment block in Volgograd, but only 28 of those received flats which met 'existing sanitary norms concerning living-space'. Fourteen families were given apartments with too much space for their needs, while 50 families found themselves squeezed into apartments that were too small. This happened, the journalist argued, because the housing department was concerned only with matching the appropriate number of people to the apartment block as a whole.[45]

In general, women suffered considerable discrimination in housing distribution. Because of the demographic peculiarities of the post-war period, they formed a disproportionate share of the long-term single, and hence of long-term hostel residents; according to one of my respondents, many single women lived in hostels for most of their lives.[46] Yet even having a family did not ensure that a woman received equal treatment. V. M. Polishchuk complained in *Rabotnitsa* in 1958 that she had been denied a new apartment, despite the fact that she met all the appropriate criteria: she was recognised as an excellent worker; she and her large family (she had four children) lived in very inadequate housing; and she had worked in the same factory for eight years. The president of the factory committee justified his decision on the grounds that he only assigned apartments to 'heads' of families, and since Polishchuk was married, he insisted that she could not be the head of her family. It was up to her husband to 'take care of the apartment situation' through his place of work.[47] Being dependent on one's husband for one's accommodation had inevitable repercussions if the marriage broke down. As noted in another *Rabotnitsa* article, 'It can happen that a woman wants to leave an alcoholic husband, but she has nowhere to go. It was he who was assigned the apartment, and he is not prepared to go anywhere else.'[48]

A woman who had children but no husband fared no better in obtaining an apartment. A fatherless family, of which there were inevitably many in the post-war period, seems not to have been considered a family at all when it came to apartment allocation. Although all apartments built after 1958 were supposedly intended only for single-family occupancy, some communal apartments were actually being established in the new apartment blocks. A 1962 article in *Trud* told of a mother and daughter who were allocated a room in a new apartment which already had a resident, an elderly woman. She was clearly not happy about sharing the apartment with strangers, and began by locking them out; then, when forced to let them back in, she presented them with a list of draconian rules concerning their use of the 'common' areas. Eventually they bought an electric hotplate and withdrew to their own small room. The article's author, M. Moisyuk, complained not about the fact that strangers were still being placed together in the new apartments, but that the old woman had brought 'her old norms and habits with her'.[49] It would seem that the mere fact that the apartments were new, whether or not they were self-contained, was meant to result in improved attitudes in their residents.

Housing policy as a socialist phenomenon

The term 'communal apartment' had a socialist ring to it, even if in reality it was euphemistic. It is difficult to see how the move to single-family housing could be construed as a socialist housing policy. Yet it was accompanied by much socialist rhetoric. The heterogeneity of residents was continually stressed: government ministers, professors, factory workers, actors, teachers, engineers and writers apparently lived happily alongside one another, offering mutual support and friendship.[50] One article in *Sovetskaya zhenshchina* told how retired residents imparted their knowledge and skills to their new neighbours. A former dancer, for example, set up a dance circle for the children in her block, and her (female) neighbours sewed the costumes for their shows; a former gardener became 'chief gardening consultant' for his block, helping his neighbours decorate their apartments and balconies with plants.[51] An article in *Trud* urged residents to put to good use their 'variety of interesting professions' by devoting an hour or two per week to chatting with neighbours about their work, and helping younger residents to make their career choices.[52] According to *Rabotnitsa*, in some cases residents had so many professional skills to put at each other's service that it was seldom necessary for anyone to call out a plumber or electrician. Neighbours also took it in turns to clean and paint the entranceways and stairwells of their buildings.[53]

The 'communal apartment', then, had been replaced by the 'communal apartment block'.

The 'self-build' initiative was also heavily promoted in the early years of the Khrushchev era. This consisted of workers forming amateur building brigades and constructing their own houses in their free time. This had actually begun on a small scale in the Stalin era,[54] but the Khrushchev reforms apparently inspired such a 'high socialist consciousness'[55] in workers that in some towns these amateur brigades produced more than a third of the annual total of new residential housing.[56] Financial arrangements differed from city to city. The land was generally provided by the factory or enterprise, which in some cases also paid professional builders to give advice and assistance. Other expenses were usually shared between the factory or enterprise and the local authorities, but in some cases the workers had to arrange bank loans and make a contribution towards the cost of their future homes. This did not entitle them to ownership, however. An article in *Trud*, arguing that the amateur builders should be paid for their work, justified this by explaining that 'the houses built by them belong to the enterprises and the state. And everyone who receives living space in them will have to pay rent.'[57]

While there were some references in the press to women joining the building brigades, this was presented as a novelty, and the phenomenon was overwhelmingly male.[58] Since the new housing went to the builders themselves, this meant that few women could acquire a 'self-build' apartment in their own right, and were, again, reliant on their husbands.

In the later Khrushchev period, a new socialist angle appeared in the housing programme, in the form of the 'micro-district' (*mikroraion*). This was to be a complete community, built outside of the city, which would meet all of its residents' domestic and recreational needs. In addition to apartment blocks there would be schools, crèches and kindergartens, shops, public dining rooms, sports and leisure facilities such as libraries and cinemas, and shaded garden areas.[59] In some apartment blocks the ground floor would accommodate a *dom khukhnya* (apartment block kitchen), producing ready-prepared meals which housewives could take home to their families. In short, the micro-district would be a reincarnation, in miniaturised form, of the 'socialist city' which had assumed such importance in the First Five-Year Plan. As Ruble put it: 'Apologists for the micro-district argued that individual apartment units were merely the smallest part of an all-encompassing system.'[60]

Micro-districts had a number of defects, particularly for women. Despite pledges to the contrary, few provided even basic services and amenities, at least in the early years of their existence. As Barkhin admitted, 'Social buildings were hardly even worked into the projects, and were not built.'[61] Residents had to make gruelling journeys to the nearest city – my respondents talked of having to walk more than 40 minutes to the nearest bus or tram stop[62] – just to take care of their basic domestic needs, and guests from the city had to bring huge bags full of essential items with them when they came to visit.[63] Crèches and kindergartens, which were supposed to be an integral part of the micro-district, were in reality not seen as priorities,[64] and some women were forced to give up work because they had nowhere to leave their children.[65] The laundries and other domestic facilities that were supposed to appear alongside the apartment blocks failed to materialise, while the apartment blocks themselves sometimes lacked the most basic services: one *Rabotnitsa* journalist, L. Travkin, found that women in some new districts outside Orel not only had to do their family's washing by hand, they also had to haul the water up to their apartments from standpipes.[66]

The geography of the new apartment

According to an article in *Rabotnitsa*, the optimum size for a one-room apartment was 18–20 square metres; of a two-room apartment, 30 square metres; and a three-room apartment, 36–40 square metres. Accordingly, the more rooms an apartment had, the smaller each would be. These figures did not include the space required for the kitchen (which should be 6 square metres), nor the bathroom.[67] Architects L. Bumazhnyi and A. Zal'tsman proposed that room size ultimately be reduced still further, to 10 or 11 square metres. This would make it possible to have more rooms in the apartment without increasing its overall size, which would enable the family 'to save the living room of the apartment from being used as a sleeping area; [and] to have separate bedrooms for the parents and children'.[68] This would create 'more normal conditions for raising children and for leisure activities for the older members of the family' – a coded suggestion, perhaps, that sexual activities could be carried out in private.[69]

Corridors were kept to a minimum. As well as saving space, this made it easier to assemble the apartments from prefabricated sections. However, cutting down on corridor space had a major drawback; it often resulted in the largest room, which functioned as the family's living room, being directly linked to the other rooms, with the result that everyone had to walk through that room to get to their own sleeping quarters, as well as the kitchen and the bathroom. Since a 'common use' room which did not double as a bedroom remained a utopian dream, the privacy of the family members who slept in this 'walk-through room' was severely compromised.

In the three-generational family consisting of a married couple, their children and a grandmother or one set of grandparents, the married couple generally slept in the walk-through room, and depending on the number of rooms the apartment had, they were likely to share it with one or more children. Of my respondents, Mariya Efimovna, slept with her husband and baby in the walk-through room, while her mother-in-law and older son slept in the only other room. Her conjugal life effectively came to an end, she said, since her mother-in-law would enter their room whenever she pleased and without warning. Galina Mikhailovna and her husband also slept in the walk-through room, but she found it less disturbing; her mother, who had the neighbouring room, was more considerate, and in any case, 'this was Russia', she explained, 'and people were used to living all together'. In Genrikh Pavlovich's family there was no set rule as to who slept where; if he had to get up early he slept in the walk-through room so that he would not disturb the others, but it was as often used as the child's bedroom. As years passed, it became common for people to reconstruct their apartments and separate the walk-through room from its neighbours by creating extra corridor space, even though this made the rooms themselves even smaller.[70]

Furnishing and decorating the new apartment

The new apartment needed furnishing and decorating, and the magazines offered copious advice on how this should be done, invariably addressed to the 'housewife'. As Susan Reid makes clear in her chapter in this volume, simplicity was the keyword. 'Excess' in furnishings, as in architecture, was denounced as a petty-bourgeois tendency, and women were urged to keep nothing in the apartment that served no practical function.[71] Some commentators accepted that they might want to stamp their own personalities on their apartments, and suggested they display a small amount of their own handiwork;[72] after all, 'the majority of girls and women love to do needlework – to embroider, sew, decorate textiles, sew on lace'.[73] Others were more nervous about encouraging dangerous individualism. *Rabotnitsa* readers were even urged by one writer to replace their handmade quilts with mass-produced alternatives imported from China, which 'are more beautiful because they are simpler and more practical'.[74]

In the experience of my respondents, furnishing the apartment was the woman's responsibility.[75] The home environment was primarily her domain, and while it generated extra work, it also afforded her some sense of control. 'I was the matriarch' exulted Galina Mikhailovna when I asked who had chosen the furniture in her apartment.

Yet if it was the woman's task to create the nest, her husband, seemingly, simply had to enjoy it. As one *Trud* reader pointed out, much of the work that men traditionally did, such as chopping wood and fetching water, was unnecessary in a well-equipped city home.[76] The self-contained apartment created a more conducive environment for entertaining, and judging from articles and stories in the press, one of the man's principal contributions to domestic life was to invite the guests. A *Rabotnitsa* journalist, visiting a new apartment block in Leningrad, found a mother and daughter worrying about how best 'to make things cosy'; hanging up curtains would make a crucial difference but they would have to wait until 'Papa [can] help us on Sunday'. Little did they know that Papa had no intention of helping them; he was 'giving up his beloved fishing' on Sunday, but 'in order to invite friends over for a housewarming gathering'.[77]

If inviting guests was largely a male prerogative, tending to their needs was still the woman's duty. An article in *Sovetskaya zhenshchina* discussed the range of beautiful table settings, cutlery and crockery which would help women entertain more elegantly: 'Every housewife wants to set the table beautifully when guests are coming ... and this wish is being satisfied now by the increased variety of beautiful things being introduced by many factories. ... '[78] A *Trud* commentator was less enthusiastic about the new trend for entertaining, complaining that women were expected to drop everything and produce food and drink whenever their husbands turned up with guests.[79] A short story in *Rabotnitsa* offered a particularly chilling scenario, of a man inviting friends over to celebrate International Women's Day. Although this was supposed to be the woman's special day, his wife had to cook and serve their food, and although the guests raised their glasses to her, she could not drink herself because she did not like vodka and her husband had not thought to buy any wine. The story ended with one guest so drunk that she had to put him to bed with her husband, leaving her with nowhere to sleep.[80]

Domestic appliances and services

In the Khrushchev era some effort was put into dispelling the notion that women had a genetic predisposition for housework, and both *Rabotnitsa* and *Trud* published articles complaining about men's refusal to help their wives in the home and discussing ways to encourage them to do so.[81] However, in general they were fatalistic about men's ability to change, and saw labour-saving domestic appliances as the only practical way of lightening women's workload. Accordingly, *Rabotnitsa* reported in 1959 on a new government resolution 'On measures to increase the production and range and improve the quality of appliances for domestic use' which would 'lighten and simplify the domestic work of millions of women'.[82]

The press also made much reference to the increase in domestic services available within the community. As well as reducing the time women had to spend on housework, providing more public services was also, as Susan Reid has indicated, an attempt to counteract the increasingly privatised nature of family life. As one of my respondents noted, 'this was socialism, so there were many communal things'.[83]

Particular attention was paid to alternatives to home cooking. Public dining rooms were strongly recommended,[84] with *Trud* claiming that the Communist Party had set itself the task of ensuring that within 10–15 years it would be more common for people to eat in public dining rooms than at home.[85] For those who could not be lured out of the home, takeaway meals were available from some dining rooms and the 'apartment block kitchens' in the new micro-districts,[86] and ready-made meals and washed and chopped vegetables were now on sale in new delicatessen sections of food shops.[87] The press also drew attention to the growth in the number of public laundries, some of which were actually located in the new apartment blocks,[88] and to 'the fairy-tale growth' in the number of childcare facilities.[89]

Yet as the more candid commentators acknowledged, the supply and quality of labour-saving devices and services remained inadequate.[90] The public dining rooms, so celebrated in the press, were unpopular since 'the food is unappetising and expensive'.[91] There were too few laundries, and they had a reputation for tearing sheets and clothes.[92] Furthermore, despite the supposed 'fairy-tale' growth in the number of crèches and kindergartens, in reality many women had to give up their jobs to look after their children, or else leave them unsupervised while they were at work.[93]

The new micro-districts were particularly poorly served by domestic services.[94] L. Travkin, writing in *Rabotnitsa*, complained that laundries were sometimes not even included in the original architectural plans, and that women workers had no choice but to spend their one free day per week doing the family's washing instead of enjoying the leisure activities which were supposed to be a central part of Soviet life.[95]

It could also be argued that in some respects the new domestic appliances, and in general the state's new interest in the domestic realm, threatened to increase women's workload by raising expectations about the quality of their housekeeping. The director of the Institute of Experimental Planning of the USSR Academy of Builders and Architects, Boris Rubanenko, asked in an interview in *Rabotnitsa* about what was being done to alleviate women's domestic workload, replied that the Institute of Residential Life (Institut zhilishch) was preparing a series of books and brochures full of domestic tips, in which housewives 'will find out how best to equip their work place in the kitchen, how to create a children's corner, how to make a beautiful window display, how to select wallpaper and material for upholstery – in a word, everything that will help them to equip and beautify their apartments with taste and convenience'.[96] This seems to be aimed less at lightening the workload than turning it into a hobby. Entertaining guests was also presented by some writers as a female hobby, even if their husbands were likely to have done the inviting. R. Chaikovskaya, writing in *Sovetskaya zhenshchina*, portrayed the increased availability of beautiful crockery, place settings and so on as a boon for women.[97] We have already noted that a single-family apartment was more conducive to entertaining than a *kommunalka* (something which was, arguably, encouraged by articles such as Chaikovskaya's), and that this inevitably created more work for women.

My respondents agreed that women did all the domestic work, even before they had any appliances or services to help them. Yet even when these were available, they did not save as much time and effort as anticipated. The new public dining facilities were seen as a last resort, to be avoided if at all possible. Galina Mikhailovna did not need them since her mother, who lived with them, did the cooking. Mariya Efimovna did try the *dom khakhnya* in her new district, but was not impressed. Emma Aleksandrovna insisted that the food from her local house kitchen actually made people ill; the only person she knew who ate it on a regular basis was an alcoholic living in her husband's communal apartment, and she was ill anyway on account of the alcohol.

They also had reservations about the washing machines and laundries available at that time. The early models of washing machine were very labour intensive since the wet laundry had to be transferred by hand from the washing tub to a separate drying tub. Accordingly, several of my respondents felt that taking the washing to a laundry took less time than using their own machines, especially since many of the laundries offered an ironing service.[98] However, their reputation for tearing clothes was well founded, and some of the time the women saved by having their clothes washed and ironed for them was then spent on repairing them. Accordingly, many women only took less destructible items like sheets to the laundry, and washed their family's clothes themselves. This meant that they had the inconvenience both of travelling to the laundry, and using their own inadequate machines. In short, the new domestic appliances and services, which were greeted with such enthusiasm in the press, had rather less favourable responses from the women whose lives they were meant to be improving.

Conclusion

The Khrushchev housing and domestic goods programmes were part of a genuine campaign to address and improve the living conditions of Soviet citizens. However, both fell short of their original intentions. The housing programme did not fulfil its main pledge, to provide all families with their own self-contained apartments within two decades; indeed, the 'communal apartment' remains a significant feature of the Russian urban landscape more than four decades later. All the same, the programme's effect on the urban population should not be underestimated. In the six years between 1957 and 1963, 75 million people moved home, a third of the total Soviet population.[99] My respondents made it clear that getting their own apartments was a matter of huge importance to Soviet citizens.

This was, supposedly, a socialist society, and families were not supposed to close their doors and disappear into their own private space. Accordingly, the housing programme was accompanied by much rhetoric about new forms of communal feeling and mutual support. Yet neighbourliness and a sense of community did not figure strongly in my respondents' recollections of life in their new homes. They laid more stress on the pleasures of privacy, however limited that was in the multi-generational, 'small-dimensioned' Khrushchevian apartment. Not having to share cooking and washing facilities with strangers was a huge relief. Despite the party's attempts to present the move to single-family housing as a new form of socialist living, in reality it resulted in a more privatised form of family life. However, there had been no genuine sense of community in the communal apartments; on the contrary, there had been a determined attempt to create as much privacy as was possible within that environment. The move to single-family accommodation, then, indulged an existing desire for private family life rather than creating it.

As we have noted, women were the primary homemakers, and the home was generally held to be their domain. Hence responsibility for creating a homely atmosphere and meeting the domestic needs of their families, both in the communal apartment and the single-family apartment, lay firmly with the woman. Accordingly, moving to a single-family apartment was portrayed, both in the press and by my respondents, as more important to women than to men. In *Trud*, for example, one male resident of a new apartment block in a mining community was quoted as saying: 'It is difficult to convey how glad we all were – especially our wives.'[100] In another article, a woman talked of the delight of feeling herself 'to be completely the boss. For a woman housekeeper, that, to speak honestly, means a lot.'[101] *Sovetskaya zhenshchina* noted that 'children and husbands are simply pleased' at the prospect of moving to their own apartment, while women took a much more active interest in details.[102] One of my male respondents, Vladimir Borisovich, acknowledged that for him the home had represented above all a source of relaxation and recuperation; it was 'a place to sleep' after a hard day at work, as he put it.[103] For women it was, conversely, a second work environment, but it also gave them a sense of control; in a patriarchal society, it was the one place in which, as Galina Mikhailovna noted, the matriarch held sway. Given that the home was more important to women, then, it is ironic that they had little chance of actually obtaining an apartment in their own right. They may have felt they had some power over the home environment, but in general they were reliant on their husbands to actually provide them with that environment.

Women were not portrayed in the Khrushchev era solely, or even primarily, as housewives and homemakers. Indeed, Khrushchev professed his determination to tackle gender inequalities in the workplace and improve women's showing in the higher reaches of professional hierarchies, and women's magazines continued to stress the importance of women having a professional and public life.[104] Yet this was offset by the privatisation of the family brought about by the move to single-family accommodation, which inevitably facilitated and encouraged a pride in housekeeping. My female respondents, without exception, said that the home and work were both of crucial importance to them. Yet it can be argued that the housing programme encouraged a shift in the balance in women's lives between work and home, with home claiming a more prominent position.

Appendix

Interviews were conducted with the following people.

Mariya Efimovna, interviewed 29 March 2002. Widowed, with two adult sons. Originally from Ukraine, her family moved to Moscow in 1930 to escape the famine. At first her family of six (parents and four children) lived in a hostel, then in one room in a communal flat. When she married she moved into her husband's communal flat; they got their own flat, which they shared with his mother, in the Lenin Hills in 1960.

Vladimir Borisovich, and his sister *Nina Borisovna*, interviewed 30 March 2002. Vladimir B. is married with one adult son. Nina B. has never been married. They grew up in Zhukovskii, a small town outside of Moscow, built in the mid-1930s. They lived in various communal flats until 1948, when the family was assigned a self-contained flat on account of their father's excellent work record. Their parents separated in 1955 and the father moved out. Nina B. left Zhukovskii to work in another city in 1961. In 1962 Vladimir B. married and his wife moved in with him and his mother. His wife's parents moved to Moscow in 1971, where they lived in two rooms in a four-room communal apartment. Two years later, through a complicated process of apartment exchanges, Vladimir B. and his family – by now they had a son – moved into the other two rooms.

Lyudmila Ivanovna, wife of Vladimir Borisovich, interviewed 30 March 2002. She also grew up in Zhukovskii, in various communal apartments, though during the war the family was evacuated to Kazan. She moved to Moscow when she started university. She lived for one year with a friend's family; then for another year with an aunt, a school-teacher whose husband had been the director of the same school before he was killed in the war, and who had her own flat in the school grounds; and for the next two years in a university hostel, sharing a room with five other people. She finished university in 1955 and moved back with her parents, who at that time were still in a communal apartment in Zhukovskii. Later that same year they were assigned a single-family apartment. Lyudmila I. moved to the new apartment with them, but was only there for a few months before she went off to work in the Urals for a year, where she lived in a communal apartment which she shared with a large Tatar family. When she left the Urals she moved back in with her parents in Zhukovskii, though she got a job in Moscow and had to commute two hours each way every day. In 1962 she married Vladimir Borisovich and moved in with his family.

Galina Mikhailovna, interviewed 1 April 2002. She lived in a communal apartment in Moscow until 1963, sharing one room with her parents, husband and child. Her parents were assigned their own small apartment that year and moved out; Galina M., her husband and child remained in the communal flat for a few more months, until her father died, when they exchanged their room and the mother's apartment, for a larger self-contained apartment where they all lived together.

Elena Mikhailovna, interviewed 2 April 2002. Married with two children. She began life in a communal apartment, but when she was only a year old her family moved to Fili, a settlement outside Moscow, where they had been assigned more space: two rooms for a family of four (parents and two children). They were evacuated to Tatarstan during the war but later returned to the same house in Fili. They received a self-contained flat on Moscow's Lomonosov prospect, near the university, in 1954. Elena M. married in 1960 and she and her husband moved into a communal apartment with his parents. They had two rooms between them, which in due course also had to accommodate two children and a nanny. In 1966 Elena M., her husband, children and nanny moved into a three-room 'cooperative apartment', which they received on account of her husband's army service.[105]

Genrikh Pavlovich, and his wife *Emma Aleksandrovna*, interviewed 7 April 2002. Genrikh P. lived in a university hostel for 13 years, which included all the years he was studying (as an undergraduate and postgraduate), and the first two years in post as a university researcher. As an undergraduate student he had to share a room with three others, but when he started his postgraduate studies he moved to a two-person room. In the late 1950s he got his own room in a communal apartment, a room originally designed for a housekeeper and created from a section of corridor. He shared the apartment with three families, all of which had some connection with the university. In the early 1960s he was given a room in a three-room apartment in a new apartment block. He married shortly afterwards and his wife moved in with him; but when she was pregnant, in 1964, they were assigned their own apartment, near Moscow's Taganskaya metro station. This was a 'second-stage' Khrushchev apartment block and hence higher than those of the 'first stage'; theirs had nine storeys. When they had a second child, they and Emma A.'s family exchanged their respective apartments for one larger one, which accommodated Genrikh P., Emma A., their two children, and Emma A.'s mother and grandmother. Genrikh P.'s mother was also registered to live there, but in reality she lived with her widowed son-in-law in the winter and in a dacha in the summer.

Emma A. lived in a communal apartment in Fili as a child; it had originally been part of a large country estate which consisted of three buildings, the main manor house and two small side buildings which had housed the staff. All three buildings had been divided into communal apartments, and Emma A.'s family of three (her and her parents) lived in one of the side buildings, which they shared with another family with five children. Emma A.'s parents divorced and her father got a room in a communal flat in Moscow. In 1958 Emma A., her mother and an unmarried aunt were assigned a self-contained two-room apartment in Moscow.

Notes

1   Khrushchev later described it *the* main problem of the post-war period. N. Khrushchev, *Khrushchev Remembers* (London, 1974), p. 95.

2   E. Zubkova, *Russia after the War: Hopes, Illusions, and Disappointments, 1945–1957* (London, 1998), pp. 102–3, referring to a 1956 survey.

3   See R. Medvedev, *Khrushchev* (Oxford, 1982), pp. 51–2.

4   A. Sobel (ed.) *Russia's Rulers: the Khrushchev Period* (New York, 1971), p. 243 (quoting from the TASS translation of the Party Programme).

5   The Seven-Year Plan was dropped on 13 March 1963 on the grounds that it had been rendered out of date by the new economic changes ordered by the Central Committee in November 1962. See Sobel, op cit., p. 328.

6   A. Werth, *The Khrushchev Phase* (London, 1961), p. 139.

7   The new slogan was: 'build quickly, cheaply, and well' (*stroit' bystro, deshevo, khorosho*). See, for example, two small articles in *Trud*, 1 September 1957, both with this slogan as their title.

8   See, for example, G. Gradov, 'Sovetskuyu arkhitekturu na uroven' novykh zadach', *Arkhitektura SSSR*, no. 2, 1955, p. 5; 'Zabota o cheloveke – osnova sovetskogo gradostroitel'stva', editorial article, *Arkhitektura SSSR*, no. 6, 1960, pp. 1–3; and Werth, op cit., p. 142.

9   Gradov, op cit., pp. 4–8.

10   In fact, the use of concrete was not as widespread as was desired. Engineer M. Taub noted that in 1956 only 10–11 per cent of Moscow buildings were made out of large concrete panels: see 'Doma iz krupnykh blokov', *Trud*, 9 May 1957. According to Ruble this had risen to just over a quarter by 1965, and to half a decade later. See B. A. Ruble, 'From Khrushcheby to Korobki', in W. C. Brumfield and B. A. Ruble, *Russian Housing in the Modern Age: Design and Social History* (Cambridge, 1993), p. 243.

11   Towards the end of Khrushchev's time in power, technological improvements reduced costs, resulting in far higher blocks.

12   See, for example, 'Pravil'no, nauchno reshat' problemy tipizatsii zhilykh domov', *Arkhitektura SSSR*, no. 5, 1956, pp. 1–4, editorial; B. Olenko, 'V novom, "malometrazhnom" dome', *Trud*, 26 March 1957; T. Druzhinina, 'Vse dlya sovetskogo cheloveka', *Rabotnitsa*, no. 11, 1958, pp. 21–2.

13   Khrushchev, op cit., p. 101.

14   Gradov, op cit., pp. 4–8.

15   Khrushchev, op cit., p. 102.

16   See Appendix for details of interviewees.

17   See R. Stites, *Revolutionary Dreams* (Oxford, 1989), pp. 200–4.

18   L. Attwood, *Creating the New Soviet Woman: Women's Magazines as Engineers of Female Identity* (London, 1999), pp. 38–9.

19   S. Kotkin, 'Shelter and Subjectivity in the Stalin Period', in Brumfield and Ruble, op. cit., pp. 182–3.

20   Attwood, op. cit., pp 104–10.

21   Elena Mikhailovna spent the first year of her life in an eight-room *kommunalka* in the Arbat district of Moscow, in a beautiful art nouveau building. The former owner's family retained three rooms for themselves, while each of the other five rooms housed a different family.

22   Alexander Werth was told by the head of Glavmosstroi (the Moscow organisation responsible for building work) that the principle of one-family-one-flat had begun to be applied in 1958, but that 'even so, not all flats built in 1958 were one-family flats'. Werth, *The Khrushchev Phase*, p. 141. See also B. Borisov and V. Segalov, 'V novom dome', *Trud*, 13 July 1961, who state that in Taganrog it had only been two years since construction had switched to small-scale single-family flats.

23   S. Boym, *Common Places: Mythologies of Everyday Life in Russia* (Cambridge, Mass., 1994), pp. 123–4.

24   G. Rykin, 'Skandal'nykh del masteritsa', *Rabotnitsa*, no. 10, 1955, p. 29.

25   L. Novogrudskii, 'My khotim, chtoby v novykh domakh novogo stala zhizn'!', *Trud*, 12 July 1961.

26   I. Utekhin, *Ocherki kommunal'nogo byta* (Moscow, 2001).

27   Rykin, 'Skandal'nykh', p. 29.

28   'Apartment hooliganism' was the term used in the Stalin era. See, for example, L. Veselova, 'Uvazhat' chelovecheskuyu lichnost'', *Rabotnitsa*, no. 26, 1940, pp. 14–15.

29   From the TASS translation of the draft 1961 Communist Party Programme, introduced at the XXII Party Congress in October 1961; quoted in Sobel, op. cit., p. 243.

30   M. G. Barkhin, *Gorod 1945–1970: praktika, proekty, teoriya* (Moscow, 1974), p. 58. See also M. Kostandi and E. Kapustyan, 'Tipy zhilykh domov dlya eksperimental'nogo zhilogo raiona Moskvy', *Arkhitektura SSSR*, no. 4, 1961, pp. 17–28, in which they identified three types of housing which would meet all needs.

31   Barkhin, op. cit., p. 58.

32   See L. Lopovok, 'Gorod, dom, kvartira', *Trud*, 7 October 1961. Lopovok, an architect himself, rails against his colleagues' insistence on designing apartments for the 'average' three-person family: 'It must ... be clear that

a small self-contained flat, built completely in accordance with the "average" family of three people, will not suit a family of seven to eight people.'

33   Ruble, op. cit., pp. 252–3.

34   I. Mendzheritskii, 'Zdes' byla derevnya', *Sovetskaya zhenshchina*, no. 3, 1963, p. 12.

35   V. Borovoi and L. Balanovskii, 'Eksperimental'nyi krupnopanel'nyi zhiloi dom novogo tipa', *Arkhitektura SSSR*, no. 5, 1963, pp. 3–7.

36   Almost all of my female respondents complained about the size of the kitchen in the new self-contained apartment.

37   Werth, op. cit., footnote, pp. 136–7.

38   Kostandi and Kapustyan, 'Tipy zhilykh domov', pp. 17–28.

39   L. Bumazhnyi and A. Zal'tsman, 'Perspektivnye tipy zhilykh domov i kvartir', *Arkhitektura SSSR*, no. 1, 1959, p. 6. This was echoed by B. Svetlichnyi, 'Zaboty gradostroitelei', *Novyi mir*, no. 10, 1958, pp. 211–23, who suggested that for young and single people it might be 'more convenient to live in house communes with all services provided for their domestic needs'. E. Tsuglulieva told of one factory which turned some of its new apartments into hostels for its female workers. See 'V dom v"ekhali zhil'tsy', *Rabotnitsa*, no. 10, 1954, p. 3.

40   This was how Mariya Efimovna's family received its own apartment, in 1960; their communal apartment, in which her husband had lived since his birth, was in a decrepit wooden building with such inadequate heating that buckets of water would freeze over in the winter.

41   Vladimir Borisovich estimated this to be around 90 per cent.

42   See, for example, F. Potashnikov, 'Komu predostavit' kvartiry?', *Trud*, 30 July 1959, response to a letter from a reader about how new flats are assigned. Also K. Olechov, 'Schastlivoe novosel'e', *Trud*, 7 November 1959, extended caption accompanying a photograph of a family which had just been moved into a new flat; A. Levina, 'Order na kvartiru', *Rabotnitsa*, no. 10, 1961, pp. 15–17; and Tsuglulieva, 'V dom v"ekhali zhil'tsy', p. 3.

43   See, for example, 'Komu predostavit' kvartiry?', *Trud*, 30 July 1959, response by F. Potashnikov to a letter from a reader about how apartments are assigned.

44   See, for example, V. Sevryukov, 'Kto budet zhit' v novom dome?', *Trud*, 3 December 1957; D. Makarov, 'Novosel'e ne sostoyalos'', *Trud*, 12 November 1961; G. Sukhov, 'Kakim budet novyi dom?', *Trud*, 15 December 1961. A light-hearted short story in *Rabotnitsa* also hints that factory housing committees were not always sufficiently diligent in checking the circumstances of applicants: in this tale, a young worker had his mother and three supposedly orphaned nephews move in with him until he was assigned a new apartment, when his 'dependants' suddenly disappeared. Vasilii Kukushkin, 'Novosel'e', *Rabotnitsa*, no. 12, 1954, pp. 19–21.

45   Sukhov, 'Kakim budet novyi dom?', *Trud*, 15 December 1961.

46   Interview with Emma Aleksandrovna.

47   L. Pozdnyakova, 'Mozhet li zhenshchina byt' glavoi sem'i'?', *Rabotnitsa*, no. 10, 1958, p. 23.

48 Elena Kononenko, 'Obuzdat' p'yanits! (Po pis'mam chitatelei)', *Rabotnitsa*, no. 9, 1964, pp. 23–4.
49 M. Moisyuk, 'Pokhititeli radosti', *Trud*, 10 May 1962. See also R. Izmailova, 'Klub interesnykh vstrech', *Sovetskaya zhenshchina*, no. 9, 1960, pp. 24–8, which refers to one new apartment which housed both a widow and her daughter, and a lathe operator from the neighbouring factory.
50 See, for example, T. Molilevskaya and B. Pokrovskii, 'Nash dom', *Sovetskaya zhenshchina*, no. 7, 1960, pp. 14–17; and Izmailova, 'Klub interesnykh vstrech', pp. 24–8.
51 Molilevskaya and Pokrovskii, 'Nash dom', p. 16.
52 M. Akolupin, from Novosibirsk, 'Chem ogorchen novosel', *Trud*, 28 December 1960.
53 M. Voskresenskaya, 'Dom, v kotorom ty zhivesh'', *Rabotnitsa*, no. 8, 1962, p. 25.
54 See M. Guterman, 'Sobstvennyi dom rabochego', *Trud*, 23 November 1957.
55 M. Kryglova, 'Na narodnoi stroike', *Trud*, 4 September 1957.
56 See Elena Mikulina, 'My stroim dom – svoimi silami', *Novyi mir*, no. 4, 1958, p. 4.
57 'Stroitel'stvo zhilishch – vazhnoe obshchenarodnoe delo', *Trud*, 6 August 1957.
58 See, for example, A. Levina, 'Svoimi silami', *Rabotnitsa*, no. 4, 1957, pp. 9–10.
59 See, for example, T. Druzhinina, 'Vse dlya sovetskogo cheloveka', *Rabotnitsa*, no. 11, 1958, pp. 21–2; Izmailova, 'Klub interesnykh vstrech', pp. 24–8.
60 Ruble, op. cit., p. 250
61 Barkhin, op. cit., p. 60.
62 Interviews with Mariya Efimovna and Emma Aleksandrovna.
63 Interview with Emma Aleksandrovna.
64 L. Burmistrova, 'Trudnosti? Net, ravnodushie!', *Rabotnitsa*, no. 9, 1964, pp. 26–7.
65 Interview with Emma Aleksandrovna. This point is echoed by articles in the press: see, for example, L. Burmistrova and M. Buzhkevich, 'Pavlodar – gorod novostroek', *Rabotnitsa*, no. 7, 1959, pp. 9–11; and Burmistrova, 'Trudnosti?', *Rabotnitsa*, no. 9, 1964, pp. 26–7.
66 L. Travkin, 'Gde vystirat' bel'e?', *Rabotnitsa*, no. 4, 1959, p. 26.
67 T. Druzhinina, 'Vse dlya sovetskogo cheloveka', *Rabotnitsa*, no. 11, 1958, pp. 21–2.
68 L. Bumazhnyi and A. Zal'tsman, 'Perspektivnye tipy zhilykh domov i kvartir', *Arkhitektura SSSR*, no. 1, 1959, pp. 2, 3, 6, 9.
69 Ibid.
70 Personal conversation with Sasha Breigin, son of Mariya Efimovna.
71 See L. Kamenskii, 'O vkusakh i bezvkusitse', *Trud*, 1 June, 1957; A. Gol'dshtein, 'Chto takoe uyut', *Rabotnitsa*, no. 1, 1959, p. 30.
72 Architect Irina Voeikova was particularly sympathetic to the notion of personal taste. See her articles 'Oboi dlya kvartiry', *Sovetskaya zhenzhchina*, no. 10, 1954, p. 43; 'Kak obstavit' svoyu komnatu', *Rabotnitsa*,

no. 9, 1955, p. 30; 'Vasha kvartira', *Rabotnitsa*, no. 9, 1962, p. 30; and 'Uyut – v prostote', *Rabotnitsa*, no. 10, 1964, pp. 30–1.

73　I. Voeikova, 'Kak obstavit' svoyu komnatu', *Rabotnitsa*, no. 9, 1955, p. 30. See also Z. Supishchikova, 'Chtoby bylo uyutno', *Rabotnitsa*, no. 11, 1961, p. 29, who holds that embroidery is the favourite pastime of many Soviet women. See also N. Lazareva, 'Veshchi rasskazyvayut', *Rabotnitsa*, no. 4, 1964, p. 27, who admitted that mass-produced factory furniture, combined with the standardised room layout in the new apartments, did make for a certain monotony. She suggested that this could be counteracted by a 'modest' display of folk art.

74　Gol'dshtein, 'Chto takoe uyut', p. 30.

75　There was one exception: for Emma Aleksandrovna and her husband it was a mutual decision.

76　'Dela nashi semeinye', *Trud*, 21 August 1960.

77　I. Golovan, 'V novom dome', *Rabotnitsa*, no. 5, 1953, pp. 7–8.

78　R. Chaikovskaya, 'Dlya domashnego khozyaistva', *Sovetskaya zhenshchina*, no. 11, 1954, pp. 44–5.

79　A. Protopova, 'Muzh', *Trud*, 19 March 1960.

80　N. Il'ina, 'Kak ya provela prazdnik', *Rabotnitsa*, no. 2, 1963, pp. 15–16.

81　See M. Romanova, 'Muzh prishel domoi', *Trud*, 4 August 1959; Protopova, 'Muzh', *Trud*, 19 March 1960; 'Dela nashi semeinye', *Trud*, 21 August 1960, extracts from readers' letters on the Protopova article. For a discussion of the *Rabotnitsa* articles, see L. Attwood, 'Celebrating the "Frail-figured Welder": Gender Confusion in Women's Magazines of the Khrushchev Era', *Slavonica*, vol. 8, no. 2, 2002, pp. 158–76.

82　I. I. Gorgeev, 'Dlya vas, zhenshchiny!', *Rabotnitsa*, no. 11, 1959, p. 22.

83　Interview with Emma Aleksandrovna.

84　See, for example, Protopova, 'Muzh', *Trud*, 19 March 1960; G. Spiridonov, 'Vkusno kormit', khorosho obsluzhivat'', *Trud*, 21 February 1960.

85　V. Zakharov, 'Chtoby luchshe, chem doma', *Trud*, 9 December 1961.

86　Ibid., and L. Bernaskoni, 'Domovaya kukhnya', *Trud*, 29 May 1959. According to Zakharov, in the Russian Federation these increased in number from 40 in 1956 to 600 in 1961.

87　'Dlya domashnykh khozyaek', *Trud*, 5 March 1959.

88　See, for example, A. Levina, 'Sluzhba byta, deistvui!' *Rabotnitsa*, no. 9, 1962, pp. 20–1, and M. Angarskaya, 'V domovoi prachechnoi', *Rabotnitsa*, no. 8, 1955, p. 31.

89　Protopova, 'Muzh', *Trud*, 19 March 1960, and P. S. Ivanov, 'V tret'em godu semiletki', *Rabotnitsa*, no. 1, 1961, pp. 4–5.

90　See, for example, B. Kosharovskii and E. Cherepakhova, 'Eto – delo sovnarkhozov', *Rabotnitsa*, no. 7, 1958, p. 21.

91　'Dela nashi semeinye', *Trud*, 21 August 1960.

92　Ibid.

93　Ibid.

94　See, for example, L. Voronkova et al., 'Obedy – na dom', *Trud*, 12 November 1959; L. Bernaskoni, 'Domovaya kukhnya', *Trud*, 29 May 1959; G. Voskresenskii, 'Na vykhoda iz doma', *Trud*, 12 June 1960.

95　L. Travkin, 'Gde vystirat' bel'e?', *Rabotnitsa*, no. 4, 1959, p. 26.

96 'Bystro, deshevo, dobrotno!', *Rabotnitsa*, no. 9, 1957, pp. 1–3. Rubanenko also took part in a round table discussion organised by *Sovetskaya zhenshshina:* see Izmailova, 'Klub interesnykh vstrech', pp. 24–8.

97 Chaikovskaya, 'Dlya domashnego khozyaistva', pp. 44–5.

98 Lyudmila Ivanovna said that the journey to the laundry took half an hour each way, hence two hours in total. Doing the same amount of washing and ironing herself at home, even though she had her own washing machine, would take four hours. Mariya Efimovna was so disappointed in her first washing machine that she hardly ever used it and continued to take all her family's washing to the laundry. Galina M., however, only went to the laundry with sheets because she did not want her clothes damaged. Elena Mikhailovna also took only sheets to the laundry until she was in a position to buy a good West European washing machine. Emma Aleksandrovna's family could not afford a washing machine, and since 'laundries were not good, and they ruined the clothes', her mother continued to wash the clothes by hand and take only the sheets to the laundry.

99 See K. Zhukov, 'Bol'shoe novosel'e i bol'shie zadachi, *Novyi mir,* no. 2, 1963, pp. 230–8; I. Mendzheritskii, 'Zdes' byla derevnya', *Sovetskaya zhenshchina,* no. 3, 1963, pp. 9–12.

100 V. Liverko, 'S novosel'em!',*Trud,* 15 November 1957.

101 'Dom, v kotorom my zhivem', *Trud,* 1 January 1959.

102 Mendzheritskii, 'Zdes' byla derevnya', pp. 9–12.

103 When asked which he felt was more important to him, work or home, his first response was an emphatic 'work!' However, he then reconsidered and said that they were probably of equal importance, but that the home was primarily a place to sleep. My female respondents, in contrast, felt that work and home were equally important aspects of their lives.

104 Attwood, 'Celebrating the "Frail-figured Welder"', pp. 158–76.

105 Cooperative apartments began in the late Khrushchev era but became more widespread with Brezhnev in power, and were a way of tapping people's savings for use in the housing programme. A group of people, often work colleagues, would form a cooperative and would put down a deposit of 40 per cent of the building costs so that work on a new apartment block could commence; the state would put up the rest of the money, which would be paid back by the residents in monthly payments. This did not give the residents full ownership rights, even though they were paying much more than the residents of ordinary state-owned apartments; but cooperative apartment blocks were generally better built and had better security.

10
Demystifying the Heavens: Women, Religion and Khrushchev's Anti-religious Campaign, 1954–64

Irina Paert

In 1964 a Soviet propaganda pamphlet, 'Communism and Religion', evaluated the impact of the first woman in space, Valentina Tereshkova, on religious beliefs: 'The mysterious heavens that used to mystify the imagination of every believer have now been conquered by an ordinary young woman Communist who grew up in the society where atheism has become a mass phenomenon!'[1]

As was the case with Yuri Gagarin, whose smiling face decorated anti-religious posters from 1962, the party used Tereshkova's space odyssey not only to demonstrate Soviet technological superiority over the West, but also to propagandise atheism to domestic audiences. In Tereshkova's case, however, the anti-religious message had a gender dimension. Soviet propaganda presented the first woman astronaut as a beneficiary of communist ideology and social policies promoting real equality between men and women. Ultimately, the combination of supertechnology and atheism made 26-year-old Tereshkova a model of new womanhood.[2] Anti-religion was inseparable from the Soviet presentation of women's emancipation in the Khrushchev period.

Both Soviet and Western scholars have addressed the theme of women and religion in the Soviet post-war era.[3] In contrast to previous studies which focused on Soviet patterns of secularisation in general, this chapter will analyse the gender dimension of religion and atheism during the Khrushchev era. During this period the party employed an array of ideological and political methods to combat popular religious affiliation, and at the same time emphasised the benefits of the Soviet way of life for women. Thus this chapter aims to explore the connection between two major discourses of the Khrushchev period: women's

emancipation and atheism. It addresses the question of the female preponderance in religious communities, focusing on the social dimensions of this phenomenon. It analyses the methods, rhetoric and
impact of Khrushchev's anti-religious campaign, which targeted
women in particular. It does not claim to provide a complete account
of the subject, but will hopefully help to generate a fruitful discussion
on the gender aspects of Soviet anti-religious policy.

The chapter is based on party circulars, anti-religious journals and
pamphlets, film scenarios and on the documents of the key institutions
responsible for the regulation and control of religious groups and institutions, the Council for Church Affairs and the Council for Religious
Cults Affairs, both of which came under the auspices of the Council of
Ministers (Sovmin). Much of the discussion is based on material collected from Estonian archives. Since Estonia became part of the Soviet
Union only in 1939 after its annexation by Stalin, its religious profile
cannot be seen as characteristic for the whole of the Soviet Union, yet
it renders an important case study since it provided a home for one of
the major female convents in the post-war era and attracted a large
number of women from other parts of the Soviet Union as nuns or
pilgrims.

Background

Following the liberalisation of Church–state relations during the war,
the position of the Russian Orthodox Church improved. The number
of parishes grew from 9829 in 1943 to 14,187 in 1948; 1270 of these
were opened with the approval of the state.[4] The number of clergy
increased from 9254 in 1946 to 11,827 in 1948.[5]

In the recently occupied territories of Western Ukraine and the
Baltic States, Russian Orthodoxy was in a stronger position than the
non-Russian religions, which lost a large number of church leaders
and clergy to emigration and repression. This was due to the patriotic
role of the Orthodox Church in the Second World War, which the
state promoted as a protector of Great Russian interests in the borderlands in the post-war period.[6] All the same, there was more room for
manoeuvre for most established religions in the USSR after the war.[7]
The Council for Church Affairs, presided over by Colonel G. G.
Karpov, and the Council for Religious Cults Affairs, led by I. V.
Polyanskii, regulated the relationship between the religious organisations and Soviet institutions and authorities. The councils served as
mediators between the party and the religious leadership, handling

complaints and petitions, developing religious legislation, and informing the party of recent developments on the ground.[8] The central councils also had representatives (*upolnomochennye*) in the regions; for example, the Council for Church Affairs employed 112 staff in 1946.[9] The relationship between the Church and the state soured in the last years of Stalinism: between 1948 and 1953 a number of clergy were arrested for anti-Soviet agitation, only a small number of petitions to reopen the churches received a positive response, and the local authorities arbitrarily closed some local churches. Yet despite this backlash, in comparison with the 1920s and 1930s the late Stalin period produced a favourable environment for the religious revival that followed Stalin's death in 1953.

The relaxation of religious policies during the war, the reopening of churches and the general atmosphere of liberalisation led to a growth in popular devotion. This was expressed in a large increase in church attendance, especially during major feast days, mass pilgrimages to holy springs and shrines, and a growth in sacraments such as baptisms and weddings.[10] The booming popular devotion can also be measured by calculating the Church's improved financial position: its income increased between 1947 and 1955 from 180 million to 347 million rubles.[11] Notwithstanding the popularity of the Orthodox Church, other religious denominations also experienced a boom in the late 1940s and 1950s, as did non-church evangelical groups: Evangelical Christians and Baptists both increased their membership after the unification in 1944.[12] Most established churches still enjoyed a strong presence in rural areas, whereas the non-established groups, such as Evangelical Christians (Baptists, Pentecostalists, and smaller groups such as Seventh-Day Adventists, Methodists and Jehovah's Witnesses), were becoming predominantly urban.[13] Stimulated by urbanisation, the latter groups enjoyed a steady growth in post-Stalinist Russia.

The feminisation of religion?

Women had traditionally formed a large and active contingent in religious congregations,[14] and their role in these congregations increased in the Soviet Union. According to the 1937 census, 77 per cent of women declared themselves believers compared to 45 per cent of men.[15] In the 1950s and 1960s women constituted at least two-thirds of the members of Orthodox congregations.[16] Orthodox congregations appear to be slightly more 'feminised' than non-Orthodox congregations, largely due to demographic reasons, but the difference is not significant.[17] The authorities in Estonia have also described Methodist and Baptist congregations as 'feminised'.[18] In 1955 women thus made up 80 per cent of Baptists (Evangelical Christian-Baptists), 84 per cent of Adventists, and 83–85 per cent of the Methodist congregations in Estonia.[19]

Soviet sociologists have suggested a number of explanations for the preponderance of women in these congregations.[20] Some sympathetic surveys have emphasised the role of religion as a compensation for the trauma of bereavement or loneliness. Other studies have pointed out that the majority of female believers had little education and were often unemployed.[21] Thus, patterns of economic activity were also deemed important for religious attendance and observation of religious ritual. Also, in accordance with the traditional Bolshevik discourse of religion as a 'survival of the past', female believers have also been represented as old women.[22]

The preponderance of women in the city-based sects and religious denominations also suggests that women were more likely to be affected by the anomic situation produced by post-war reconstruction and development.[23] The massive flow of people between the country and the city and between the different regions of the USSR led to the breakdown of traditional social networks that provided security, a sense of order and moral regulation for individuals. Many single female migrants experienced displacement not only as a liberation from patriarchal structures, but also as a loss of moral guidance and social support, and they also suffered exposure to sexual aggression.[24] Thus religious groups, especially those with more emphasis on their social mission, such as Baptists, provided a new moral community for the displaced women who experienced moral confusion and crises of identity.

For some women religion was an expression of resistance to the regime. In the post-war Soviet Union, women circulated eschatological rumours and prophecies, implicitly criticising state institutions and political leaders.[25] While overt resistance may have receded with the death of Stalin and liberalisation, the negative attitude to Soviet institutions, including the Communist Party and communist youth organisations, prevailed among sectarians and many traditionalist Orthodox believers.[26] Soviet ideology and culture were perceived as a threat to the traditional moral order in the family and rural communities, which were generally based on shared religious beliefs. Women often outstripped men in their zealousness to defend religious tradition.[27]

Despite the party's claim to provide Soviet women with equal access to public life and leadership roles, religious congregations often allowed more opportunities for female activism than society at large. Ironically, the repressive policies and laws directed against the clergy enabled women to take a more active role in the Church's administration. Women read and chanted in church, formed church choirs, and looked after the parish finances and buildings. Women dominated the parish councils, and had the right to appoint and discharge priests. Women were employed in the Orthodox Church as accountants, readers (*psalomshchiki*), secretaries, security guards and cleaners. Restrictions on women entering the clergy and obtaining a theological education, however, remained unchallenged.

The return of the male clergy from the Gulag in 1956–57 as a result of a mass amnesty may have led to the shift in the balance of power in congregations previously dominated by women. Their suffering gave these returning priests and ministers more authority than the female-dominated parish councils. Yet ordinary women continued to be the backbone of the Church, virtually running it on a day-to-day basis by selling candles, supervising church services and supporting their priests morally and financially.

The family was a key institution for ensuring the survival of religion in Soviet Russia. Sociologists noted that members of religious groups were linked not only by shared beliefs, but also by blood ties.[28] As long as formal religious education and the catechisation of children and adults were banned in the Soviet Union, the family was the only institution which could transmit religious beliefs.[29] Women promoted religious culture in the family through the maintenance of rituals, festivities and diet. The celebration of Christmas and Easter, made special by traditional cuisine, remained central for Russian Orthodox families throughout the Soviet period.

There was some gender differentiation in the socialisation of children in religious families, with more emphasis placed on the religious education of girls than boys. Surveys of children's attitudes in the 1920s and 1930s demonstrated that girls were more likely than boys to know prayers by heart, and girls outnumbered boys at church services.[30] The surveys also suggest that the party and other Soviet institutions were less concerned about bringing girls and young women into line with party expectations, of which an atheistic outlook was a major part, than they were with boys and young men. In the post-war Soviet Union, then, the party had to face the persistence of religion, which was believed to be sustained by women on an everyday basis.

The female religious – a case study of Pyukhtitsy convent[31]

Some women did see religion as a full-time commitment, and were not satisfied with the role of ordinary parishioners. Monasticism for many women was a vocation similar to that of the clergy, to which they were denied access. In the post-war period there were 75 functioning celibate communities, of which the majority were convents. The Pyukhtitsy convent in north-east Estonia, founded in 1888, remained active after the occupation of Estonia by Soviet troops. After 1945 the monastery started active recruitment of novices. By 1956 the convent had 121 members, including 85 nuns and 36 novices. However, the number of applicants was twice as high. The mother superior Rafaila (Migacheva) claimed that if she had enough resources she could easily raise the number of sisters to 200 or more.[32] Between 1949 and 1955 the convent accepted 48 new members, the majority of whom were between 19 and 40 years of age. Nuns aged 55 and over made up about the half of the membership, thus making an equal balance between the young and physically able, on the one hand, and the experienced but physically inactive, on the other.[33]

At least half of the younger women who were accepted into the convent between 1954 and 1955 had never married, had between four and seven years of schooling and worked at factories prior to entering the convent.[34] Most of them stated in their application forms that they had always wanted to become nuns. This fact contradicted the traditional view of religious women as aged, illiterate and bereaved. These younger women had exemplary personal histories as Soviet women workers, but they had chosen to climb the ladder of spiritual rather than social advancement. The prevalence of working-class and peasant women among the newly recruited novices was partly a result of the selection process. As agriculture was the main occupation of the nuns, the mother superior gave preference to younger, physically strong women, many of whom came from rural families. Some women had degrees in medicine and agronomy, but they were in the minority. The novices came from different parts of the Soviet Union: Moscow, Leningrad, Voronezh, Orel, Rostov and Pskov, and also the republics of Karelia and Latvia.

The monastic lifestyle was characterised by self-sufficiency and communalism. In 1953 the nuns cultivated 20.1 hectares of land, and made use of 49.4 hectares of meadows and 13.5 hectares of forest-land.[35] In addition the convent kept 19 cows and 7 horses. The output was intended for the nuns' own consumption, however, and the Soviet authorities complained about the low productivity of the convent, which used minimal technology and relied on traditional peasant methods.

The convent maintained good relations with the local authorities. The local *sovkhoz* (state farm), suffering a shortage of labour, relied on the convent's help at harvest time: the mother superior would send a 'team' of 30 younger novices to help the state farmers with the potato harvest. In exchange the *sovkhoz* administration leased tractors and other technical equipment to the nuns to plough the convent's land.[36]

During the late 1950s and 1960s the convent also benefited from the reputation of its mother superior. Mother Angelina (Lyudmila Afanas'eva) was born in 1894 to a St Petersburg craftsman and a midwife. She lost both of her parents as a child, and was brought up by her grandmother. After school, at the age of 18, she became a novice in Pyukhtitsy. During the First World War she was evacuated, together with other sisters, to Rostov, where they stayed during the revolution and the Civil War. Meanwhile, on the orders of her mother superior and the patroness Princess Shakhovskaya, Angelina went to Tallinn to study pharmacology in 1917, but came back to Rostov in 1918, where she remained with another 12 sisters, while other nuns returned to the newly independent Estonia. Angelina worked as a nurse in Rostov and kept her monastic vows even after the closure of the monastery. In 1927 she went to Leningrad, where she remained during the blockade of 1941–45, working in a hospital. She received several official awards and was decorated with medals 'For the defence of Leningrad' and 'For selfless labour' for her work during the war. She returned to Pyukhtitsy in 1947 and became the abbess in 1955. It is likely that the authorities approved the choice of Angelina as the abbess for her loyalty and patriotism.[37]

The convent enjoyed a good reputation. There were no expressions of religious exaltation, such as *klikushestvo*, which was believed to be demonic possession, which annoyed the authorities so much, and no proselytising to the local population.[38] During the 1950s the authorities tolerated the growth of the convent in line with the official encouragement of Russian migration to Estonia, since the majority of the nuns were of Russian origin.

The convent was organised along very traditional lines. The younger nuns and novices had to do menial work before they were assigned a more challenging and fulfilling occupation. The younger sisters worked in the fields and stables, in the sewing workshop and the kitchen. Most nuns and novices had several occupations, including singing in church, helping in the church and looking after guests.[39] The level of education or social origin was not the deciding factor in a nun's position in the monastic hierarchy; rather, it was the extent of her experience of monastic life.

Most women who joined the convent in 1945–55 took their vows within one to three years. In the choice of monastic names, Pyukhtitsy nuns gave preference to male saints or prophets, thus becoming Aleksiya, Mefodiya, Romana, Efrema, Sofroniya, Siluana, Savvatiya and so on. Only a minority of women chose the names of female saints, such as Svetlana, Veronika, Magdalina, Lyudmila and Evdoksiya. Apart from the fact that there were more male saints in the Orthodox calendar, the preference for male names suggests an ascetic approach to monastic spirituality, which traditionally placed its emphasis on manliness.[40] Yet the feminine aspect was important: the monastery was dedicated to Mary (the Mother of God in the Orthodox tradition), whose apparition in the area of Pyukhtitsy was witnessed by local peasants in the sixteenth century, and its central feast was the Dormition ('Falling asleep') of the Mother of God.

The administration of the monastery had a hierarchical structure: the abbess ruled with the help of a team consisting of a treasurer, economist and a number of supervisors. The Bishop of Tallinn tried to implement collegial rule in the convent through a council of elected sisters, possibly in response to some financial mismanagement by the abbess Rafaila. However, the council gathered only four times in 1955, and with the election of the new abbess it was dissolved by the bishop.[41]

The process of de-Stalinisation had some effect on the convent. Following Stalin's death, nuns as well as male clergy returned from the Gulag. The presence in the convent of nuns who had experience of the Stalinist camps provided an important spiritual experience for younger nuns. However, the spirit of de-Stalinisation also had damaging effects on traditional monastic discipline. Some novices grumbled about the dominant role of older nuns. One novice complained to the representative of the Council for Church Affairs, Kapitonov, that the younger women were forced into total dependence on the older ones:

> in all circumstances the older nuns are always right, and no one takes seriously the suggestions, however reasonable, made by younger sisters. This contradicts the spirit of Christianity, and also does not accord with the new social relations in the Soviet state where criticism and self-criticism are respected and the young people have their say [*molodym daetsya doroga*].[42]

Thus the spirit of the era as characterised by iconoclasm and challenging the authorities had some impact on the traditional convent.

It is clear that the Pyukhtitsy convent provided an alternative to mainstream society: women devoted themselves wholeheartedly to prayer, celibacy and monastic practices. At the same time, the convent was not totally opposed to society at large: it was in the convent that the spirit of collectivism and the emphasis on unpaid work found its ultimate expression. In this all-women collective, the women enjoyed economic self-sufficiency and self-rule. Power in this single-sex organisation was distributed in accordance with age and experience rather than gender and education. Yet their autonomy was limited: bishops, priests and the party officials oversaw the activities of the convent to ensure its loyalty and propriety.

Anti-religious campaigns

The thaw in Church–state relations initiated during the war came to an end in 1958–59. Khrushchev and his ideological advisers, M. A. Suslov and L. F. Il'ichev, celebrated their victory over the Stalinist opposition, promising to restore Leninist principles on religion and revive the anti-religious campaigns of the 1920s.[43] The party removed the old staff of the councils, including Karpov, who had established amiable relations between the Church and the state. It criticised the local authorities for the lack of atheistic propaganda, and it introduced a new taxation policy that aimed to squeeze the pockets of parishioners.[44] The party adopted a number of proposals in secret circulars between 1958 and 1961 that criticised the local and central authorities for leniency towards the growth of religious activism and proposed a programme for a clampdown on religion. After 1961, when Khrushchev announced that Soviet citizens were standing on the threshold of communism, religion was held to play the part of an ideological adversary. The materialist outlook was promoted as an essential element in the 'moral code of the builder of Communism'. Religion was once again held to be a 'survival of the past', which prevented Soviet citizens from 'fully developing their creative powers'.[45] Press, school, local authorities, Soviet intelligentsia, artists, secret police and medical workers were held responsible for helping Soviet citizens to purge from themselves this 'survival of the past'. Women, children and young people in general were explicitly targeted in what can be seen as a 'battle for souls'. Khrushchev supported the revival of the anti-religious propaganda which had been suppressed during late Stalinism.[46] The 1960s saw the emergence of an explicitly atheistic journal, *Nauka i religiya* (Science and Religion), in 1962, a party-sponsored Society for the Dissemination of Political and Scientific Knowledge, and a network of local groups for atheistic propaganda (*otdel politprosveshcheniya*).[47]

As in the 1920s, the party started the campaign with an attack on popular pilgrimage and the monasteries. Secret instructions of 1959 commanded that pilgrimages to holy places were to be halted and limits were to be placed on monasticism in the Soviet Union. While the Roman Catholic and Old Believer monasteries were to be closed immediately, the Orthodox monasteries and convents were to be gradually suppressed.[48] Some Orthodox convents were less lucky than others. For example, the authorities in Zhitomir oblast' in Ukraine closed the local Obruchskii convent in less than 24 hours, providing vans and police enforcement; 62 nuns had to leave the convent immediately, with no idea as to where they could go. On the morning after this expulsion, the authorities opened a children's clinic in the former convent.[49] In other places, the authorities encountered a robust resistance. In Moldavia, people living near Rechul'skii convent anticipated the actions of the authorities and organised a 24-hour patrol around the convent. When the police approached, the crowd attacked them with pitchforks and stones. Some people were injured, and one was killed.[50]

The authorities promised to resettle the nuns in other convents which were to remain open, but they rarely did so. In 1959 the Vilnius authorities transferred 28 nuns from Mariinskii convent to the neighbouring Svyatodukhovskii monastery, situated in the centre of Vilnius, where nuns had to share the buildings with monks. However, the fear of creating a larger and more dangerous religious organisation in the centre of the city prompted Vilnius communists to send nuns to the Pyukhtitsy convent in neighbouring Estonia.[51] The reason for the failure to reaccommodate all the nuns from the closed convents, despite the promise made to the Church, was that the party was really aiming at the eventual closure of all monasteries in the Soviet Union.

Pyukhtitsy convent remained under the threat of closure during the entire six years of Khrushchev's campaign. However, it survived perhaps because it was used as the 'show-monastery' for foreign visitors who had to be persuaded that there was no religious persecution in the Soviet Union.[52] Yet Pyukhtitsy convent also suffered from Khrushchev's crackdown on religion. It could not accept any new novices between 1959 and 1964, it had to pay increased taxes, and it lost some of its land. In 1963 the representative of the Council for

Church Affairs, Yakov Kanter, alerted the leadership of the Estonian republic to the economic cooperation between the convent and the local *sovkhoz*, pointing out that the convent provided an extra work-force for the *sovkhoz*, while the latter sent their tractors to the convent's fields: 'What a sweet partnership!', he stated with irony. 'The *sovkhoz* helps the convent with its agriculture, and by doing this it helps it to continue its [religious] "activities". This is an abnormal and unacceptable situation!'[53] The *sovkhoz*'s attitude to the nuns changed dramatically after the party's dressing down. In 1964 the new leader-ship of the *sovkhoz* announced a plan to cut off a portion of the convent's land and use the site for a kindergarten, perhaps hoping that the sight of children would remind the nuns of their more 'natural' duties as mothers and wives. This plan did not succeed, however, because of the energetic interference of Kanter, who was more con-cerned about the potential dangers of such an arrangement for the children who would be in close proximity to the convent.[54]

Khrushchev's campaign affected not only the female religious, but also lay women. The secret party instructions to the local authorities emphasised that religious organisations should not have any special activities in relation to women, including prayer groups, women-only meetings, charities and choirs.[55] Special attention was paid to religious families. Il'ichev argued that the family was the primary institution responsible for the survival of religion.[56] To act as a counterweight, schools had to ensure that children had a sufficient dose of anti-religious propaganda.[57] Children were not allowed to attend church services, and police raided churches to check whether people under the age of 18 were present. An Old Believer priest, now in his fifties, remembers that during these raids he and other children used to hide under a heap of coats in the church.[58] Pressure was placed on priests not to carry out baptisms,[59] and nurses and doctors in local maternity clinics made pregnant women promise that they would not baptise their infants.[60]

Anti-religious propaganda targeted religious mothers, pointing out that women were responsible for religious education in the family.[61] Khrushchev's campaigns made it clear that the religiousness of women and children were two sides of the same coin. The propaganda placed little emphasis on the role of fathers and other male members of the family in the religious education of children. This accords with the per-sistence of the identification of women with the private sphere in the Soviet Union under Khrushchev. The harmful influence of religious mothers (not all of whom could be isolated from their children) was to be confronted with the positive influence of the socialist collective. The Soviet school was to serve as a healthy counterweight to the mother–child relationship. Yet in the 1960s, as presented by anti-religious propaganda, it was not teachers who served as the main anti-religious campaigners in schools, but an egalitarian collective of school students who were intent on 'liberating' their fellow schoolmates from the 'web of religion'. *Nauka i religiya* told of a teenage girl, Mariya Strunnikova, who disappeared from her school and became a secret nun in the sect of the Wanderers, hidden in the cellar of her mother's house. The case was uncovered by the girl's classmates, resulting in her release from the clutches of her sectarian family.[62] A similar line was pursued in V. Tendriakov's novel *An Emergency* (*Chrezvychainoe*), in which a vigilant Komsomol member, Sasha Ivanov, appalled when he came across the diary of his God-fearing fellow student, alerted the anti-religious campaigners in his school, whose activities were reminiscent of Stalin's 'witch-hunts' of the 1930s, to cases of religious belief among students and teachers. Tendriakov also stressed the importance of the Soviet collective in protecting its members. The modern, rational, open and collectivist society was placed in opposition to the private, secretive and traditional family.[63]

De-Stalinisation was characterised by an unrestrained zeal concerning society's transformation. The anti-religious activists did not aim to cast believers out, but wanted to bring them back into society. Journals and films told of former sectarians and committed churchgoers who abandoned this way of life and became normal, optimistic and socially active Soviet citizens. The female characters in these Pygmalion stories served to emphasise the natural female predisposition towards life, society, happiness and love. *Nauka i religiya* told the story of Liza Fenyushkina, a building site worker, who joined an evangelical sect after an accident left her severely disabled. The article explained Liza's involvement with the sect as the result of a lack of social support on the part of her fellow workers. Liza, however, was transformed after a meeting with the local female journalist who had launched a campaign to bring the woman back to the collective. The methods, such as adult education classes, getting her to read atheistic novels and watch anti-religious films, as well as one-to-one conversations, proved successful, and Liza abandoned the sect and started a new life.[64]

The 1960s saw an orchestrated movement of the clergy and laymen publicly renouncing their beliefs. Although these included both women and men, the majority of renegades who produced narratives of their 'conversions' were men.[65] Yet given the focus of anti-religious propaganda on female religiousness, one would expect more stories of this kind to come from women than from men. Perhaps men found themselves more at ease with the self-searching exercise, in which the journey from religion to atheism was presented as a process of obtaining a more authentic masculinity.

Propaganda presented young religious women, such as Liza Fenyushkina, not as enemies, but rather as victims. The cinema of the 1960s produced a narrative pattern that featured in several film scenarios addressing the theme of religion. This emerged after the success of the film *Clouds over Borsk* (*Tuchi nad Borskom*) and can be summarised as follows. An idealistic young woman is a member of a sect or a convent. Her faith is sincere. She may have a broken heart. A young man, who is in love with the female protagonist, is in conflict with his environment. The sect leaders plan to marry the woman to someone she does not love, demand her to sacrifice her love to the young hero, or plan to use her as a human sacrifice. In due course, the young woman experiences a crash of ideals, discovering hypocrisy, lies or greed on the part of the leaders of the sect or Church. She protests against her environment and abandons the sect or convent. Her protest, sometimes accompanied by the tragic deaths of innocent members of the religious community, leads other members of the community to re-evaluate their beliefs.[66]

Propaganda films served to discredit religion and provide legitimacy for the onslaught against Pentecostalists, Jehovah's Witnesses, Baptists and Roman Catholics. The films reinforced the image of a young idealistic female character who yearned for truth, love and fulfilment, but was trapped in a harmful environment. This image evoked sympathy rather than rebuke. The idealism of the protagonist had an affinity with the images of young Komsomol men and women of 1960s cinema, whose religion was communism, not Christianity.

The view of women as victims of religion and the traditional way of life was also a theme of articles and films about Asian women. The 1960s saw a renewed campaign against the shariah law in Central Asian republics, especially against arranged marriages and the veil.[67] In this case, the propagandists accused local men of being perpetrators of the patriarchal laws. They cited cases of bigamy, sexual assault and the misuse of Soviet legislation on marriage, and argued that shariah laws made women more vulnerable to male sexual aggression.[68] An Uzbek poetess, Zul'fiya, appealed to her compatriot women to take off their veils: 'I am appalled by the spiritual deformations that are developing under this seemingly innocent cover, which many still see an exotic oriental feature, as necessary in the Asian setting as the *chaikhana* (tea-house) and *aryk* (well).'[69] Thus the Khrushchev era revived the earlier Soviet campaigns which challenged traditional attitudes and beliefs and promoted the emancipation of women as a symbol of modernity. As in the earlier campaigns, women were presented as victims of patri-archal society and the objects of male manipulation.[70]

The anti-religious discourse addressed in particular the issue of female religiousness, which allows us to analyse the dominant percep-tions about women in the Khrushchev period. In order to explain female piety, the authors of anti-religious brochures argued that apart from the usual lack of education and the age factor, a lack of emotional fulfilment was an important cause for women's attraction to religion. The authors pointed to the prevalence of unmarried women or single mothers in religious communities, explaining this as the result of demographic factors or the irresponsible behaviour of men.[71] Religion was represented as a compensation for trauma and bereavement. Although the authors denied natural causes for female religiousness, they nevertheless emphasised that women had, by nature, a 'height-ened emotional perception' and a desire for beauty.[72] According to them, the clergy and sectarians used these aspects of women's nature to attract them to religion, for example, by drawing women into church choirs. The Soviet response to this was to encourage amateur artistic groups (*khudozhestvennaya samodeyatel'nost'*) which could provide an outlet for women's need for aesthetic fulfilment.

How did women respond to the anti-religious campaigns? During the official attempt to close the Rechul'skii convent, many local women joined the crowds challenging the authorities. Mothers resisted anti-religious propaganda by taking their children out of schools.[73] Sometimes anti-religious propaganda achieved the opposite ends to those intended: women and men used anti-religious literature to educate themselves and to reinforce their beliefs. Ul'yana Glukhova (b. 1931), an Old Believer from a Urals village, learned about world religions and the history of the Church by reading books and brochures intended for the promotion of atheism. She put her knowl-edge to use in the catechisation of other women in the local Old Believer community, as well as in debates with Baptist preachers.[74] The dissident Christian movement of the 1970s produced a rich literature written in a polemical and uncompromising tone, which to some extent replicated the tone and argument of its ideological opponents.[75] Thus, Khrushchev's promotion of atheistic propaganda stimulated the revival of religious debate and catechisation.

Conclusion

The anti-religious campaign receded after Khrushchev was deposed in 1964. By and large, Khrushchev did not manage to achieve his promise to show the Soviet citizens 'the last priest' (*poslednii pop*). The six-year campaign, however, had a lasting impact on Soviet culture, the education system and Church–state relations, leading to a polarisation of the boisterous dissident movement and the tamed church leadership. The party paid special attention to the prevalence of women in congregations in the 1950s and 1960s. Dissatisfied with conventional demographic or existential explanations, Khrushchev's ideologists made a bold attempt to remove religion from the lives of Soviet women.

Material concerns, such as consumption and living standards, were central to the regime's search for legitimacy.[76] Yet in the atmosphere of the XXI Party Congress (1961), ideological aspects of communism were as important as material welfare. The party emphasised the importance of creating a new person who would inherit the perfect society of the future.[77] The New Man and Woman of Khrushchev's utopia were concerned not only with technological advancement and the rationalision of private and public space. They were expected to have spiritual values (*dukhovnye tsennosti*), social ideals and a moral code. The anti-religious campaigns of 1958–64 suggest that the Khrushchev regime was searching for an ideological basis for its existence.

The focus on women during this campaign had pedagogical and disciplinarian dimensions. The party made a commitment to fight religion as a remnant of social injustice and oppression and to bring women to a fulfilling and meaningful life outside the religious fold. Thus by emphasising their liberation from 'the web of religion', Khrushchev's regime asserted a revolutionary role.

Despite the representation of religion as conservative and backward, religious organisations displayed signs of change in the post-war era. The growth of female-dominated non-established religious groups was a response to urbanisation and migration. De-Stalinisation had a stirring effect on traditional hierarchies within communities. The Church's encouragement of female religious activism can be seen as a response to the secular discourse on women's emancipation.

The anti-religious campaign was a logical extension of the iconoclasm of de-Stalinisation, aimed at erasing religion from the culture of the 1960s, which had elements of demystification and carnival. When the 'mysterious heavens' were 'conquered' by a mortal woman astronaut, the last veil was removed from the face of the world. Yet the self-presentation of Soviet society did not reflect the diversity of female experience in this period. The image of an agnostic, emancipated woman striving for human happiness and professional fulfilment, produced by the secular culture of the Khrushchev era, competed with images maintained by religious institutions and popular memory. These images of self-denying saints, devout nuns and humble mothers and wives seeking spiritual experience and redemption retained their appeal to women in the age of space travel and communist utopia.

Notes

1　I. Ermakov, *Kommunizm i religiya* (Moscow, 1964), p. 82.
2　She was contrasted with Jerrie Cobb, the American woman pilot who was training to become an astronaut around the same time as Tereshkova. The Soviet press scoffed at Cobb's piety as presented in the American book *A Woman in Space*: 'One of the photographs in the book portrays the woman pilot at prayer. She kneels before the crucifix. The Bible lies on the table in front of her. Jerrie prays for good luck.' Tereshkova, when shown the photograph, apparently said: 'Jerrie and I have different wings, that's all.' Although never explicitly atheistic, Tereshkova, who had an exemplary biography as a proletarian girl, never deviated from the party line on religion. She had a civil wedding blessed by Khrushchev rather than by a priest, and she did not baptise her daughter, as many women did at that time. M. G. Pismannik, *Otnoshenie religii k zhenshchine* (Moscow, 1964), p. 24.
3　A number of Soviet sociological studies discussed the gender aspects of popular devotion and religious structure. See I. P. Timchenko, *Zhenshchina, religiya, ateizm* (Kiev, 1981); N. P. Krasnikov (ed.), *Voprosy preodoleniya religioznykh perezhitkov v SSSR* (Moscow, 1966); J. Anderson, 'Out of the Kitchen, out of the Temple: Religion, Atheism and Women in the Soviet Union', in C. Ramet (ed.), *Religious Policy in the Soviet Union* (Cambridge, 1993).
4　T. Chumachenko, *Gosudarstvo, pravoslavnaya tserkov', veruyushchie* (Moscow, 1999), p. 78.
5　Ibid., p. 79.
6　Compare this with Chumachenko's argument about the Church being a 'bearer of national traditions'. Chumachenko, op. cit., p. 123.
7　Stalin continued the persecution of dissenting groups within the Russian Orthodox Church, such as the IPKh (*istinno-pravoslavnye khristiane*) who did not recognise the legitimacy of the Russian patriarch cooperating with the state.
8　Chumachenko, op. cit., pp. 24–6.
9　Ibid., p. 29.
10　According to M. Shkvarovskii, *Russkaya Pravoslavnaya Tserkov' pri Staline i Khrushcheve* (Moscow, 1999), p. 357, at least one-third of all infants born in the RSFSR were baptised in the 1950s. On the growth of religious sentiment

in post-war Russia, see E. Zubkova, *Russia after War: Hope, Illusions and Disappointments, 1945–57* (Armonk, 1998).

11 Shkvarovskii, op. cit., p. 357.

12 C. Lane, *Christian Religion in the Soviet Union* (London, 1978), pp. 140–1 and Appendix A.

13 Ibid., p. 149.

14 On female devotion in nineteenth-century Russia, see B. Meehan Waters, *Holy Women of Russia* (New York, 1996).

15 V. B. Zhiromskaya, I. N. Kiselev and Yu. A. Polyakov, *Polveka pod grifom 'sekretno'. Vsesoyuznaya perepis' naseleniya 1937g.* (Moscow, 1996), p. 104.

16 Teplyakov, cited in Anderson, op. cit., p. 208. Our data do not support Anderson's argument that more women were found in Orthodox than Baptist congregations.

17 Again, our data do not support Anderson's argument that a higher proportion of women were found in Orthodox congregations than non-Orthodox groups.

18 Partei Arhiiv (Estonian Communist Party archive), f. 1, n. 163, s. 11, l. 161.

19 Riigiarhiiv (Estonian National Archive), R-1989, n. 2s, s. 16, ll. 28–32. Anderson, op. cit., p. 208.

20 For a summary of the Soviet argument see Anderson, op. cit., pp. 209–11.

21 Ibid., p. 210.

22 Ibid.

23 I am using here the argument of C. Lane that the anomic situation of the developing society stimulated the growth of Baptism, and applying it to women.

24 See B. Engel, *Between the Fields and the City: Work, Women and Family in Russia, 1861–1914* (Cambridge, 1994).

25 IPKh was an especially active eschatological rumour-mill. GADPRPO, f. 1, op. 1, d. 10391.

26 I. Korovushkina Paert, 'Memory and Survival in Stalin's Russia: Old Believers in the Urals during the 1930–50s , in P. Thompson and D. Bertraux (eds), *On Living through Soviet Russia* (Routledge, forthcoming).

27 A. Kefeli, 'The Role of Tatar and Kriashen Women in the Transmission of Islamic Knowledge, 1800–70', in R. Geraci and M. Khodarkovsky (eds), *Of Religion and Empire: Missions, Conversion and Tolerance in Tsarist Russia* (Ithaca, NJ, 2001), pp. 250–73.

28 Lane, op. cit., p. 163. About 70 per cent of all Baptist membership had blood ties.

29 On the role of the family in maintaining Old Believer faith see I. Korovushkina Paert, 'Popular Religion and Local Identity during the Stalin Revolution: Old Believers in the Urals (1928–41)', in D. Raleigh (ed.), *Provincial Landscapes: the Local Dimensions of Soviet Power* (Pittsburgh, 2001).

30 GASO, f. R-233, op. 1, d. 1278, ll. 69–70. I am using the results of the surveys carried out at schools in the Urals in 1929.

31 The title for the convent 'Pyukhtitsy' (both 'Pyukhtitsa' and 'Pyukhtitsy' are acceptable) originates from the Estonian word *Püha* – holy.

32 Partei Arhiiv, f. 1, n. 163, s. 12, l. 4.

33 Ibid., l. 1.

34 Ibid., l. 3.

35 Prior to 1953 the convent possessed 178.9 hectares of land, including 29.4 as ploughed fields, 48.3 as hayfield, 54.1 as pasture land and 12.5 as woodland. Ibid., 1. 4.

36 Ibid., l. 20. N. N. Sokolova, *Pod krovom vsevyshniago* (Novosibirsk, 1998), p. 290.

37 Riigiarhiiv, f. R 1961, n.1, s. 115, l. 4.

38 Partei Arkhiiv, f. 1, n. 163, s. 12, l. 10. On *klikushi* and the phenomenon of *klikushestvo* see C. Worobec, *Possessed: Women, Witches and Demons in Imperial Russia* (Illinois, 2001).

39 Riigiarchiiv, f. R-1961, n. 1, s. 68, ll. 66–8.

40 See the discussion of the ascetic concept of manliness in I. Korovushkina Paert, 'Gender and Salvation: the Old Believers in Imperial Russia' in L. Edmondson (ed.), *Gender in Russian History and Culture, 1880–1990* (Basingstoke, 2001).

41 Riigiarhiiv, f. R-1961, n. 1, s. 68, l. 17.

42 Ibid., l. 21.

43 Chumachenko, op. cit., pp. 180–1.

44 Ibid., pp. 197–200.

45 *Pravda*, 18 October 1962. See also D. A. Lowrie and W. C. Fletcher, 'Khrushchev's Religious Policy, 1959–64', in R. H. Marshall (ed.), *Aspects of Religion in the Soviet Union, 1917–67* (Chicago, 1971), pp. 133–4.

46 D. Peris, *Storming the Heavens: the Soviet League of the Militant Godless* (Ithaca, 1998).

47 For more on this, see Lowrie and Fletcher, op. cit., pp. 135–43.

48 Riigiarhiiv, R-1989, n.2, s. 23, l. 7, Chumachenko, op. cit., p. 201.

49 Chumachenko, op. cit., p. 203.

50 Ibid., p. 204.

51 Riigiarhiiv, f. R-1961, n. 1, s. 131, l. 22.

52 Ibid., l. 6. For example, in 1962 and 1963 the convent had received several foreign delegations, including those from the Protestant churches in France, Church of Brethren from the USA, the delegation of the Constantinople Patriarchy, Malabar Church in India and the representatives of the South-East Asian Christian Conference from Indonesia. The convent invited the guests to participate in church services, treated them with dinners and rang all the bells to greet them.

53 Ibid., l. 13.

54 Ibid., l. 24.

55 Riigiarhiiv, f. R-1989, n. 2, s. 25, l. 58.

56 Pismannik, op. cit., p. 32.

57 Lowrie and Fletcher, op. cit., p. 135.

58 Interview with Fr Leontii (Nizhnii Tagil, 8 November 1999).

59 Lowrie and Fletcher, op. cit., pp. 138–9.

60 Data from interview with Old Believer women in Nizhnii Tagil (November 1999).

61 Pismannik, op. cit., pp. 32–3.

62 A. Romanov, 'Bez vesti propavshie', *Nauka i religiya*, no. 5, 1963, pp. 60–4.

63 Compare with the rhetoric of rationalising domesticity, S. E. Reid, 'Cold War in the Kitchen: Gender and the De-Stalinization of Consumer Taste in the Soviet Union under Khrushchev', *Slavic Review*, vol. 61, no. 2, 2002, pp. 242–9.

64 'Trudnym putem', *Nauka i religiya,* no. 7, 1963, pp. 71–4.

65 See articles in *Nauka i religiya,* and single volumes of the 'conversion' stories.

66 A number of films produced in the 1960s were inspired by *Tuchi nad Borskom* (Mosfilm, 1960), dir. Vasilii Ordynskii; *Greshnitsa* (Mosfilm, 1962), dir. F. Filippov; *Tsvetok na kamne* (Dovzhenko, 1962), dir. S. Paradjanov; *Obmanutye* (Riga, 1961), dirs A. Neretniek, M. Rudzitis; *Armageddon* (Moldova-film, 1962), dir. M. Izrailev.

67 Kh.-M. Khashaev, *Perezhitki shariata i vrednykh adatov* (Makhachkala, 1963), p. 14. On earlier communist unveiling campaigns in Soviet Central Asia, see D. T. Northrop, '*Hujum:* Unveiling Campaigns and Local Responses in Uzbekistan, 1927', in Raleigh, op. cit., pp. 125–45.

68 Khashaev, op. cit., pp. 14–15.

69 Zul'fiya, 'Snova o zhenshchine v parandzhe', *Nauka i religiya,* no. 11, 1961, pp. 34–5.

70 G. Massell, *The Surrogate Proletariat: Muslim Women and Revolutionary Struggle in Soviet Central Asia, 1919–29* (Princeton, 1974).

71 Pismannik, op. cit., p. 30.

72 Ibid., pp. 31–2.

73 Ibid., p. 35.

74 Interview with Ul'yana Glukhova (the names are changed) (14 July 1998) Elovo, Perm' oblast'.

75 On Christian dissident literature see M. Meerson-Aksenov and B. Shragin (eds), *The Political, Social and Religious Thought of Russian Samizdat: an Anthology* (Belmont, Mass., 1977).

76 Reid, op. cit., p. 212.

77 *Programma Kommunisticheskoi partii Sovetskogo Soyuza,* part 2, v, 1. *Pravda,* 30 July 1961.

11
The Cold War and the Cosmos: Valentina Tereshkova and the First Woman's Space Flight

Sue Bridger

On 12 April 1961, Soviet scientists stamped their undisputed supremacy on the race to conquer space with the successful launch of the world's first manned spacecraft. The single orbit of the Earth by a craft in which Yuri Gagarin never actually took the controls captured world imagination and propelled its hero on a ceaseless tour of international capitals. Two years later adulatory crowds were still turning out to greet the 'Columbus of Space', the Russian with the extraordinary smile, when his equally charming compatriot hit the headlines. On 16 June 1963, Valentina Tereshkova, a textile worker from the ancient town of Yaroslavl, became the first ever woman to fly in space.

The American response to Gagarin's triumph was immediate. In the Cold War climate of the time, space research, however much it might appear to be a matter of human endeavour and personal glory, had massive military implications. American dismay at Soviet technical superiority in the field of rocket science was instantly translated into dollars. Just seven weeks after Gagarin's flight, President John F. Kennedy was using his State of the Union address to announce a gigantic expansion of the US space programme. Making an 'urgent request for funding' – no less than 9000 million dollars over the next five years – Kennedy announced that there would be no half measures in America's battle to put a man on the Moon. The determination to invest whatever it took to outstrip Soviet advances was backed by an immediate NASA announcement that they were now aiming to send a three-man team to the Moon by 1967.[1]

In Kennedy's epoch-making speech to Congress, any antagonistic implications of this decision were tempered in the light of his imminent meeting with Khrushchev in Vienna. Assuring the USSR of America's good intentions, Kennedy took the moral high ground in a passage complete with biblical quotations:

> We will make it clear that America's concern is for both freedom and peace; that we are anxious to live in harmony with the Russian people; that we seek no conquests, no satellites, no riches; and that we seek only the day when 'nation shall not lift up sword against nation, neither shall they learn war any more'.[2]

A week later in Vienna, Kennedy outlined to Khrushchev a proposal for a joint Soviet–American expedition to the Moon. Yet, in the grave climate of crisis over the future of Berlin which lay at the heart of this summit, Khrushchev was quick to refuse.

As the international temperature rose, Kennedy's statements on the subject became markedly less conciliatory. In the public arena, away from the solemnity of Congress, and with the crowd at his feet roaring on its approval, the US President did not flinch from employing language which was far more gung-ho:

> For the eyes of the world now look into space: to the Moon and to the planets beyond. And we have vowed that we shall not see it governed by a hostile flag of conquest, but by a banner of freedom and peace. We choose to go to the Moon, we choose to go to the Moon, we choose to go to the Moon in this decade, and do the other things, not because they are easy, but because they are hard.[3]

The deep mistrust of the Soviet Union and all it stood for implicit in these words was still, in the early 1960s, a pronounced feature not merely of foreign but also of domestic policy within the United States. Though the worst excesses of the McCarthy era might be over, anti-communist hysteria was far from being a thing of the past: as Kennedy was returning from the Vienna summit with Khrushchev, the US Supreme Court was ruling that individual Americans could be prosecuted merely for membership of the Communist Party. In such a climate of intense and potentially deadly rivalry between East and West, it was inevitable that the question of sending women into space would be caught up in moves both to enflame and to defuse the Cold War.

The space race and the spectre of annihilation

In the immediate aftermath of the Second World War and the use against Japan of the first American atom bombs, the USSR, massively damaged by the war itself, had nonetheless poured resources into the development of its own nuclear weapons. With the testing of the first Soviet nuclear device in August 1949, the arms race moved into a second gear as both the USA and USSR raced to develop the hydrogen bomb, a feat achieved by both sides by 1953. Throughout the 1950s work continued on the research and development of delivery systems for the new nuclear armoury. By the mid-1950s, the Americans had developed a substantial force of bombers, such as the B52 and B47, based in Western Europe. The Soviet Union, meanwhile, had, since the late 1940s, placed great emphasis on the development of intercontinental ballistic missiles, a fact which was to become apparent from the very beginnings of the space race. In October 1957 the USSR put its first Sputnik into orbit, an event whose significance went well beyond its historic breaking of the silence of space. For the Americans, the launch of Sputnik 1 had staggering implications: only an extremely powerful missile, one equally capable of delivering a nuclear bomb directly onto American soil, could have propelled Sputnik into orbit. From the very first day of the era of space exploration, the potential military applications of its technology were fearful.

From the mid-1950s, a series of proposals to control the development of nuclear arms or halt nuclear testing were made by both sides, culminating in conferences on both the prevention of surprise attacks and the cessation of nuclear testing towards the end of 1958. Whatever fears had been generated by the nuclear arms race thus far, there was, however, still no consensus that, in the event of nuclear war, there could be no victors. Within the USSR, this was a concept which only began to be aired in the pages of the national press from 1960. Towards the end of the first nuclear decade, East–West negotiations to rein back the awesome power of the new weaponry were ending in stalemate, although the USSR had suspended its own nuclear testing from the spring of 1958. All negotiations in this area, however, were soon to be overtaken by a chain of events which would bring about the most grave occurrences of the Cold War.

Disregarding warnings from the United States, Khrushchev in November 1958 announced that he considered the Potsdam Agreement on the occupation of Berlin by the Big Four to be obsolete. The crisis in international relations triggered by this declaration was to reach a head in the summer of 1961 with the construction of the Berlin Wall and the resumption of nuclear testing by the USSR. Meanwhile, in the same week that the Soviet Union was enjoying the triumph of Gagarin's flight, the United States' new, young President was suffering the indignity of watching the US-backed Bay of Pigs invasion descend into fiasco. This ill-conceived attempt to overthrow Cuba's Fidel Castro was to form the opening chapter in events around this Caribbean island which, in October 1962, would push the world to the very brink of nuclear war. In the wake of the Cuban Missile Crisis, talks on disarmament were rapidly resumed. The spectre of mutual annihilation prompted negotiations for the setting up of the so-called 'hot line' between the White House and the Kremlin and discussions began on a further suspension of nuclear testing. But, within months of the near-Armageddon that was Cuba, more would be needed to assure the shaken peoples of both sides that peace was now their governments' prime concern.

The turning point which produced a sudden thaw in East–West relations and which, by the autumn of 1963, brought about the signing of a nuclear test ban treaty, took place in June of that year. Speaking at the American University in Washington, John F. Kennedy announced a unilateral moratorium on the atmospheric testing of nuclear weapons and talks in Moscow towards an early agreement on a comprehensive test ban treaty. The key indicator of change, however, came in the President's discussion of 'the new face of war' and what this must mean for international relations. The USA and USSR, Kennedy reminded Americans, had never actually been at war with each other. The Soviet people, moreover, had a very particular understanding of what war was about:

No nation in the history of battle ever suffered more than the Russians suffered in the course of the Second World War. At least 20 million lost their lives. Countless millions of homes and farms were burned or sacked. A third of the nation's territory, including nearly two-thirds of its industrial base, was turned into a wasteland – a loss equivalent to the devastation of all this country east of Chicago.[4]

Extending Americans' sympathies towards the Russians, Kennedy's speech marked a dramatic softening of approach towards a near-mortal enemy. From the Russians, a response in kind came just six days later. If the Americans had their youthful and charismatic JFK to give a lead, the Russians could offer a charm offensive of their own: 'Gagarin in a skirt', Valentina Tereshkova.[5]

The aims of 'manned' space flight: why train women?

As the name of Tereshkova was placed firmly in the history books with the launch of Vostok 6 on 16 June 1963, newspaper editors across the USSR must have greeted the first press releases on the country's latest heroine with undisguised delight. As purveyors of the Communist Party's ideological preoccupations to the nation, journalists at once discovered that Valentina Tereshkova had virtually done their job for them. She was born in 1937 on a collective farm in Yaroslavl region, her mother a dairy woman, her father a tractor driver. With her father's death on active military service at the beginning of the war, her mother struggled to care for the children in the village until, in 1945, she moved to be near relatives in the textile town of Yaroslavl itself. From a background such as this, Valentina became both the caring daughter and the exemplary young Soviet citizen. Leaving school as soon as she could to earn money for her family in the textile factory, she continued her studies part-time, joined the Komsomol and was entrusted with responsibility within its ranks and, decisively for her future career, took up the adventurous sport of parachuting. She was the textbook all-round Soviet woman: the responsible worker, the dutiful follower of the party, the loving daughter, the active participant in sports. Her biography wonderfully combined the key symbols of Soviet development: the union of the city and the village, the tragic losses of the Second World War, the diversity and opportunity of post-war Soviet lifestyles. She was virtually a walking embodiment of the progress of the working people and the equality of women under Soviet rule; to cap it all, she even lived on 8 March Street.

Yet women's space flight at the time was very far from being a product of Soviet determination to score propaganda points on the issue of gender equality. While it was undoubtedly true that the history of space exploration throughout the 1960s was dominated by the scramble to chalk up a series of firsts – the first manned flight, the first group flight, the first women's flight, the first three-man flight, the first space walk, the first moon landing – there was, equally, a longer-term goal in mind. The prize at the end of this particular race, quite apart from the military spin-offs, was the issue of the colonisation of space. If space was now seen as the new frontier with potentially unbounded riches and uses to be explored and exploited, this would, it was assumed, ultimately require humans to take up residence far beyond the Earth's atmosphere. The notion that, in due course, this would be entirely possible gave rise to the massive optimism, the sense of science marching irresistibly onwards, with which not merely the world's press but also leading scientists greeted Tereshkova's achievement. Sir Bernard Lovell, for example, senior British radio astronomer and director of the experimental station at Jodrell Bank, declared his opinion that her flight represented part of a Soviet plan to colonise another part of the solar system within 25 years. Their main object, he said, would be Mars, which had the least hostile environment. The problem of living there would be no greater than living in a jet airliner at 30,000 feet.[6]

In fact, though it was not widely advertised at the time, the Americans, evidently taking a similar view, had recruited no less than 13 women astronaut candidates in 1960, two years earlier and almost three times the size of the group training in the USSR. The advanced nature of their plans had become known to the Soviets in the spring of 1962 as General Nikolai Kamanin, head of cosmonaut training and a major Soviet advocate of women's space flight, accompanied German Titov, the Soviet Union's second cosmonaut, on a visit to the USA. Here the first American astronaut, John Glenn, invited them to his home and obligingly confirmed that the US also had women currently in training and were planning a women's flight in the second half of that year. Kamanin's response to this was to accelerate the training programme of his women's team with a view to creating a lead in the space race which would look unassailable. If Kamanin, however, regarded women's space flight as an important demonstration of the Soviet view of gender equality, his position was by no means universally supported.

Despite the USSR's remarkable history of women fighter pilots in the Second World War and the widespread participation of women in parachuting and sports aviation, there was nothing inevitable about women's inclusion in the ranks of trainee cosmonauts. Indeed, it seems doubtful that a decision would have been taken to train women at all had it not been for the conviction of Nikolai Kamanin that women would inevitably fly in space one day, in which case the first of them ought to be a citizen of the USSR. For Kamanin, such a position was at least as much about Soviet patriotism as it was about gender equality and it was from this perspective that his determined advocacy of women cosmonauts ultimately won the day. Throughout 1961, in the months following Gagarin's flight, Kamanin waged an unremitting battle against staunch opposition to secure a decision in favour of recruiting women.

In the first place, no progress could be made without the agreement of the chief designer of Soviet spacecraft, Sergei Korolev, a man who has been characterised by those around him at the time as viewing the prospect of women in space as anything from a distraction to an abomination.[7] Alongside Korolev came an entire phalanx of senior scientific, military and political figures, up to and including the Minister of Defence, Marshal Rodion Malinovsky, whom it was necessary to convince of the advantages of such a scheme. By the time the plans to recruit women cosmonauts had received the blessing of the Central Committee Presidium in December 1961, Kamanin was, not surprisingly, describing the event as 'a great personal victory for me'.[8] Finally, despite this tortuous process of gaining consent, and the efforts involved in the accelerated training of the women's team, the entire issue of sending a woman into space was again called into question as late as March 1963. This time the opposition within the Central Committee was led by no less a figure than Khrushchev's effective second-in-command, Frol Kozlov, who demanded, 'What do we need this for? Who said you could train women?' This antagonism led to what Kamanin sarcastically described as an 'inspired' fudge by the Central Committee Presidium two days later to link the women's flight to a longer and more complex flight by a man, a procedure for which neither the men nor the rockets were ready.[9]

This lack of enthusiasm from key men in the space programme and high-ranking Soviet politicians towards sending women into space was, perhaps, scarcely surprising given the embryonic state of manned space flight. In 1961, the entire programme was in its infancy and relatively little was known about the effects of prolonged weightlessness on the human body. Substantial concern had been expressed before Gagarin's flight, not least by Khrushchev himself, about the potential damage to the human mind which might be caused by the stress of isolation in space.[10] Given these understandable anxieties, politicians could be forgiven for concluding that a women's flight was simply premature: should anything go wrong the potential propaganda triumph could turn in seconds into a public relations disaster. For an administration pulling back from the brink of nuclear war it might very easily appear to be one problem too many: why risk reputations any further in a programme which, by its very nature, was constantly dealing with the unknown? Nevertheless, on 14 June 1963, Major Valery Bykovsky left the launch pad in his Vostok 5 spacecraft for what was to be the longest flight to date of any man in space: an achievement which was to be instantly overshadowed two days later with the launch of Vostok

6. Over the next three days, the excitement aroused in the international media by the USSR's latest 'group flight' was to focus almost entirely on the fact that Vostok 6 was piloted by Valentina Tereshkova, the first woman in space.

Inevitably, in the rush to greet the USSR's latest heroine, however, after her triumphant landing such reservations were rapidly forgotten and the chance to trumpet the Soviet approach to equality was eagerly seized. The concerns and prejudices of these early days did not, however, simply melt away with Tereshkova's success and they were to bedevil the future of women's space flight in the Soviet Union through the 1960s and beyond.

A 'Seagull' in orbit – harbinger of peace

As Valentina Tereshkova, 'Seagull' as she was known by her radio call sign, stood on the podium in Red Square enjoying the adulation of the crowds, her widowed mother beside her, the message of peace was already the hallmark of the entire theatrical event of which she was the centre. For the Soviet population, the day on which she took the capital by storm could scarcely have been more significant: it was 22 June, 22 years to the day since the Nazi invasion of the USSR. It was a piece of timing which provided the perfect Cold War symbolism: while a woman in space, encircling the planet with her charming smile, had displayed her nation's most peaceful intentions, the politicians were now at liberty to point out that this was not the peace of the cowardly appeaser but of the resolute defender. Those who had dared to trample on Soviet soil in 1941 had, in due course, reaped the whirlwind: the same could be expected by any power daring to threaten the country's borders a generation later. Having paid his respects to the sacrifice of Tereshkova's father, Nikita Khrushchev linked the invasion anniversary to the massive technological progress the USSR had just amply demonstrated: 'Everyone understands perfectly well, of course, that if the Soviet Union possesses rockets such as these which can orbit the Earth with such extraordinary accuracy, then the Soviet Union also possesses rockets of a different type.'[11]

The threatening implications of Tereshkova's achievement were never to be underlined, however, by the cosmonaut herself. Standing alongside her colleague in the group flight, Lieutenant-Colonel Valery Bykovsky, her simple summer dress was in stark contrast to his military uniform. Though she held the rank of junior lieutenant it had been agreed at Politburo level that she should not wear uniform and should be referred to as 'Miss Tereshkova' in briefings to the foreign press. In her carefully scripted speech in Red Square her family's experiences became symbols of the sufferings of the entire Soviet people:

> I know all too well what war means. My father died at the front defending the independence of our beloved Motherland. My mother was left to bring up three children and we experienced all the bitterness of such a great loss. ... Every person in this land knows what war is – it means grief and tears for millions. We don't want war. Soviet people are busy with peaceful, creative work.[12]

It was a theme she was to repeat again and again in the years which followed.

Two days after the celebrations on Red Square, Tereshkova was stepping onto another podium as guest of honour at the World Congress of Women on its opening day in Moscow. The theme of women and peace was, as ever, uppermost in this gathering of women from the international communist women's movement. Who better than this young textile worker, the only woman to have seen Planet Earth from space, to declare the need to protect its beauty from the madness of war?

> I looked at our wonderful Earth and thought, 'we must not let this shining blue planet be covered in black atomic dust'. And as I flew on, I thought how good it would be if my Vostok 6, this 'female' space craft, could make an invisible but powerful bridge between the hearts of all the women on Earth.[13]

The idea of the uniqueness of her experience in space giving this 'simple Russian girl', as she was constantly called, the right to plead for peace in the international arena was too good to waste on those who were guaranteed to agree with her. Charming the crowds across three continents with a vivacity only matched by Gagarin's dazzling smile, Tereshkova began to fit naturally and gracefully into the role of unofficial but highly effective goodwill ambassador.

Women in space – a model of equality?

Though the process of decision-making which had eventually sent a woman into space scarcely reflected any credit onto a state with an avowed commitment to gender equality, this was not to stop its leadership exploiting the mileage to be made from Tereshkova's achievement. While her group-flight partner, Valery Bykovsky, now held the record for the longest space flight, Tereshkova in her three days in space had failed by only seven minutes to equal the achievement of Pavel Popovich whose flight was the third-longest made to date. Her time in space of course far outstripped the records of the space pioneers, Gagarin and Titov, but, far more importantly, dwarfed the achievements of the American men. Her flight of 48 orbits in a time of 22 hours 50 minutes more than doubled the American record held by Gordon Cooper. Statistics such as these clearly delighted Khrushchev who, in his Red Square speech, indulged in a characteristic piece of gloating:

> Her flight lasted longer than all the American astronauts together have spent in space. (Applause) That's the 'weaker sex' for you. (Stormy applause) ... The name of Valentina Vladimirovna will go down in world history. She has demonstrated once again that women raised under socialism walk alongside men in all the people's concerns, both in self-sacrificing labour and in heroic feats which amaze the world.[14]

While the Soviet leadership clearly had reservations in practice about women taking their place 'alongside men', whatever the rhetoric, they could still appear remarkably radical by comparison with Western politicians. In 1963 gender equality was far from being taken for granted on the other side of the Cold War divide. Even as Vostok 6 returned to earth, discussion of the Soviet model of equality could be heard in some surprising places.

In the United States the question of equal rights was at the forefront of the political agenda in the early summer of 1963, yet it was race, not gender, which took centre stage. From the earliest months of the Kennedy presidency challenges to race discrimination across the south had produced vicious acts of retaliation by whites. In May 1961, as the President's attention was focused on defusing the tensions of the Cold War and on securing funding for the race to the Moon in the wake of Gagarin's flight, the American Nazi Party's 'Hate Bus' was touring the deep south and the Governor of Alabama was refusing to give the Attorney General, Robert Kennedy, any assurance that law and order would be maintained as mobs attacked a church where Martin Luther King was speaking. Two years on, the summer once more brought serious unrest across the south during which the black civil rights leader, Medgar Evers, was assassinated. On the day Tereshkova and Bykovsky returned to earth, Evers, the D-Day veteran shot by a sniper in Mississippi, was buried in Arlington National Cemetery with the words 'no soldier buried in this field has fought more courageously'. On this same day, John F. Kennedy presented his sweeping Civil Rights Act to Congress, paving the way for an end to 'the wrongs inflicted on Negro citizens' in employment and education.[15]

In this climate, though Kennedy had found the time to send congratulations to Khrushchev on an achievement which would 'excite the imagination of all people', the question of gender equality was some way from the top of the American political agenda. Indeed, by comparison with the Depression years, the affluence of sixties America made it tempting to characterise women's lives as completely unproblematical in a feel-good era of consumer spending and household gadgetry. It would be some time before the 'nameless, aching dissatisfaction' of apparently comfortably settled housewives and mothers described by Betty Friedan in her interviews with American women in the early 1960s translated itself into widespread action.[16] Meanwhile, in this same June of 1963, the Conservative government in Britain, buoyed for so long by a similar wave of post-war prosperity, was floundering in the extraordinary farce of the Profumo scandal and both political and spiritual leaders were preoccupied with questions of morality.

For British women of the time, the uncomfortable realities of life for the economically dependent housewife were nowhere more apparent than in the reports from the divorce courts so assiduously reported in the national press. In the very week of Tereshkova's flight, the House of Lords was faced with an unprecedented proposal to introduce the concept of no-fault divorce. In place of a detailed examination of the 'matrimonial offence' by the courts, often involving stage-managed and humiliating testimony on the presence of the husband in a hotel with 'a woman not his wife', it was suggested that prolonged separation might equally be taken as evidence of the breakdown of a marriage. The fact that this separation should be for a minimum period of seven years did not prevent the bitter opposition of the bishops to this dilution of the nation's morals. For women whose economic dependence on men was not sanctified by a wedding ring a mixture of condemnation and prurient fascination could be expected. Day after day the startling revelations of the Profumo affair with its heady mix of aristocratic high jinks and the treatment of lower-class women as sexual playthings filled the press and television, prompting calls for 'Moral Re-Armament' and a declaration by the Archbishop of York that 'the nation needs guidance'.[17]

For those determined to force this issue of the economic discrimination faced by women onto the political agenda, Valentina Tereshkova's space flight was manna from heaven. Five hours after Tereshkova descended by parachute onto the steppes of Kazakhstan, Edith Summerskill, doctor, former chair of the Labour Party and relentless fighter for women's rights for over 25 years, rose to open a House of Lords debate:

> Thousands of miles away, she said, the Russian woman cosmonaut had returned to earth with her male colleague. The relevance of this to the subject of the debate was that both would be equally feted and would be equally paid the rate for the job. If Valentina had still been in orbit and could have glimpsed into the Chamber she would have been amazed to learn that British women in the second half of the twentieth century still had to plead for the simplest justice. ... Valentina's father was a tractor driver and her mother was a textile worker. But the Soviet Union had a system whereby they recognised intelligence in individuals whether they were men or women, and did not judge them just by their reproductive glands. In Britain a girl in the same position as Valentina had no opportunity of having a scientific training.[18]

Despite the somewhat rosy view of the Soviet approach to equal pay, the illustration served well as a comparison with the dismal situation of women in the British workforce and the 'financial disabilities' of women who were not employed outside the home.

The responses to Lady Summerskill's speech made it clear that progress would not be achieved overnight. Lords both spiritual and temporal were alarmed that, in the rush for economic independence, women might be 'tempted away from their home responsibilities' and that men might be expected to attempt 'all sorts of domestic jobs'. 'You cannot run a home on tinned food', declared Lord Amwell, while the Earl of Longford, speaking up for women, helpfully offered the observation that they were 'still denied access to the main staircase of the Carlton Club'. In conclusion, Edith Summerskill expressed her gratitude for a small crumb of comfort from the government: a reforming Bill would be introduced to allow non-employed married women to keep some of the savings they made from their housekeeping allowance. It seemed safe to assume, in the light of such meagre advances, that British women would not be ascending launch pads while staircases were still posing such a problem.[19]

Whatever the ambivalence of the Soviet leadership and scientific community had been towards the reality of women in space, there was clearly a substantial potential propaganda value to their achievements. As Valentina Tereshkova embarked on tour after tour, her natural abilities as a public speaker and unofficial diplomat provided the USSR with a much-needed 'human face'. Not only could both her experiences and her public image be successfully exploited as a persuasive argument for world peace, but her private life apparently spoke volumes for the future of women's space flight. Her marriage by the end of the year to her cosmonaut colleague, Andrian Nikolaev, and the birth of her daughter in 1964 struck another blow for women's independence. Here was a woman who had dared to venture where few men had been, who had, it was constantly observed, retained all of her feminine charm, and who, patently, had emerged from her experience unscathed. Nothing, it seemed, could be more natural than to recognise her achievement by placing her at the head of the socialist bloc's major national women's organisation. In 1968, Valentina Tereshkova became the leader of the Committee for Soviet Women, an institution she was to dominate for the next two decades.

After the first flight – what next for women?

As the admiration for Tereshkova's feat continued to resound around the world, it might have been expected that women would become a fully accepted and integrated part of the Soviet cosmonaut team. Yet, even as she was engaged in a series of successful tours and public engagements through the summer of 1963, the questioning of Tereshkova's achievement and of the wisdom of further flights by women only seemed to gain in intensity. Within the inner circle of the space programme itself controversy soon erupted over the results of the medical monitoring of the flight. The conviction of the doctors that she had suffered from space sickness and that her performance had been under par placed a question mark over any subsequent flights for Tereshkova, despite her own strenuous denials of any difficulties. It was inevitable that all of this would only serve to bolster negativity towards the very concept of further flights by other members of the women's team. From Korolev's perspective, there was no mileage to be gained and potentially much to lose by continuing to schedule women's flights. Put crudely, his attitude could be summed up in his heartfelt sigh of relief to Kamanin when Tereshkova finally touched down: 'just don't let me have anything to do with broads again'.[20]

Only Nikolai Kamanin persisted in championing the women against what was to become some very vocal opposition led by an increasingly frustrated Yuri Gagarin. With his habitual stealthy persistence, Kamanin managed by 1965 to persuade all concerned to schedule a prolonged flight including the first ever women's space walk by Tereshkova's doubles, Irina Solov'eva and Valentina Ponomar'eva. But it was not to be: with Korolev's untimely death in January 1966 the entire Soviet space programme stalled and a women's flight gradually but inexorably slid down the agenda until, in 1969, the women's team was disbanded. It would be a further 13 years before a particularly single-minded test pilot, Svetlana Savitskaya, who already had a track record of taking on the prejudices of the Soviet aviation establishment, broke through to become the second ever woman in space. Curiously, in one of those turns of the circle so characteristic of East–West experiences around gender equality, it would be American women who would be the first to be fully accepted as space flight crew as the 1980s progressed. Exactly 20 years after Tereshkova's flight in the USSR and the publication of Betty Friedan's *The Feminine Mystique* in the USA, the impact of second-wave Western feminism on traditional male bastions had become unmistakable: in 1983 Sally Ride became the first American woman in space to be followed by no less than 26 of her colleagues through the years until Eileen Collins became the first woman to command a spacecraft in 1999.

As for Valentina Tereshkova herself, the new job as head of the Committee for Soviet Women promptly turned her into the dutiful mouthpiece of the Communist Party in its pronouncements on the inherent benefits to women of the Soviet model of emancipation and its preoccupations with the role of women as anti-imperialist agents of peace. By the mid-1980s her parroting of the party line had become a source of intense frustration to Western feminists who attempted to engage with her, producing some unkind, if not entirely undeserved, journalistic criticism: 'she is a triumph of Soviet human engineering, a highly tuned and perfectly programmed robot'.[21] In both the West and the USSR it seemed simply to be assumed that the well-behaved factory Komsomol secretary had been only too willing to use her position as the first woman in space to graduate effortlessly into elite party hack.

Nikolai Kamanin's diaries, however, reveal a rather different story. Summoned to the Central Committee in 1968, Tereshkova was appalled to discover the future they had in mind for her. Five years after her flight she was still working for the space programme, was studying at the Zhukovsky Military Aviation Academy, and fully intending to qualify as an engineer. Though Kamanin had attempted to steer her towards a life of public service, she continued to be entranced by space. Above all, the worldwide struggles of the women's movement simply did not interest her. When the Politburo duly rubber-stamped the decision without her consent she was devastated. Sitting in floods of tears in Kamanin's flat, there was nothing even he could do but lend a sympathetic ear: 'She kept coming back again and again to the same theme, "I've lost everything" – space, the academy, flying, her family, her daughter.'[22]

Four years after her 'cosmic father', Nikita Khrushchev, was swept from power, Valentina Tereshkova had fallen victim to her own success. The very reasons why she ultimately became the preferred candidate for the first women's space flight – her dependability and confidence when speaking in public – had put an end to her career as an engineer. With remarkable irony, the woman who for 20 years represented the ossified Soviet approach to women's emancipation had been forced to give up a career path so often used by Western feminists in those years as a shorthand symbol for progress against male domination of the world of work. Yet, for the Soviet leadership, it was an outcome so obvious as to be scarcely worth debating. As Kamanin so astutely summed the matter up, engineers were two a penny in the Soviet Union but a woman who could appear at ease in Paris or Washington was worth her weight in gold. Laying aside her military uniform for the sober suits of the party bureaucrat Tereshkova became, perhaps more than she had ever been, a serving soldier in the front line of the Cold War.

Notes

1 *The Times*, 26 May 1961, p. 14, and 27 May 1961, p. 7.
2 *The Times*, 26 May 1961, p. 14.
3 Footage of this public speech is included in *Moon Race*, BBC broadcast, 2001.
4 *The Times*, 11 June 1963, p. 10.
5 Numerous people have claimed to be the originator of this ringing phrase. It was, however, certainly employed by Nikolai Kamanin in his private diary to explain why he had formed the view that she was the most likely candidate for the first women's flight. This entry was made in November 1962, long before most people outside the Cosmonaut Training Centre had met Tereshkova. See N. P. Kamanin, *Skrytyi kosmos*, vol. 1 (Moscow, 1995), p. 188.

6   *The Times*, 18 June 1963, p. 12.

7   Korolev's view of women is repeatedly in evidence throughout Kamanin's diaries. Female eyewitnesses who describe their own good relations with him invariably refer to his reputation as someone who had little time for women in his own professional sphere. See, for example, the reminiscences of A. R. Kotovskaya in A. Yu. Ishlinskii (ed.), *Akademik S. P. Korolev: uchenyi, inzhener, chelovek* (Moscow, 1986), p. 478.

8   Kamanin, op. cit., vol. 1, p. 83.

9   Ibid., pp. 238, 240.

10 Ibid., p. 43.

11 *Uchitel'skaya gazeta*, 23 June 1963, p. 2.

12 Ibid.

13 *Pervye v mire* (Moscow, 1987), p. 125.

14 *Uchitel'skaya gazeta*, 23 June 1963, p. 2.

15 *The Times*, 20 June 1963, pp. 10, 12.

16 Betty Friedan, *The Feminine Mystique* (New York, 1963), p. 33.

17 *The Times*, 17 June 1963, p. 6.

18 *The Times*, 20 June 1963, p. 8.

19 Ibid. In the event, however, the gentlemen's clubs proved more impenetrable. Helen Sharman became the first and only British woman in space, joining the Mir expedition in 1991. To this day, Margaret Thatcher remains the only woman permitted to ascend the staircase of the Carlton Club.

20 N. P. Kamanin, *Skrytyi kosmos*, vol. 2 (Moscow, 1997), p. 187.

21 Polly Toynbee, 'I could claim this is an exclusive interview. But I am not sure if you can have an exclusive interview with a computer program', *The Guardian*, 22 October 1984, p. 14.

22 N. P. Kamanin, *Skrytyi kosmos*, vol. 3 (Moscow, 1999), p. 243.

Select Bibliography

Archives

APRK – Arkhiv Prezidenta Respubliki Kazakstana (Presidential Archive, Kazakhstan)

GADPRPO – Gosudarstvennyi arkhiv dokumentov politicheskikh repressii Permskoi oblasti (State Archive of the History of Political Repressions of Perm' Oblast)

GARF – Gosudarstvennyi Arkhiv Rossiiskoi Federatsii (State Archive of the Russian Federation)

GASO – Gosudarstvennyi Arkhiv Sverdlovskoi oblasti (State Archive of Sverdlovsk oblast)

OPDAO – Otdelenie Partiinoi Dokumentatsii Akmolinskoi oblasti (Party Archive of the Akmola region)

Open Society Archives, Budapest, Hungary

Partei Arhiiv (Estonian Communist Party Archive)

RGAE – Rossiiskii Gosudarstvennyi Arkhiv Ekonomiki (Russian State Archives of the Economy)

RGALI – Rossiiskii Gosudarstvennyi Arkhiv Literatury i Iskusstva (Russian State Archive of Literature and Arts)

RGANI – Rossiiskii Gosudarstvennyi Arkhiv Noveishei Istorii (Russian State Archive of Contemporary History)

RGASPI-m – Rossiiskii Gosudarstvennyi Arkhiv Sotsial'no-Politicheskoi Istorii-m (Russian State Archive of Social-Political History, incorporating TsKhDMO – Tsentr khranenii dokumentov molodezhnykh organizatsii – Centre for the Preservation of Youth Organisation Documentation)

Riigiarhiiv (Estonian National Archive)

TsALIM – Tsentral'nyi arkhiv literatury i iskusstva Moskvy (Moscow Central Archive of Literature and Arts)

TsAODM – Tsentral'nyi Arkhiv Obshchestvennykh Dvizhenii Moskvy (Moscow Central Archive of Social Movements)

TsKhDMO – see RGASPI-m

TsMAM – Tsentral'nyi Munitsipial'nyi Arkhiv Moskvy (Central Municipal Archive of Moscow)

Unpublished sources

Brova, S. V., 'Sotsial'nye problemy zhenskogo truda v promyshlennosti. Po materialam sotsiologicheskikh issledovanii na predpriyatiyakh Sverdlovskoi i Chelyabinskoi oblastei' (Candidate dissertation, Sverdlovsk, 1968)

Field, D., 'Communist Morality and Meanings of Private Life in Post-Stalinist Russia, 1953–1964' (PhD dissertation, University of Michigan, 1996)

Harris, S., 'Recreating Everyday Life: Building, Distributing, Furnishing and Living in the Separate Apartment in Soviet Russia, 1950s–1960s' (PhD dissertation, University of Chicago, 2003)

Korobitsyna, M. A., 'Zhenskii trud v sisteme obshchestvennogo truda pri sotsializme' (Candidate dissertation, Sverdlovsk, 1966)

Maloletova, N. P., 'Rabochie legkoi promyshlennosti SSSR v 1945–1965gg. (chislenost' i sostav)' (Candidate dissertation, Moscow, 1970)

Pohl, M., 'The Virgin Lands between Memory and Forgetting: People and Transformation in the Soviet Union, 1954–1960' (PhD dissertation, Indiana University, 1999)

Sagimbaeva, R. M., 'Problemy ispol'zovaniya resursov zhenskogo truda (na materialakh Kazakhskoi SSR)' (Candidate dissertation, Moscow, 1968)

Sakharova, N. A., 'Zhenskie reservy trudovykh resursov gorodov i rabochikh poselkov Ukrainskoi SSR' (Candidate dissertation, Kiev, 1962)

Starodub, V. I., 'Tekhnicheskii progress i trud zhenshchin' (Candidate dissertation, Leningrad, 1966)

State Department Intelligence Reports, 'The Soviet Bloc Exchange Program in 1957' (February 1958)

Newspapers, journals and serials

Akmolinskaya pravda
Arkhitektura SSSR
Current Digest of the Soviet Press
Dekorativnoe iskusstvo SSSR
Iskusstvo
Itogi
The Guardian
Kinovedcheskie zapiski
Kommunist
Komsomol'skaya pravda
Krest'yanka
Krokodil
L'Express
Ladies Home Journal
Le Monde
Life
Literaturnaya gazeta
London Daily Telegraph
Manchester Guardian
Molodoi kommunist
Moskovskaya pravda
Moskovskii khudozhnik
Moskovskii komsomolets
Nauchnye zapiski (Leningradskii Finansovo-ekonomicheskii Institut im. N. A. Voznesenskogo)
Nauka i religiya
New York Mirror

New York Times
Newsweek
Novaya gazeta
Novyi mir
Ogonek
Oktyabr'
Pravda
Problems of Communism
Rabochii krai
Rabotnitsa
Sem'ya i shkola
Sovetskaya pedagogika
Sovetskaya Rossiia
Sovetskaya torgovlya
Sovetskaya yustitsiya
Sovetskaya zhenshchina
Soviet Review
Soviet Woman
The Times
Trud
Tvorchestvo
Uchitel'skaya gazeta
Ural'skii rabochii
US World and News Report
Vestnik statistiki
Voprosy filosofii
Voprosy literatury
Yunost'
Zdorov'e
Zhenshchiny mira

Russian language sources

Abramenko, L. and L. Tormozova (eds), *Besedy o domashnem khozyaistve* (Moscow, 1959)

Abramskii, I. P., *Smekh sil'nykh. O karikaturistakh 'Krokodila'* (Moscow, 1977)

Adzhubei, A., *Te desyat' let* (Moscow, 1989)

Aimermakher, K., G. Bordyugov and I. Grabovskii, *Kul'tura i vlast' v usloviyakh kommunikatsionnoi revolyutsii XX veka* (Moscow, 2002)

Akademia nauk SSSR, *Nvravstvennye printsipy stroitel'ya kommunizma* (Moscow, 1965)

Barkhin, M. G., *Gorod 1945–1970: praktika, proekty, teoriya* (Moscow, 1974)

Bayar, O. and R. N. Blashkevich, *Kvartira i ee ubranstvo* (Moscow, 1962)

Bil'shai, V., *Reshenie zhenskogo voprosa v SSSR* (Moscow, 1956)

Bogdanova, O. S., *Zdorovyi byt sem'i* (Moscow, 1956)

Brezhnev, L. I., *Tselina* (Moscow, 1978)

Burg, D., *Oppozitsionnye nastroeniya molodezhi v godi posle 'Ottepeli'* (Munich, 1962)

Chalin, M., *Moral' stroitel'ya kommunizma* (Moscow, 1963)

Cherednichenko, T., *Tipologiya sovetskoi massovoi kul'tury* (Moscow, 1994)

Cherkasov, G. N., *Sotsial'no-ekonomicheskie problemy intensivnosti truda v SSSR* (Moscow, 1966)

Chumachenko, T., *Gosudarstvo, pravoslavnaya tserkov', veruyushchie* (Moscow, 1999)

Danilova, E. Z., *Sotsial'nye problemy truda zhenshchiny-rabotnitsy* (Moscow, 1968)

Demezer, A. A. and M. L. Dzyuba, *Domovodstvo* (Moscow, 1957)

Dmitrieva, N., *O prekrasnom* (Moscow, 1960)

Ermakov, I., *Kommunizm i religiya* (Moscow, 1964)

Estetika povedeniya i byta: metodicheskie rekomendatsii (Moscow, 1963)

Garanin, L. Ya., *Memuarnyi zhanr sovetskoi literatury: istoriko-teoreticheskii ocherk* (Moscow, 1986)

Gluzhkov, N. I., *Ocherkovaya proza* (Rostov, 1979)

Golod, S. I., *XX vek i tendentsii seksual'nykh otnoshenii v Rossii* (Moscow, 1996)

Golubtsov, V. S., *Memuary kak istochnik po istorii sovetskogo obshchestva* (Moscow, 1970)

Grushin, B. and V. Chikin, *Ispoved' pokoleniya* (Moscow, 1958)

Gryzunova, M. G., *Mezhdunarodnaya demokraticheskaya federatsiya zhenshchin, 1945–1975* (Moscow, 1975)

Gurchenko, L., *Aplodismenty* (Moscow, 1994)

Itogi vsesoyuznoi perepisi (Moscow, 1962)

Kalinina, N. P., *Usloviya truda i osnovnye napravleniya ikh uluchsheniya na pred-priyatiyakh tekstil'noi promyshlennosti* (Moscow, 1969)

Kamanin, N. P., *Skrytyi kosmos*, vol. 1 (Moscow, 1995)

Kamanin, N. P., *Skrytyi kosmos*, vol. 2 (Moscow, 1997)

Kamanin, N. P., *Skrytyi kosmos*, vol. 3 (Moscow, 1999)

Kharchev, A. G., *Sem'ya v sovetskom obshchestve* (Leningrad, 1960)

Khashaev, Kh.-M., *Perezhitki shariata i vrednykh adatov* (Makhachkala, 1963)

Khrushchev, N. S., *O shirokom vnedrenii industrial'nykh metodov, uluchshenii kachestva i snizhenii stoimosti stroitel'stva* (Moscow, 1955)

Kon, I., *Seksual'naya kul'tura v Rossii: klubnichka na berezke* (Moscow, 1997)

Korshunova, E. and M. Rumyantseva, *Prava sovetskikh zhenshchin* (Moscow, 1960)

Kosolapov, S. M. and O. N. Krutova, *Voprosy vospitaniya trudyashchiekhsya v dukhe kommunisticheskoi nravstvennosti* (Moscow, 1961)

Kozlov, A., *Kozel na sakse* (Moscow, 1998)

Krasnikov, N. P. (ed.), *Voprosy preodoleniya religioznykh perezhitkov v SSSR* (Moscow, 1966)

Kuprin, O., *Byt – ne chastnoe delo* (Moscow, 1959)

Lapin, K., *Slovo o materi* (Moscow, 1961)

Lebedeva, V. E. (ed.), *Ot shestidesyatykh k vos'midesyatykh. Voprosy sovremennoi kul'tury* (Moscow, 1991)

Lebina, N., *Povsednevnaya zhizn' sovetskogo goroda: normy i anomalii: 1920/1930 gody* (St Petersburg, 1999)

Lebina, N. and A. Chistikov, *Obyvatel' i reformy. Kartiny povsednevosi zhizni gorozhan* (St Petersburg, 2003)

Lenin, V. I., *Polnoe sobranie sochinenii*, 5th edn (Moscow, 1970), vol. 39

Lifanov, M. I., *Za kommunisticheskii byt* (Leningrad, 1963)

Luppov, I. A., 'Novym zdaniyam – novyi inter'er', in N. I. Matveeva (ed.), *Iskusstvo i byt* (Moscow, 1963)

Marks, K., *Iz rannykh proizvedenii* (Moscow, 1956)
Matveeva, N. (ed.), *Iskusstvo i byt* (Moscow, 1963)
Mervol'f, N. R. (ed.), *Molodye rezhissery sovetskogo kino: sbornik statei* (Moscow, 1962)
Mikhailyuk, V. B., *Ispol'zovanie zhenskogo truda v narodnom khozyaistve* (Moscow, 1970)
Morgun, F. (ed.), *Na zemlyakh tselinnykh* (Alma-Ata, 1955)
Narodnoe khozyaistvo SSSR za 60 let (Moscow, 1977)
Opyt i metodika konkretnykh sotsiologicheskikh issledovanii (Moscow, 1965)
Pap, A. G. et al., *Gigiena zhenshchiny* (Kiev, 1964)
Pervye v mire (Moscow, 1987)
Pismanik, M. G., *Otnoshenie religii k zhenshchine* (Moscow, 1964)
Popovskii, M., *Tretii lishnyi* (London, 1985)
Puti likvidatsii tekuchesti kadrov v promyshlennosti SSSR (Moscow, 1965)
Rabochii klass i tekhnicheskii progress. Issledovanie izmenii v sotsial'noe strukture rabochego klassa (Moscow, 1965)
Rappoport, S. Kh., *Tvorit' mir po zakonam krasoty* (Moscow, 1962)
Razzakov, F., *Seks-simvoly Rossii* (Moscow, 2000)
Rubinov, A., *Intimnaya zhizn' Moskvy* (Moscow, 1991)
Saltanova, R. and N. Kolchinskaya (eds), *Podruga* (Moscow, 1959)
Saltykov, A. ,*O khudozhestvennom vkuse v bytu* (Moscow, 1959)
Savkina, I., *'Pishu sebya...' Avtodokumental'nye zhenskie teksty v russkoi literature pervoi poloviny XIX veka* (Tampere, 2001)
Savosko, V. K. (ed.), *Narodnoe dvizhenie za osvoenie tselinykh zemel' v Kazakhstane*, (Moscow, 1959)
Senyavskii, S. L., *Rost rabochego klassa SSSR (1951–1965gg.)* (Moscow, 1966)
Shishkan, N. M., *Trud zhenshchin v usloviyakh razvitogo sotsializma* (Kishinev, 1976)
Shishkin, A. F., *Osnovy kommunisticheskoi morali* (Moscow, 1955)
Shkvarovskii, M., *Russkaya pravoslavnaya tserkov' pri Staline i Khrushcheve* (Moscow, 1999)
Slavkin, V., *Pamyatnik neizvestnomu stilyage* (Moscow, 1996)
Sokolova, N. N., *Pod krovom vsevyshniago* (Novosibirsk, 1998)
Sotsiologiya v SSSR, vol. 2 (Moscow, 1965)
State Tret'yakov Gallery, *Iskusstvo zhenskogo roda* (Moscow, 2002)
Statistika byudzhetov vremeni trudyashchikhsya (Moscow, 1967)
Strukova, L. (ed.), *Trud, sem'ya, byt sovetskoi zhenshiny* (Moscow, 1990)
Svadkovskii, I. F., *O kul'ture povedeniya sovetskoi molodezhi* (Moscow, 1958)
Sverdlov, G. M., *Sovetskoe zakonadatel'stvo o brake i sem'e* (Moscow, 1961)
Timchenko, I. P., *Zhenshchina, religiya, ateizm: iz opyta preodoleniya religioznosti zhenshchin* (Kiev, 1981)
Trud i razvitie lichnosti (Leningrad, 1965)
Trud v SSSR (Moscow, 1968)
Utekhin, I., *Ocherki kommunal'nogo byta* (Moscow, 2001)
Vail', P. and Genis, A., *60-e. Mir sovetskogo cheloveka* (Ann Arbor, 1988)
Volkov, I. M. (ed.), *Velikii podvig partii i naroda. Massovoe osvoenie tselinnykh i zalezhnykh zemel'. Sbornik dokumentov i materialov* (Moscow, 1979)
Zezina, M. R., *Sovetskaya khudozhestvennaya intelligentsiya i vlast' v 1950-e – 60-e gody* (Moscow, 1999)

Zhanrovo-stilevye problemy sovetskoi literatury (Kalinin, 1986)
Zhenshchiny goroda Lenina (Leningrad, 1963)
Zhenshchiny i deti v SSSR (Moscow, 1969)
Zhenshchiny v revolyutsii (Moscow, 1959)
Zhiromskaya, V. B., I. N. Kiselev and Yu. A. Polyakov, *Polveka pod grifom 'sekretno'. Vsesoyuznaya perepis' naseleniya 1937g.* (Moscow, 1996)
Zhurin, N., *Trudnye i schastlivye gody: Zapiski partiinogo rabotnika* (Moscow, 1982)

Non-Russian language sources

Adams, J. S., *Citizen Inspectors in the Soviet Union* (New York, 1977)
Aksenov, V., *In Search of Melancholy Baby* (New York, 1987)
Alexeyeva, L. and P. Goldberg, *The Thaw Generation* (London, 1990)
Ashwin, S. (ed.), *Gender, State and Society in Soviet and Post-Soviet Russia* (London, 2000)
Atkinson, D., A. Dallin and G. Lapidus, *Women in Russia* (Hassocks, 1978)
Attwood, L., *Creating the New Soviet Woman: Women's Magazines as Engineers of Female Identity, 1922–53* (Basingstoke, 1999)
Attwood, L. (ed.), *Red Women on the Silver Screen: Soviet Women and Cinema from the Beginning to the End of the Communist Era* (London, 1993)
Attwood, L., 'Celebrating the "Frail-figured Welder": Gender Confusion in Women's Magazines of the Khrushchev era', *Slavonica*, vol. 8, no. 2, 2002, pp. 158–76.
Barker, A. (ed.), *Consuming Russia: Popular Culture, Sex, and Society since Gorbachev* (Durham, USA, 1999)
Belfrage, S., *A Room in Moscow* (New York, 1958)
Black, C. (ed), *The Transformation of Russian Society* (Harvard, 1960)
Blekher, F., *The Soviet Woman in the Family and in Society* (New York, 1979)
Bowlt, J. and O. Matich (eds), *Laboratory of Dreams: the Russian Avant-Garde and Cultural Experiment* (Stanford, 1996)
Boym, S., *Common Places: Mythologies of Everyday Life* (Cambridge, Mass., 1994).
Breslauer, G., *Khrushchev and Brezhnev as Leaders: Building Authority in Soviet Politics* (London, 1982)
Brezhnev, L. I., *The Virgin Lands* (trans. R. Daglish) (Moscow, 1978)
Bridger, S., *Women in the Soviet Countryside: Women's Roles in Rural Development in the Soviet Union* (Cambridge, 1987)
Brine, J., M. Perrie and A. Sutton (eds), *Home, School and Leisure in the Soviet Union* (London, 1980)
Brown, D. (ed.), *The Role and Status of Women in the Soviet Union* (New York, 1968)
Brown, J., *Russia Explored* (New York, 1959)
Browning, G., *Women and Politics in the USSR: Consciousness Raising and Soviet Women's Groups* (London, 1987)
Brudny, Y., *Reinventing Russia* (Cambridge, 1998)
Brumberg, A., *Russia under Khrushchev: an Anthology from Problems of Communism* (London, 1962)
Brumfield, W. C. and B. Ruble (eds), *Russian Housing in the Modern Age: Design and Social History* (Cambridge, 1993)

Buchli, V., 'Khrushchev, Modernism, and the Fight against Petit-Bourgeois Consciousness in the Soviet Home', *Journal of Design History*, vol. 10, no. 2, 1997, pp. 161–76

Buchli, V., *An Archaeology of Socialism* (Oxford, 1999)

Buckley, M., *Women and Ideology in the Soviet Union* (London, 1989)

Buckley, M., 'The Untold Story of *Obshchestvennitsa* in the 1930s', *Europe–Asia Studies*, vol. 47, no. 4, 1996, pp. 569–86

Buck-Morss, S., *Dreamworld and Catastrophe* (Cambridge, Mass., 2000)

Burlatsky, F., *Khrushchev and the First Russian Spring: the Era of Khrushchev through the Eyes of his Adviser*, trans. D. Skillen (New York, 1991)

Chatterjee, C., *Celebrating Women: Gender, Festival Culture and Bolshevik Ideology, 1910–1939* (Pittsburgh, 2002)

Chernin, K., *In My Mother's House* (New Haven, 1983)

Clark, K., *The Soviet Novel: History as Ritual*, 3rd edn (Bloomington, 2000)

Cohen, S., A. Rabinowitch and R. Sharlet (eds), *The Soviet Union since Stalin* (Bloomington, 1980)

Courtship of Young Minds: a Case Study of the Moscow Youth Festival (New York, 1959)

Crankshaw, E., *Russia without Stalin* (New York, 1956)

Crankshaw, E., *Khrushchev's Russia* (Harmondsworth, 1959)

Crowe, D. M., Zh. Dzhunusova and S. O. Sabol (guest eds), *Focus on Kazakhstan: History, Ethnicity and Society*, Special Topic Issue, *Nationalities Papers*, vol. 26, no. 3, 1998

Crowley, D. and S. Reid (eds), *Socialist Spaces: Sites of Everyday Life in the Eastern Bloc* (Oxford, 2002)

Dallin, A. and G. Lapidus, *The Soviet System in Crisis* (Boulder, Colo., 1991)

Davies, R., *Soviet History in the Gorbachev Revolution* (London, 1989)

De George, R., *Soviet Ethics and Morality* (Ann Arbor, 1969)

Dodge, N. T., *Women in the Soviet Economy: Their Role in Economic, Scientific and Technical Development* (Baltimore, 1966)

Dunham, V. S., *In Stalin's Time: Middle-Class Values in Soviet Fiction* (Cambridge, 1976)

Edmonds, R., *Russian Vistas* (London, 1958)

Edmondson, L., *Women and Society in Russia and the Soviet Union* (Cambridge, 1992)

Edmondson, L. (ed.), *Gender in Russian History and Culture, 1880–1990* (London, 2001)

Engel, B. A., *Between the Fields and the City: Work, Women and Family in Russia, 1861–1914* (Cambridge, 1994)

Equality of Women in the USSR: Materials of International Seminar (Moscow, 1957)

Field, D., 'Irreconcilable Differences: Divorce and Conceptions of Private Life in the Khrushchev Era', *Russian Review*, vol. 57, no. 4, 1998, pp. 599–613

Filtzer, D., *Soviet Workers and De-Stalinization* (Cambridge, 1992)

Filtzer, D., *The Khrushchev Era: De-Stalinisation and the Limits of Reform in the USSR, 1953–1964* (Basingstoke, 1993)

Filtzer, D., *Soviet Workers and De-Stalinization: the Consolidation of the Modern System of Soviet Production Relations 1953–1964* (Cambridge, 2002)

Fitzpatrick, S., *The Cultural Front* (Ithaca, 1992)

Fitzpatrick, S., *Everyday Stalinism: Ordinary Life in Extraordinary Times: Soviet Russia in the 1930s* (New York, 1999)

Fitzpatrick, S. (ed.), *Stalinism: New Directions* (London, 2000)

Fürst, J., 'Prisoners of the Soviet Self? – Political Youth Opposition in Late Stalinism', *Europe–Asia Studies*, vol. 54, no. 3, 2002, pp. 353–75

Gasiorowka, X., *Women in Soviet Fiction* (Madison, 1968)

Geraci, R. and M. Khodarkovsky (eds), *Of Religion and Empire, Missions, Conversion and Tolerance in Tsarist Russia* (Ithaca, NJ, 2001)

Gilison, J. M., *The Soviet Image of Utopia* (Baltimore, 1975)

Goldman, W. Z., *Women, the State and Revolution: Soviet Family Policy and Social Life, 1917–1936* (Cambridge, 1993)

Gorsuch, A., *Youth in Revolutionary Russia* (Bloomington, 2000)

Goscilo, H. and B. Holmgren (eds), *Russia – Women – Culture* (Bloomington, 1996)

Gray, F. du P., *Soviet Women Walking the Tightrope* (New York, 1989)

Gunther, H., *The Culture of the Stalin Period* (Basingstoke, 1990)

Gunther, J., *Inside Russia Today* (New York, 1957)

Hanson, P., *Advertising and Socialism: the Nature and Extent of Consumer Advertising in the Soviet Union, Poland, Hungary and Yugoslavia* (Basingstoke, 1974)

Hansson, C. and K. Liden, *Moscow Women* (London, 1984)

Haynes, J., *New Soviet Man: Gender and Masculinity in Stalinist Soviet Cinema* (Manchester, 2003)

Henry Art Gallery (Seattle), *Art into Life: Russian Constructivism, 1914–1932*, exh. cat. (Seattle, 1990)

Hessler, J., 'A Postwar Perestroika? Towards a History of Private Enterprise in the USSR', *Slavic Review*, vol. 57, no. 3, 1998, pp. 516–42

Hindus, M., *House without a Roof: Russia after Forty-three Years of Revolution* (London, 1962)

Hodnett, G. (ed.), *Resolutions and Decisions of the Communist Party of the Soviet Union. Vol. 4: The Khrushchev Years 1953–1964* (Toronto, 1974)

Hoffman, D. and Y. Kotsonis (eds), *Russian Modernity: Politics, Knowledges, Practices* (Basingstoke, 2000)

Holland, B. (ed.), *Soviet Sisterhood: British Feminists on Women in the USSR* (London, 1985)

Holt, A. (ed. and trans.), *Selected Writings of Alexandra Kollontai* (New York, 1977)

Ilič, M., *Women Workers in the Soviet Interwar Economy: From 'Protection' to 'Equality'* (Basingstoke, 1999)

Ilič, M. (ed.), *Women in the Stalin Era* (Basingstoke, 2001)

Inkeles, A., *Social Change in Soviet Russia* (Cambridge, Mass., 1968)

Inkeles, A. and K. Geiger (eds), *Soviet Society: a Book of Readings* (London, 1961)

Johnson, P. and L. Labedz (eds), *Khrushchev and the Arts: the Politics of Soviet Culture, 1962–1964* (Cambridge, Mass., 1965)

Juviler, P., *Revolutionary Law and Order* (New York, 1976)

Karlsson, K-G., *Historia som vapen. Historiebruk och Sovjetunionens upplösning, 1985–1995* (Stockholm, 1999)

Kassof, A., *The Soviet Youth Programme* (Cambridge, Mass., 1965)

Kay, R., *Russian Women and their Organizations: Gender, Discrimination, and Grassroots* (London, 2000)

Keep, J., *Last of the Empires* (Oxford, 1995)

Kelly, C., *Refining Russia: Advice Literature, Polite Culture and Gender from Catherine to Yeltsin* (Oxford, 2001)

Kelly, C. and D. Shepherd (eds), *Constructing Russian Culture* (Oxford, 1998)

Kettering, K., '"Ever More Cosy and Comfortable": Stalinism and the Soviet Domestic Interior, 1928–1938', *Journal of Design History*, vol. 10. no. 2, 1997, pp. 119–36

Kharkhordin, O., 'Reveal and Dissimulate: a Genealogy of Private Life in Soviet Russia', in J. Weintraub and K. Kumar (eds), *Public and Private in Thought and Practice* (Chicago, 1996), pp. 333–63

Kharkhordin, O., *The Collective and the Individual in Russia: a Study of Practices* (Berkeley, 1999)

Khrushchev, N. S., *Khrushchev Remembers*, trans. Strobe Talbot (London, 1971)

Khrushchev, N. S., *Khrushchev Remembers: the Last Testament* (Boston and London, 1974)

Khrushchev, S., *Khrushchev on Khrushchev* (London, 1990)

Khrushchev, S. N., *Nikita Khrushchev and the Creation of a Superpower* (Pennsylvania, 2000)

Kosmarskaya, N. 'Russian Women in Kyrgyzstan: Coping with New Realities', *Women's Studies International Forum*, vol. 19, nos 1–2, pp. 125–32

Kotkin, S., *Magnetic Mountain: Stalinism as a Civilization* (Berkeley, 1995)

Kulavig, E., *Dissent in the Years of Khrushchev* (Basingstoke, 2002)

Lahusen, T. and E. Dobrenko (eds), *Socialist Realism without Shores* (London, 1997)

Lane, C., *The Rites of Rulers: Ritual in Industrial Society – the Soviet Case* (Cambridge, 1981)

Lane, C., *Christian Religion in the Soviet Union* (London, 1978)

Lapidus, G. W., *Women in Soviet Society: Equality, Development, and Social Change* (Berkeley, 1978)

Liegle, L., *The Family's Role in Soviet Education* (New York, 1975)

Liljeström, M., *Emanciperade till underordning. Det sovjetiska könssystemets uppkomsi och diskursiva reproduction* (Turku, 1995)

Liljeström, M., 'Regimes of Truth? Soviet Women's Autobiographical Texts and the Question of Censorship', in M. Kangaspuro (ed.), *Russia: More Different than Most* (Helsinki, 2000)

Liljeström, M., E. Mäntysaari and A. Rosenholm (eds), *Gender Restructuring in Russian Studies* (Tampere, 1993)

Liljeström, M. et al. (eds), *Models of Self: Russian Women's Autobiographical Texts* (Helsinki, 2000)

Linden, C., *Khrushchev and the Soviet Leadership, 1957–1964* (Baltimore, 1966)

McAuley, A., *Women's Work and Wages in the Soviet Union* (London, 1981)

McCauley, M. (ed.), *Khrushchev and Khrushchevism* (Basingstoke, 1987)

Mace, D. and V., *The Soviet Family* (London, 1963)

McLaughlin, S., *The Image of Women in Contemporary Soviet Fiction* (Basingstoke, 1989)

Madison, B., *Social Welfare in the Soviet Union* (Stanford, 1968)

Marsh, R. (ed.), *Women and Russian Culture* (Berghahn, 1998)

Marshall, R. H. (ed.), *Aspects of Religion in the Soviet Union, 1917–67* (Chicago, 1971)

Massell, G., *The Surrogate Proletariat, Muslim Women and Revolutionary Struggle in Soviet Central Asia, 1919–29* (Princeton, 1974)

Matthews, M., *Class and Society in Soviet Russia* (London, 1972)

Mayne, J., *Kino and the Woman Question* (Columbus, Ohio, 1989)

Medvedev, R., *Khrushchev* (Oxford, 1982)

Medvedev, R. and Zh. Medvedev, *Khrushchev: the Years in Power* (New York, 1978)

Meehan Waters, B., *Holy Women of Russia* (New York, 1996)

Meerson-Aksenov, M. and B. Shragin (eds), *The Political, Social and Religious Thought of Russian Samizdat: an Anthology* (Belmont, Mass., 1977)

Miller, W., *Russians as People* (London, 1960)

Naiman, E., *Sex in Public: the Incarnation of Early Soviet Ideology* (Princeton, 1997)

Nove, A., *Stalinism and After* (London, 1975)

Nove, A., *An Economic History of the USSR* (Harmondsworth, rev. edn, 1982)

Oja, M., 'From *Krestianka* to *Udarnitsa*: Rural Women in the *Vydvizhenie* Campaign, 1944–41', *Carl Beck Papers in Russian and East European Studies*, no. 1203 (Pittsburgh, 1996)

Paert, I. K., 'Memory and Survival in Stalin's Russia: Old Believers in the Urals during the 1930–50s', in P. Thompson and D. Bertraux (eds), *On Living through Soviet Russia* (London, forthcoming)

Peris, D., *Storming the Heavens: the Soviet League of the Militant Godless* (Ithaca, 1998)

Petrone, K., *Life has Become More Joyous, Comrades: Celebrations in the Time of Stalin* (Bloomington, 2000)

Pilkington, H., *Russia's Youth and Its Culture: a Nation's Constructors and Constructed* (London, 1994)

Pohl, M., '"It Cannot Be that Our Graves Will Be Here": the Survival of Chechen and Ingush Deportees in Kazakhstan, 1944–1957', *Journal of Genocide Research*, vol. 4, no. 3, September 2002, pp. 401–30

Raleigh, D. (ed.), *Provincial Landscapes: the Local Dimensions of Soviet Power* (Pittsburgh, 2001)

Ramet, C. (ed.), *Religious Policy in the Soviet Union* (Cambridge, 1993)

Ransell, D., *Village Mothers: Three Generations of Change in Russia and Tataria* (Bloomington, Ind., 2000)

Rau, S. R., *My Russian Journey* (New York, 1959)

Reid, S., 'Destalinization and Taste', *Journal of Design History*, vol. 10, no. 2, 1997, pp. 177–202

Reid, S., 'All Stalin's Women: Gender and Power in Soviet Art of the 1930s', *Slavic Review*, vol. 57, no. 1, 1998, pp. 133–73

Reid, S., 'Masters of the Earth: Gender and Destalinisation in Soviet Reformist Painting of the Khrushchev Thaw', *Gender and History*, vol. 11, no. 2, 1999, pp. 276–312

Reid, S. E., 'Cold War in the Kitchen: Gender and the De-Stalinization of Consumer Taste in the Soviet Union under Khrushchev', *Slavic Review*, vol. 61, no. 2, 2002, pp. 211–52

Reid, S., 'Khrushchev in Wonderland: the Pioneer Palace in Moscow's Lenin Hills, 1962', *The Carl Beck Papers*, no. 1606 (Pittsburgh, 2002)

Reid, S. and D. Crowley (eds), *Style and Socialism: Modernity and Material Culture in Post-War Eastern Europe* (Oxford, 2000)

Salisbury, H., *To Russia – and Beyond* (London, 1960)

Scanlan, James P., *Marxism in the USSR: a Critical Survey of Current Soviet Thought* (Ithaca, 1985)

Schrand, T., 'Soviet "Civic-Minded Women" in the 1930s: Gender, Class, and Industrialization in a Socialist Society', *Journal of Women's History*, vol. 11, no. 3, Autumn 1999, pp. 126–48

Scott, H., *Women and Socialism: Experiences from Eastern Europe* (London, 1976)

Shlapentokh, D. and V. Shlapentokh, *Soviet Cinematography, 1918–1991: Ideological Conflict and Social Reality* (New York, 1993)

Shlapentokh, V. *Soviet Intellectuals and Political Power: the Post-Stalin Era* (Princeton, 1990)

Shrayer, M. D., 'Why Are the Cranes Still Flying?', *Russian Review*, vol. 56, 1997, pp. 425–39

Simmons, C., 'Lifting the Siege: Women's Voices on Leningrad (1941–1944)', *Canadian Slavonic Papers/Revue Canadienne des Slavistes*, vol. XL, nos 1–2, March–June 1998, pp. 43–65

Sobel, A. (ed.), *Russia's Rulers: the Khrushchev Period* (New York, 1971)

Sosnovy, T., 'The Soviet Housing Situation Today', *Soviet Studies*, vol. 11, no. 1, 1959, pp. 1–21

Soviet Legislation on Women's Rights: Collection of Normative Acts (Moscow, 1978)

Starr, S. F., *Red and Hot: the Fate of Jazz in the Soviet Union, 1917–1980* (New York, 1983)

Stites, R., *Revolutionary Dreams* (Oxford, 1989)

Stites, R., *Russian Popular Culture* (Cambridge, 1992)

'Summary of XXI (Extraordinary) Party Congress', *Soviet Studies*, vol. 11, no. 1, 1959

Tatarinova, N., *Women in the USSR* (Moscow, 1968)

Tatu, M., *Power in the Kremlin* (London, 1968)

Taubman, W., *Khrushchev: the Man and His Era* (London, 2003)

Taubman, W., S. Khrushchev and A. Gleason (eds), *Nikita Khrushchev* (New Haven, 2000)

Tompson, W., *Khrushchev: a Political Life* (Basingstoke, 1995)

Trifonov, Yu., *The Long Goodbye: Three Novellas* (Ann Arbor, 1978)

Troitsky, A., *Back in the USSR* (Boston, 1988)

Viola, L., '*Bab'i bunty* and Peasant Women's Protest during Collectivization', *Russian Review*, vol. 45, 1986, pp. 23–42

Werner, C., 'The Dynamics of Feasting and Gift Exchange in Rural Kazakhstan', in I. Svanberg (ed.), *Contemporary Kazaks: Cultural and Social Perspectives* (New York, 1999), pp. 47–72

Werth, A., *The Khrushchev Phase* (London, 1961)

Werth, A., *Russia under Khrushchev* (New York, 1962)

White, A., *De-Stalinization and the House of Culture* (London, 1990)

Woll, J., *Real Images: Soviet Cinema and the Thaw* (London, 2000)

Women and Children in the USSR: Brief Statistical Returns (Moscow, 1963)

Women and Russia: First Feminist Samizdat (London, 1980)

Women in the USSR: Brief Statistics (Moscow, 1960)

Wood, E., *The Baba and the Comrade* (Bloomington, 1997)

Woodward, K. (ed.), *Identity and Difference* (London, 1997)

Worobec, C., *Possessed: Women, Witches and Demons in Imperial Russia* (Dekalb, Ill., 2001)

Yedlin, T., *Women in Eastern Europe and the Soviet Union* (New York, 1980)

'Youth has Its Say on Love and Marriage', *Soviet Review*, vol. 3, no. 8, 1962

Zizek, S., *The Sublime Object of Ideology* (London, 1989)

Zorkaya, N., *The Illustrated History of Soviet Cinema* (New York, 1991)

Zubkova, E. (trans. H. Ragsdale), *Russia after the War: Hopes, Illusions, and Disappointments, 1945–1957* (London, 1998)

Index

abortion, 9, 88, 118, 119
Adventists, 205–6
aesthetics, 156, 167, 168, 170
agriculture, 1, 2, 7, 14–15, 18, 52–74, 88, 208–9
    see also collective farms, Virgin Lands, tractor drivers
All-Russian Congress of Working and Peasant Women, First (1918), 132, 134, 138, 139
anti-religious campaigns, 3, 204, 213–17
apartment house kitchen, 187, 191–2
    see also public dining
Arkhitektura SSSR, 178, 183, 184
atheism, 203, 204
    and films, 215
    and novels, 214
    propaganda of, 212, 215
autobiography, 2, 131–45
    see also memoirs, *ocherkovyi* genre, oral testimonies
awards to women, 6, 8

Ballad of a Soldier (1959), 2, 115, 120, 124–7
Baptists, 205–6, 215
Barkhin, M. G., 182, 188
Bed and Sofa aka *3 Meshchanskii Street* (1927), 162
Beechey, V., 44
Belfrage, S., 82
birth rate, 6, 179
    see also 'demographic crisis', sex imbalance
Boym, S., 171, 180
Brezhnev, L. I., 54
bride abduction, 64
Brova, S. V., 36
Browning, G., 160
Buchli, V., 154–5, 168
Buckley, M., 1
Bumazhnyi, L., 188
Butler, J., 143

Bykovsky, V., 228, 229
byt/everyday life, 97, 152–5, 159, 160, 161, 162, 167, 170–1

canteens, *see* apartment house kitchen, public dining
Castro, F., 225
Cavarero, A., 142–3
censorship, 143
Certeau, M. de, 135
Central Asia, 13, 14, 19, 53, 64, 215–16
Chaikovskaya, R., 192
Chernin, K., 78, 84, 90
childcare, 6, 9, 10, 11, 16, 18, 96–113, 159, 183, 184, 187, 191
child rearing, 2, 96–109, 155, 188
Circus (1936), 86
Clouds over Borsk (1961), 215
Cold War, 3, 19, 81, 154, 161, 222, 223, 224, 229, 231, 236
collective farms, 7, 14–15, 16, 53, 57, 65, 124, 179, 226
Commissions on the Affairs of Minors, *see* minors' commissions
Committee of Soviet Women, 18, 234–5
communal apartment, 177, 178, 179–82, 183, 184, 186, 192, 193, 195–7, 198 n. 21, 199 n. 40
communal services, 160
    see also public services
'communist morality', 96–7, 119, 123, 156
Communist Party Congresses
    XX (1956), 9, 14, 114, 119, 133, 134, 154, 157
    XXI (1959), 8, 16, 18, 217
    XXII (1961), 139, 141
Communist Party Programme, *see* Party Programme
Constitution (1936), 17, 118
consumer goods, 3, 45, 67, 69, 100, 156, 165, 168, 191–3
    see also domestic appliances

249